BITCOIN FOR THE BEFUDDLED

BITCOIN FOR THE BEFUDDLED

by Conrad Barski and Chris Wilmer

San Francisco

Printed on demand in USA.

ISBN-10: 1-59327-573-0
ISBN-13: 978-1-59327-573-0

Publisher: William Pollock
Production Editor: Serena Yang
Cover Illustration: Conrad Barski
Interior Design: Octopod Studios
Developmental Editor: Tyler Ortman
Technical Reviewer: Patrick Fuller
Copyeditor: Anne Marie Walker
Compositor: Alison Law
Proofreader: Paula L. Fleming
Indexer: Nancy Guenther

For information on distribution, translations, or bulk sales, please contact No Starch Press, Inc. directly:

No Starch Press, Inc.
245 8th Street, San Francisco, CA 94103
phone: 415.863.9900; info@nostarch.com
www.nostarch.com

Library of Congress Control Number: 2014951031

About the Authors

Conrad Barski has an M.D. from the University of Miami and nearly 20 years of programming experience. Barski is a cartoonist, programmer, and the author of *Land of Lisp* (No Starch Press). He's been using Bitcoin since 2011.

Chris Wilmer holds a Ph.D. in chemical engineering from Northwestern University and is a professor at the University of Pittsburgh. Wilmer's first purchase with Bitcoin was a bag of honey caramels from a farm in Utah. They were delicious.

BRIEF CONTENTS

Preface xv

Chapter 1: What Is Bitcoin? 1

Chapter 2: Bitcoin Basics 7

Chapter 3: Storing Your Bitcoins Safely, Securely, and Conveniently 31

Chapter 4: Buying Bitcoins 49

Chapter 5: Lost at Sea: A Cryptographic Adventure 73

Chapter 6: Why Bitcoin Is a Big Deal 109

Chapter 7: The Cryptography Behind Bitcoin 129

Chapter 8: Bitcoin Mining 161

Chapter 8.5: The Strange World of Altcoins 181

Chapter 9: Understanding the Different Types of Bitcoin Wallets 185

Chapter 10: Bitcoin 2030 199

Appendix A: Hello Money! A Simple JavaScript Program 213

Appendix B: Bitcoin Programming with BitcoinJ 225

Index 241

CONTENTS IN DETAIL

PREFACE **xv**
Acknowledgments . . . xvi

1
WHAT IS BITCOIN? **1**
Why Bitcoin Now? . . . 2
The Benefits of Using Bitcoin . . . 3
The Complexity and Confusion of Bitcoin . . . 4
What's in This Book? . . . 5

2
BITCOIN BASICS **7**
How Bitcoin Works in Simple Terms . . . 8
Bitcoin Units . . . 9
The Bitcoin Address . . . 10
The Private Key . . . 11
The Bitcoin Wallet . . . 12
Creating Your First Bitcoin Wallet with Electrum . . . 14
Acquiring Bitcoins in Your Wallet . . . 16
Spending Bitcoins with Your Wallet . . . 17
Bitcoin Addresses Generated by Your Bitcoin Wallet Program . . . 19
The Blockchain . . . 19
The Blockchain Lottery . . . 21
Blockchain Forking . . . 23
Transaction Confirmations, Double Spending, and Irreversibility . . . 25
Mining Bitcoins . . . 26
The Complexity of the Bitcoin System . . . 27

3
STORING YOUR BITCOINS SAFELY, SECURELY, AND CONVENIENTLY **31**
Storing Your Private Key(s) . . . 33
Hot Storage vs. Cold Storage . . . 33
Personal vs. Hosted Wallets . . . 34
Safety, Security, and Convenience . . . 35
Storing Small Amounts of Bitcoins . . . 35
Online Hosted Wallet Services . . . 36
Online Personal Wallet Services . . . 37
Personal Hot Wallet . . . 37

Storing Large Amounts of Bitcoins 38
Paper Wallets. 39
Encrypted Paper Wallets 39
Offline Transaction Signing 40
Fragmented Private Keys and Multi-Signature Addresses 41
Special Mention: The Bitcoin Hardware Wallet 42
Special Mention: The Bitcoin Brain Wallet. 45
Choosing the Storage Method That's Right for You. 46

4
BUYING BITCOINS 49

Why Not Just Mine Bitcoins? 50
Ways to Buy Bitcoins 51
Buying Bitcoins the Easy Way 52
Authentication Factors 54
The Hassle of Converting Dollars (or Other Currencies) into Bitcoins 55
Buying Bitcoins with Coinbase 58
Buying Bitcoins the Efficient Way. 62
Buying Bitcoins from a Currency Exchange 65
Buying Bitcoins the Fun and Futuristic Way 67
Step 1: Finding Someone to Buy From. 67
Step 2: Deciding on a Meeting Place 68
Step 3: Handing Over the Money and Getting Your Bitcoins 68
Satoshi Square 70
Still Don't See a Buying Option That Works for You? 71

5
LOST AT SEA: A CRYPTOGRAPHIC ADVENTURE 73

6
WHY BITCOIN IS A BIG DEAL 109

A Brief History of Digital Currencies 110
The Dawn of Bitcoin. 112
Bitcoin's First Four Years 113
Bitcoin's Early Impact 115
The Future Potential of Bitcoin 116
What Are the Existential Risks to Bitcoin?. 117
What Role Might Bitcoin Play in the Future? 121
The Dangers of Decentralized Digital Money 123

7
THE CRYPTOGRAPHY BEHIND BITCOIN 129

A Brief Cryptography Overview. 130
One-Way Functions. 131
Cryptographic Hash Functions Verify Information 132
Public Key Cryptography 133

Digital Signatures 135
Using Digital Signatures. 136
Why Bitcoin Needs Cryptography 137
Authorizing Transactions with Digital Signatures 137
Verifying the Validity of the Transaction History 138
Proof-of-Work in Bitcoin Mining 138
Extra Protection for Bitcoin Private Keys 139
Cryptographic Methods Used in Bitcoin 139
Cryptographic Hash Functions: SHA256 and RIPEMD160 140
Crowley and the Unfortunate Jelly-Filled Donut Incident. 141
Moving Around on a Line 145
Elliptic Curve Digital Signature Algorithm (ECDSA) 146
Signing a Bitcoin Transaction Using ECDSA. 154
The Security of Bitcoin's Cryptography 158
Pseudocode for Elliptic Point Summation and Point Multiplication 159

8
BITCOIN MINING 161

Why Is Bitcoin Mining Needed? 162
A Parable of Two Generals 162
Applying the Parable to Bitcoin. 164
Preventing Attacks with Mining. 166
Distributing New Currency with Mining 167
How Does Bitcoin Mining Work? 168
How Miners Solve a Block 171
Anatomy of a Block. 171
Pooled Mining 175
Bitcoin Mining for Profit 176
Theoretical Hash Rate Limits 178
Decentralization in Bitcoin Mining 179

8.5
THE STRANGE WORLD OF ALTCOINS 181

9
UNDERSTANDING THE DIFFERENT TYPES OF BITCOIN WALLETS 185

Wallet Software Design Fundamentals 186
Offline vs. Online Transaction Signing. 186
Random Key Generation vs. Deterministic Key Generation (vs. Single Key Generation) 187
Full vs. Simplified Payment Verification 191
Other Common (and Not So Common) Bitcoin Wallet Features 195
Future Wallets 197
Which Wallet Is Right for You? 197
Additional Wallet Considerations. 197

10
BITCOIN 2030 199

What Will a Bitcoin Be Worth in 2030? 200
Bitcoin Mining in 2030 201
A Day in the Life of a Bitcoiner in 2030 202
The Bitcoin End Game 210

A
HELLO MONEY! A SIMPLE JAVASCRIPT PROGRAM 213

The Meaning of "Easy" 213
Three Ways to Write Bitcoin Software 214
General Security Notes on Bitcoin Programming 215
Some Upbeat Notes on Bitcoin Security 216
Writing Your First Bitcoin Program in JavaScript 217
Why Use JavaScript? 217
Bitcoin Core vs. Bitcoind 217
Preparing Your Machine for JavaScript Bitcoin Programming 218
Installing Node.js 218
Installing node-bitcoin 218
Starting Bitcoin Core 218
For Mac Hackers 219
For Linux Folks 219
Hello Money! 220
Part 1: Initializing the Connection with Bitcoin Core 220
Part 2: The Main Loop 221
The Bitcoin Core JSON-RPC API 222
Running the Hello Money! App 222
Limitations of Writing Bitcoin Programs That Use JSON-RPC 223

B
BITCOIN PROGRAMMING WITH BITCOINJ 225

The Best Programming Language for Connecting to the Bitcoin Network 225
Installing Java, Maven, and the BitcoinJ Library 226
Step 1: Installing Java 226
Step 2: Installing Maven 227
Step 3: Installing Git 227
Step 4: Installing BitcoinJ 227
Creating a Starter Project for hello-money 228
Writing the Code for hello-money 230
Declarations at the Top of the Program 231
Initializing Our Java Objects 231
Connecting to the Bitcoin Network 233
Listening for New Money 234

Running and Testing the hello-money Java Program 235
Bye-Bye Money 236
Importing a Private Key 237
Sending the Money 238
Ensuring the Money Transmission 238
Running bye-bye-money 238
Gotchas When Using Wallets in BitcoinJ 239
Conclusion 240

INDEX **241**

PREFACE

In writing this book, we wanted to explain the concept and potential of Bitcoin in a more-or-less timeless manner. Boy, was that hard. It would have been much easier to write a book called *The State of Bitcoin Right Now: Please Disregard Everything in This Book One Year After Its Publication*. The core technology behind Bitcoin, as well as the larger technological infrastructure around it, is rapidly evolving as this book goes to press. The debates about the legality, price volatility, and merchant adoption of Bitcoin may already be out of date by 2015, and who knows how they will sound in 2025.

To keep this book relevant for the future, we did our best to focus on those aspects of Bitcoin that will remain important forever, and we tried to cover them in a way that is fun. We hope you will enjoy our approach to this fascinating subject.

Acknowledgments

Chris Wilmer would like to thank his wife Emily Winerock and his family for their patience and early feedback. Conrad Barski would like to thank his wife Lauren Barski and daughter Ava Barski for their support as he was working on this book and for their patience during all the weekends and evenings he spent to get it done.

Special thanks go to Richard Ford Burley, for substantial editorial help in the early drafts of this book, and to Patrick Fuller, for reviewing the programming sections. Many of the great people at No Starch Press helped us to get this book into shape, including Serena Yang, Tyler Ortman, Bill Pollock, and others.

1

WHAT IS BITCOIN?

In the simplest terms, Bitcoin is just another currency. The term *Bitcoin* refers to the entire currency system, whereas *bitcoins* are the basic units of the currency.[1] As with dollars, euros, yen, and gold coins, you can save bitcoins, spend them on goods and services, and exchange them for other currencies. However, Bitcoin is the world's first currency that is both digital and decentralized.

A *digital currency* is one that can be easily stored and used on a computer. By this definition, even dollars can be considered a digital currency, since they can be easily sent to others or used to shop online, but their supply is controlled by a centralized bank organization. In contrast, gold coins are *decentralized*, meaning that no central authority controls the supply of gold in the world. In fact, anyone can dig for gold, create new coins, and distribute them. However, unlike digital currencies, it's not easy to use gold coins to pay for goods (at least not with exact change!), and it's impossible to transfer gold coins over the Internet. Because Bitcoin combines these two

1. Similar to how *renminbi* is name of the Chinese currency, but the *yuan* is the basic unit.

properties, it is somewhat like digital gold. Never before has there been a currency with both these two properties, and its impact on our increasingly digital, globalized world may turn out to be significant.

Sometimes called a stateless currency, Bitcoin is not associated with any nation. However, you should not consider Bitcoin to be in the same category as *private* currencies, hundreds of which have existed in various forms in the past.[2] Private currencies, whether issued by a person, a company, or a nonstate organization, are centrally controlled and run the risk of collapse due to bankruptcy or other economic failure. Bitcoin is not a company, nor does a single person or organization issue or control bitcoins; therefore, it has no central point of failure. For this reason, nobody can inflate the currency supply and create hyperinflation crises, such as those that occurred in post–World War I Germany and more recently in Zimbabwe.[3]

Many people are asking about the motive behind the creation of Bitcoin, so let's explore the currency's purpose.

Why Bitcoin Now?

Until recently, people could not send *digital cash* back and forth to each other in a reliable way without a central mediator. A trusted central mediator such as PayPal can track payments and money transfers in a privately held account ledger, but it wasn't clear how a group of strangers who *do not* trust each other could accomplish the same transactions dependably.[4] Sometimes referred to as the Byzantine Generals' Problem, this fundamental conundrum also emerges in computer science, specifically in how to achieve consensus on a distributed network.

---

2. For example, in the mid-1800s, banks, companies, churches, and individuals issued hundreds of private currencies in the United States. Eventually, most of these private currencies lost all their value.

3. Between 1921 and 1924, the value of the German mark fell by a factor of more than 10 trillion due to overprinting by the government. In 2008, the government of Zimbabwe printed so much of its currency that in a single year, a loaf of bread increased from $1 to $100 billion. In both cases, any savings that people had in the form of national currency were completely destroyed.

4. To say that something is *decentralized* is more or less equivalent to saying that it is run by a group of strangers who don't necessarily trust each other.

In 2008, the problem was elegantly solved by Bitcoin's inventor, known pseudonymously as Satoshi Nakamoto. Satoshi's significant breakthrough made it possible for a digital currency to exist without relying on a central authority. Satoshi described the solution to the Byzantine Generals' Problem and the invention of Bitcoin in a white paper titled "Bitcoin: A Peer-to-Peer Electronic Cash System." But the creation of the software that demonstrated the concept in practice was released a year later.

Although the first version of the software was written by Satoshi, it quickly became a community project as the software was improved and maintained by hundreds of volunteers. Currently, the software is open source, and anyone can read and contribute to it. In January of 2009, the first bitcoins were distributed using the early Bitcoin software, and since then transactions have been running smoothly. Slowly but surely, an increasing number of people have started using Bitcoin, and what began as an experiment is now a multibillion dollar economy that processes hundreds of thousands of transactions per day (and is growing quickly).

The Benefits of Using Bitcoin

Bitcoin is an inherently international currency; anyone can send bitcoins to anyone else in the world, in any amount, almost instantly. In addition, it is becoming increasingly possible to travel the world and spend bitcoins without having to change them into the local currency. Because no middleman is involved, transaction fees are negligible. Unlike with credit cards, which require giving online merchants your personal information, you can use bitcoins to shop online while maintaining your privacy. There is no risk of losing your savings due to runaway inflation because bitcoins were designed to have a fixed supply. Bitcoins are also fundamentally impossible to counterfeit.

As a merchant, you can start accepting bitcoins as payment immediately without filling out tedious paperwork (compared to setting up the credit card transaction process). You can also own bitcoins without anyone else knowing, and no third party or government can seize your money. (The privacy this feature entails may protect the security and freedom of political dissidents living under repressive regimes, for example.)

Thanks to all of its benefits, Bitcoin continues to increase in popularity; however, anyone familiar with Bitcoin will agree the technology behind it is difficult to explain and understand. At first blush, it's hard to grasp how bitcoins are stored, how they are used, or even where they come from.

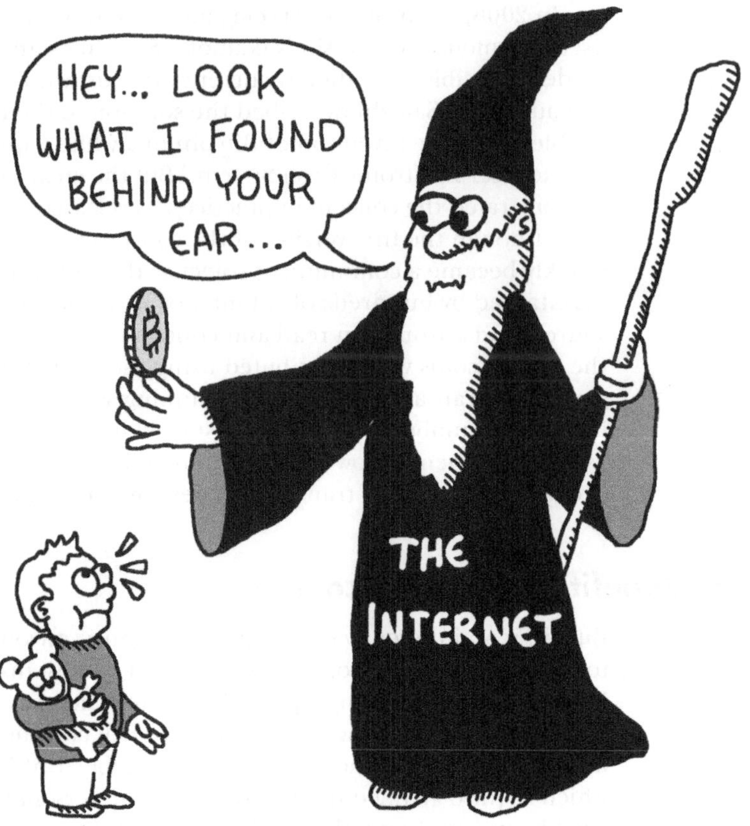

The Complexity and Confusion of Bitcoin

Rarely do we get to see the creation of a new currency, let alone one that is so different from previous currencies. This creates major challenges in comprehension and comfort for most people.

Bitcoin can be compared to the advent of paper currency years ago when everyone was using gold and silver coins. Then, it must have seemed strange and confusing to attribute value to little pieces of paper instead of precious metals. Today, paper currency feels fairly safe, and trading paper for a purely digital asset like bitcoins seems odd. Furthermore, the economic and social consequences of switching to a decentralized digital currency are still unclear. Even Satoshi and the early volunteers who helped develop the concept could not have imagined precisely how Bitcoin would be used and valued by society, much as the creators of the Internet in the 1980s could not have predicted how transformative it would become.

Confusion also stems from the fact that Bitcoin is a truly complex technology. It relies not only on Satoshi's breakthrough to achieving consensus on a distributed network but also on modern cryptographic techniques, such as digital signatures, public/private key pairs, and secure hashing. (These cryptographic concepts are covered in detail in Chapter 7.) The issuing of new currency occurs through a cryptographic lottery called mining that anyone can participate in. Mining simultaneously processes transactions made by Bitcoin users. To resist abuse from those who might want to destroy the network, Bitcoin's design uses game theory to align the incentives of those who maintain the network and those who want to act in their own selfish interest. (Bitcoin mining and game theory is explained in detail in Chapter 8.)

Put simply, you cannot learn and completely understand Bitcoin in a single afternoon. However, we hope this book will help you understand the basics of Bitcoin as quickly as possible.

What's in This Book?

To make sense of the Bitcoin technology and phenomenon, you must view it from multiple perspectives. This book is organized around those perspectives.

- First, we'll look at Bitcoin from the perspective of a basic user. In Chapters 2–4 we describe how Bitcoin works and how you can acquire, spend, and safely store bitcoins—so you can actually start using Bitcoin.
- Next, in Chapters 5 and 6, we take a philosophical perspective on Bitcoin. Chapter 5 is an adventure story told from the perspective of Crowley the cryptographer. Crowley gets stranded on an island and needs to figure out how to efficiently exchange goods with inhabitants of other distant islands. Crowley knows about Bitcoin from a chance encounter with Satoshi but has significant doubts about the currency. In the story, he works through his doubts (which may be similar to yours) by giving Bitcoin a chance.

  Chapter 6 continues in this philosophical vein by looking at the potentially broader impact of Bitcoin and the potentially uneasy relationship of Bitcoin and its users with nation states whose currencies compete with Bitcoin.
- Then, we'll look at Bitcoin from the perspective of an advanced user. Chapters 7–9 describe the cryptographic methods behind Bitcoin, the details of bitcoin mining, and the nuances of various third-party wallet software solutions.
- Finally, in Chapter 10, we'll look at what the distant future might look like in a world where Bitcoin has gone mainstream.
- For programmers and developers who are new to Bitcoin, the appendices show you how to write your own programs to send and receive bitcoins.

As you read this book, keep in mind just how new Bitcoin is as a technology. For fields like particle physics, Egyptian history, or constitutional law, we can turn to authority figures that have devoted the better part of their lives to studying those subjects; by comparison nobody is really an expert on Bitcoin. Just as there were no electricians before the discovery of electricity or programming gurus before computers were invented, arguably no Bitcoin experts exist today. We are all Bitcoin beginners, and no one can predict with any clarity how Bitcoin will evolve, even a year or two into the future.

On the upside, this means that if Bitcoin becomes widely used in the future, the potential exists for *you* to become one of the early experts in Bitcoin, since you are studying this technology at such an early stage. We hope you will be inspired by the ideas behind Bitcoin and will make your own contributions to this wonderful technology in years to come.

Now, let's learn some Bitcoin basics.

2

BITCOIN BASICS

In our experience, the simplest way to get a person excited about Bitcoin is to have him purchase something with it. That's how we got hooked ourselves. In this chapter, we'll help you perform your first Bitcoin transaction, without worrying about too much technical stuff. Along the way, though, we'll discuss how Bitcoin works. After reading this chapter, you'll understand the basics of Bitcoin—enough to chat about it at any cocktail party.

How Bitcoin Works in Simple Terms

In the Bitcoin system, everyone cooperates to keep track of everyone else's money, and as mentioned in Chapter 1, no central authority (e.g., bank or government) is involved. To best understand how the system works, let's walk through an example using dollars first.

Imagine only $21 million exists in the world, and there also exists a detailed list of all the people who possess that money. Everyone, including you (even though you have only $5), has a copy of this list. When you give $2 to your friend, you must subtract $2 from your entry on the list and add $2 to her entry. After informing her of the transaction, she updates her list as well. In fact, everyone in the world needs to update the list; otherwise, the list would be inaccurate. Therefore, not only do you need to notify your friend, but you also need to publicly announce that you are updating the list. If you tried to cheat the system and send your friend $1000, your cheating attempt would be easy to catch because everyone knows you have only $5 to give.

Now, imagine that all transactions are carried out on computers that communicate via the Internet, and replace *dollars* with *bitcoins*. This is how Bitcoin works. Pretty simple actually. So why does Bitcoin seem so complex?

The answer is threefold: First is the tricky question of how the units of any new currency system (whether bitcoins or seashells) should be valued. Should a haircut be worth 5000 bitcoins or 0.005 bitcoins? Second, many small details are involved in implementing and using Bitcoin, even though the overall concept is fairly straightforward. For example, how do you obtain a copy of the list, and how are bitcoins initially distributed? Third, an entire lexicon of new and unfamiliar words (e.g., mining) is used in the Bitcoin world.

We'll leave the first point about the value of bitcoins for a later chapter. In this chapter, we'll address the last two points by explaining the major concepts used in Bitcoin, namely the Bitcoin address, the private key, the Bitcoin wallet, and the blockchain. We'll also briefly discuss Bitcoin mining and walk you through the process of receiving and sending your first bitcoins so you can see how the system works. But first, you need to understand the Bitcoin units in more detail.

Bitcoin Units

As explained in Chapter 1, Bitcoin refers collectively to the entire currency system, whereas bitcoins are the units of the currency. Although the total currency supply is capped at 21 million bitcoins, each one can be subdivided into smaller denominations; for example, 0.1 bitcoins and 0.001 bitcoins. The smallest unit, a hundred millionth of a bitcoin (0.00000001 bitcoins), is called a *satoshi* in honor of Satoshi Nakamoto. As a result, goods can be priced in Bitcoin very precisely, and people can easily pay for those goods in exact change (e.g., a merchant can price a gallon of milk at 0.00152374 bitcoins, or 152,374 satoshis).

Rather than writing the term *bitcoins* on price tags, merchants commonly use the abbreviated currency code *BTC* or *XBT*; 5 bitcoins would be written as 5 BTC. Despite the fact that the BTC abbreviation has been widely used since the beginning of Bitcoin's development, more recently some merchants and websites have started using XBT because it conforms better to certain international naming standards.[1] As bitcoins have appreciated in value, it has become increasingly common to work with thousandths or even millionths of bitcoins, which are called *millibitcoins (mBTC)* and *microbitcoins (μBTC)*, respectively. Many people have suggested simpler names for Bitcoin's smaller denominations, and one that has gained traction is referring to microbitcoins (quite a mouthful) as simply as *bits*.

1 bitcoin = 1 BTC or 1 XBT

1 BTC = 1,000 mBTC

1 mBTC = 1,000 μBTC

1 μBTC = 100 satoshis = 1 bit

---

1. The standard for currency codes (ISO 4217) uses the first character in the code to refer to the country issuing the currency. However, since Bitcoin is a nongovernmental currency, the standard suggests that its name should start with *X*, as is the case with gold or silver, whose codes are XAU and XAG, respectively.

Now that you know the terms for various Bitcoin units, you need to increase your Bitcoin vocabulary, so let's talk about what is meant by a Bitcoin address.

The Bitcoin Address

Bitcoin uses a public ledger that indicates the number of bitcoins and their owners at any given time. But instead of associating names of people with accounts, the ledger only lists *Bitcoin addresses*. Each address can be thought of as a pseudonym for a person (or group of people, business, etc.), and the use of pseudonyms is why people can use bitcoins without revealing personal information. The following is an example of a Bitcoin address:

```
13tQ1fbTMB6GxUJfMqCSDgivc8fvkHEh3J
```

Like a bank account number, a Bitcoin address consists of a string of letters and numbers (usually beginning with the number 1). To send bitcoins to others (e.g., an online merchant, a friend, or a family member), you only need to know their Bitcoin address. In turn, when you share your address with others, they can send you bitcoins. Because Bitcoin addresses are cumbersome to type, many people use *quick response (QR) codes* to represent their address (see Figure 2-1).[2] For convenience, you can put your Bitcoin address, either typed or as a QR code (or both), on your business card, personal website, or storefront (if you're a merchant). Although you need an Internet connection to *send* bitcoins, you don't need to be connected to *receive* them. For example, if you work for a charity and pass out thousands of business cards containing your Bitcoin address and a statement like "Please consider donating in bitcoins," your organization can collect bitcoins while you sleep.

Figure 2-1: QR codes can be used to represent arbitrary data. They are easy to scan with smartphones and so are convenient for sharing the long strings of characters used for Bitcoin addresses.

2. The QR code is just one of many ways to easily share a Bitcoin address. Another method is to use a *first bits* scheme in which you share only the first few characters of your Bitcoin address, which has been abbreviated by a Bitcoin address–shortening services (similar to a URL-shortening service). Starting with version 0.9 and later, Bitcoin also supports *human-readable* Bitcoin addresses that replace the traditional ones—much as a website address such as toys.com replaces the less user-friendly IP address of 123.100.101.111.

As you know, in traditional banking, moving money from one account to another means that the bank would update its privately held ledger that listed every account at that bank. If a fire or other disaster destroyed that ledger, information about who owned the assets at the bank might be lost forever. Although Bitcoin also uses a ledger, identical copies of it are distributed across millions of computers around the world. Consequently, no central point of failure exists, and transactions recorded on the Bitcoin ledger are permanent and impossible to erase. Moving bitcoins from one address to another is equivalent to sending an instruction to all of the computers on the Bitcoin network to update each ledger in the same way.

Because all transactions on the Bitcoin ledger are *public information,* maintaining privacy (if that is desired) can be a challenge. Although no personal information is on the ledger, if you share your Bitcoin address with your friends or post it in a public place that others can associate with your identity, your Bitcoin balance at that address will be known to everyone (including all incoming and outgoing transactions). To enhance your privacy, you can use many Bitcoin addresses but publicly share only some of them.[3]

So how do you move bitcoins from one address to another (i.e., spend them)? Well, this action requires a private key.

The Private Key

A *private key,* like a Bitcoin address, is a long string of numbers and letters (usually beginning with the number 5). As with Bitcoin addresses, QR codes are often used to represent private keys because of their length. Each private key is paired with a single Bitcoin address and is able to *unlock* the bitcoins at that address (i.e., move them elsewhere).[4] The following is an example of a private key:

```
5J2ae37Jwqzt7kSp9rE17Mi2LbkHXx4tzNSzbq7xDp2cQJCzhYo
```

Whereas a Bitcoin address is similar to a bank account number, a private key is more like a PIN: You need it to authorize a withdrawal or an expenditure. When a transaction is broadcast to the Bitcoin network, instructing bitcoins to be moved from one address to another, computers on the network check whether the transaction is authorized before making any updates to the public ledger. Specifically, they check whether the transaction has been *digitally signed* using a private key. A digital signature is extra data appended to a transaction that can only be created by

3. In general, maintaining complete privacy while doing online transactions is very difficult, with or without Bitcoin. Although the use of Bitcoin helps protect privacy when compared to using a credit card, it is not a complete solution. Other tools and precautions might need to be used as well (for example, using the online privacy-protecting TOR browser).

4. Although every private key is associated with a single Bitcoin address, the reverse is not always true. A Bitcoin address can require multiple private keys to unlock the bitcoins at that address (in this case, the Bitcoin address will begin with the number 3 instead of the usual 1). However, this advanced feature isn't used for most common transactions.

someone possessing the corresponding private key. Similar to a PIN, a private key should be kept secret. If someone obtains your private key, he will be able to spend your bitcoins.

Note that although a private key can be used to produce a digital signature, a digital signature cannot be used to obtain a private key. Digital signatures also cannot be reused to make new transactions; therefore, broadcasting a signed transaction to the Bitcoin network is not a risk. This action is fundamentally different from making an online payment with a credit card. When you use a credit card, you provide your credit card number to someone to authorize a transaction. That number can then be reused (maliciously) to authorize more transactions that you never intended.

Unlike a PIN, which both you and the bank know, *only you know the private key*. The risk you take in this circumstance is if you lose the private key to an address in which you've stored bitcoins, those bitcoins will remain locked in that address forever. Clearly, it is extremely important not to lose your private key! Fortunately, you can easily make digital backups of your private keys or write them on a piece of paper and keep them in a safe place. Losing your Bitcoin address is not a problem, however, as it can be recovered from the corresponding private key (Bitcoin wallet programs, described later in this chapter, can do this for you automatically).

Although it's possible to use Bitcoin with only a single address and private key, in practice most people use many addresses, each with its own private key, and store them in a digital wallet.

The Bitcoin Wallet

A *Bitcoin wallet* is a collection of addresses and private keys owned by one person. Having multiple Bitcoin addresses can help you organize your money. You may want separate addresses for paying rent, for shopping online, and for saving bitcoins to pay for a house in the future. So a person could have two bitcoins in his wallet that are distributed among many different Bitcoin addresses (see Figure 2-2).

Using multiple addresses, in the form of a wallet, also helps you maintain privacy. This is because the public ledger maintained by Bitcoin, which anyone can look at, has no way of knowing that any two addresses are in the same wallet and are owned by the same person (as long as that person hasn't done anything to show that the two addresses are linked, such as making a single purchase using bitcoins from both accounts).

To manage several addresses and private keys, people use Bitcoin *wallet programs*.[5] Whereas a Bitcoin wallet is an abstract concept, referring to a group of Bitcoin addresses, a wallet program is a concrete tool that helps users with common Bitcoin tasks, such as creating new Bitcoin addresses, sending bitcoins to others, backing up private keys, and many others. But be aware that the terminology surrounding Bitcoin wallets is not always

5. Also called *Bitcoin wallet clients.*

used consistently. Often, Bitcoin wallet programs are called *Bitcoin wallets* for short, confusing these two distinct concepts. When you save a Bitcoin wallet (perhaps to make a backup copy), you create a *wallet file*, which contains information for multiple Bitcoin addresses. Later, you can load your wallet files into a Bitcoin wallet program.

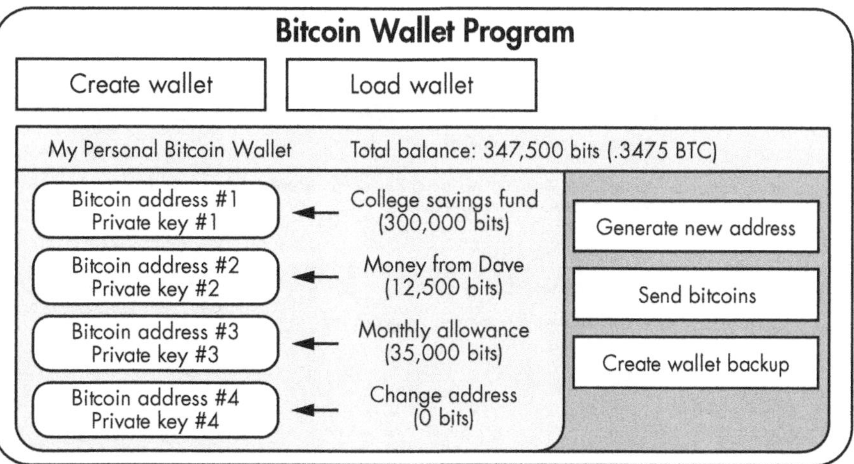

Figure 2-2: A Bitcoin wallet is an organized collection of addresses and their corresponding private keys. Bitcoin wallet programs exist to help perform common tasks like sending bitcoins and managing the bitcoins in your wallet.

Many Bitcoin wallet programs are available to choose from; most are free downloads and can be run on your laptop or phone, or even in your web browser. We'll explore the various Bitcoin wallet programs in Chapter 3, but in this chapter we'll use the Electrum wallet, which is open source, cross platform, and very simple to use.

GETTING SOME "STARTER MONEY" TO LEARN ABOUT BITCOIN

You'll need a small amount of Bitcoin (less than $1 USD) to work through this chapter. If you have a friend who's a bitcoiner, consider asking her to give you a little change to use for practice. Otherwise, go to *http://newbiecoins.com/*, which is a site we (the authors) will maintain as a public service and which will list other sites that are giving away small amounts of free Bitcoin. There are usually *some* reputable sites giving out coins for newbies, but the situation for such giveaways is fluid, with sites going up or down daily, so we can't cover specific ones in this book.

Creating Your First Bitcoin Wallet with Electrum

To follow along in this section, download and install Electrum (*http://electrum.org/*). If you choose to use a different Bitcoin wallet program, most of the instructions on the following pages should apply to it as well.

When you run Electrum the first time, you'll be asked to create a new wallet (or restore an old wallet, which we'll ignore for now), as shown in Figure 2-3.

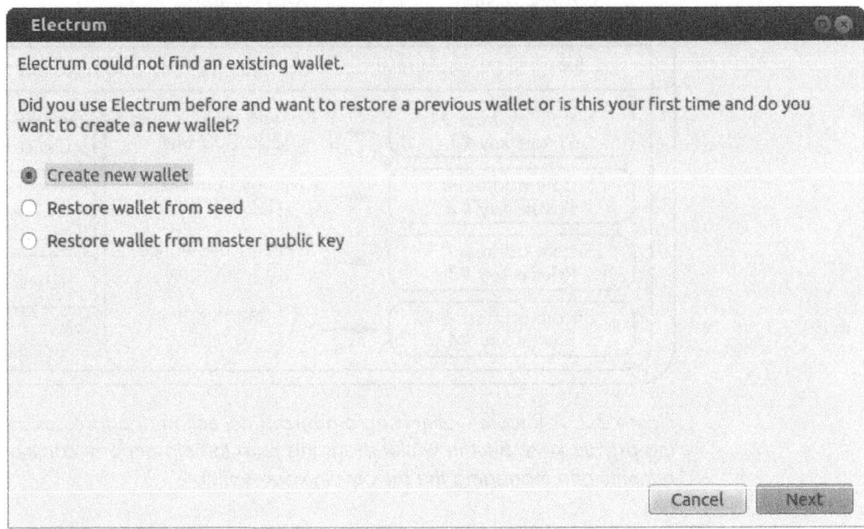

Figure 2-3: Creating a new Bitcoin wallet with Electrum

The next step is specific to Electrum; that is, it is not a standard feature of most Bitcoin wallet programs. The application presents you with a *seed*, which consists of 12 randomly chosen words, and asks you to write them down (see Figure 2-4). Electrum uses this seed to create your Bitcoin addresses and private keys; therefore, the seed must be kept secret, similar to your private keys. Because we'll be dealing with only small amounts of bitcoins in this chapter, you don't need to be too careful just yet. However, you should start keeping these security details in mind. A major benefit of a seed is that if you lose your computer (say, in a fire or theft), everything—your wallet, your Bitcoin address, your private keys, and (most importantly) your money—can be recovered from the seed.

The next step gives you the option of creating a password. Although the password is optional, it is very important. If your computer is stolen or somehow falls into the wrong hands, the password prevents others from spending your bitcoins. Because Electrum (and other Bitcoin wallet programs) uses the password to store your Bitcoin wallet on your computer in an encrypted form, the wallet is useless without the password. With many other Bitcoin wallet programs if you forget your password, you could permanently lose access to your wallet. But with Electrum, you can restore the wallet from your seed (without needing the password).

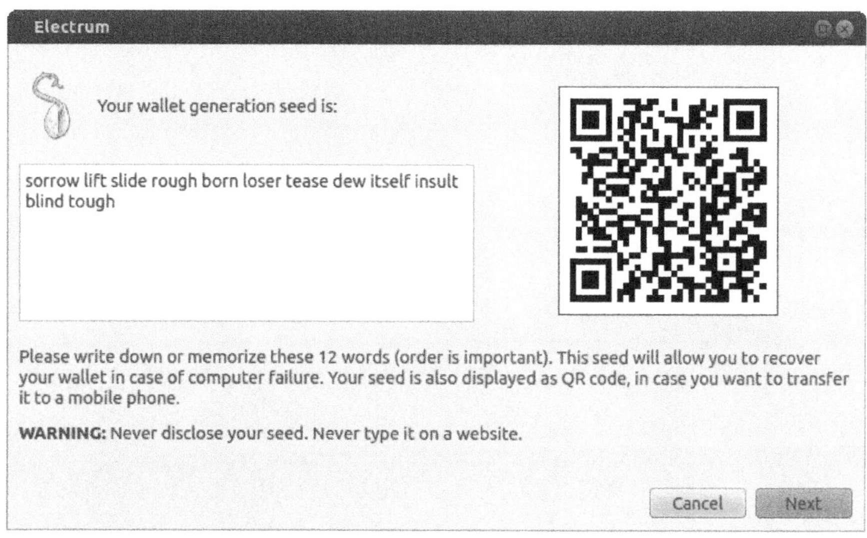

Figure 2-4: Electrum presents you with a seed.

In the final step, Electrum requests instructions on how to connect to a remote server. Select **Auto connect** and then click **Next** (see Figure 2-5).

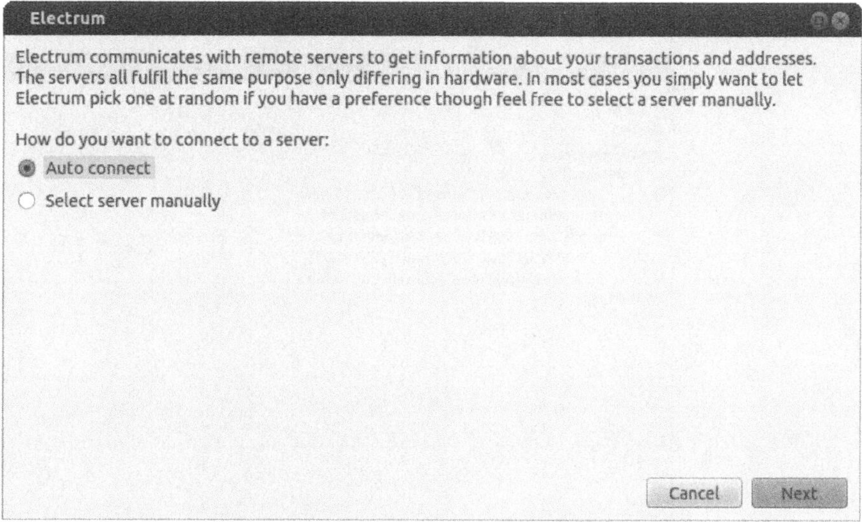

Figure 2-5: Selecting your server connection

You should see a screen similar to the one in Figure 2-6. The green dot in the bottom-right corner indicates that you are connected to the Bitcoin network. Congratulations! You've just set up your first Bitcoin wallet! Now you can fill the wallet with bitcoins.

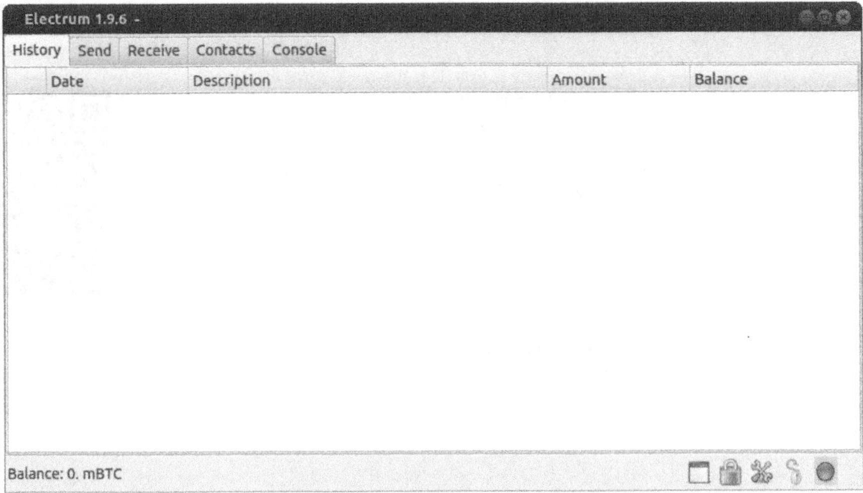

Figure 2-6: Here is your first Bitcoin wallet!

Acquiring Bitcoins in Your Wallet

On the Receive tab (see Figure 2-7), you should see a list of several Bitcoin-receiving addresses.

Electrum 1.9.6 -
History Send Receive Contacts Console

Address	Label	Balance	Tx
▾ Main account		0.	
▾ Receiving			
1PxXxv6L8JaDKWs3dAkj3XUf6SYL15vhwz		0.	0
1EHQsMJWj2CHPYyzNbPqBs9rRBephQmMqW		0.	0
1Bd2iBWBbiSmQ1UbPZP4587ywBdUScAtrC		0.	0
1sPWNNhZWeygyCnEdgyjwkuQg5UTP5cni		0.	0
1JUZeu46RUBbR56oaTbgzAXHu9oUjU2uq5		0.	0
▸ Change			

Balance: 0. mBTC

Figure 2-7: The Receive tab

You can share these addresses with your friends so they can send you some starting bitcoins—one way to acquire bitcoins! At this point, if you want to put significant money into bitcoins, refer to Chapter 4 where we discuss how to do this in detail (but be sure to first read Chapter 3, for security reasons).

To get a small quantity of bitcoins into your wallet—whether from a friend or from a site listed on *http://newbiecoins.com/*—you'll have to give that friend or website one of your public Bitcoin addresses. At the time of this writing, a small amount of Bitcoin for testing would be about 0.5 millibitcoin (mBTC). If at the time you are reading, 0.5 mBTC is a lot of money, then feel free to use a smaller amount. A few minutes after your friend (or the site) sends these coins, you should see a balance of 0.5 mBTC in your Electrum wallet. (Actually, your balance will usually update instantaneously.) Well done! You now own bitcoins, which enables you to look into your future! How? Read on.

NOTE *Importing private Bitcoin keys into a wallet can be hazardous. You should only import money using private keys when small sums of money are involved, and never use this method as part of a strategy for managing larger sums of money unless you're an advanced bitcoiner. The comic at the end of this chapter illustrates why working with raw private Bitcoin keys can be very dangerous.*

Spending Bitcoins with Your Wallet

Although thousands of merchants now accept bitcoins, you can't buy much with 0.5 mBTC. You'll need to scour the Internet for good deals!

Alternatively, for the deal of the century, you can have your fortune read online for the low, low price of 0.1 mBTC.

Visit *http://befuddled.org/* to access our fortune-telling website, which we've linked directly to a crystal ball. When you send 0.1 mBTC to the server's Bitcoin address, the server transmits a *fortune request* to the crystal ball, and it predicts your future.

To get your fortune, use Electrum's Send function and paste the website's Bitcoin address into the *Pay to* field. In the *Amount* field, specify **0.1 mBTC** (if your units are set to BTC, enter 0.0001; change the default units by choosing Tools ▸Preferences ▸Base Unit). Bitcoin transactions also require a fee. In the *Fee* field, enter **0.1 mBTC** as well (this amount may be more than is necessary, but let's not worry about that for now). Your screen should look something like Figure 2-8.

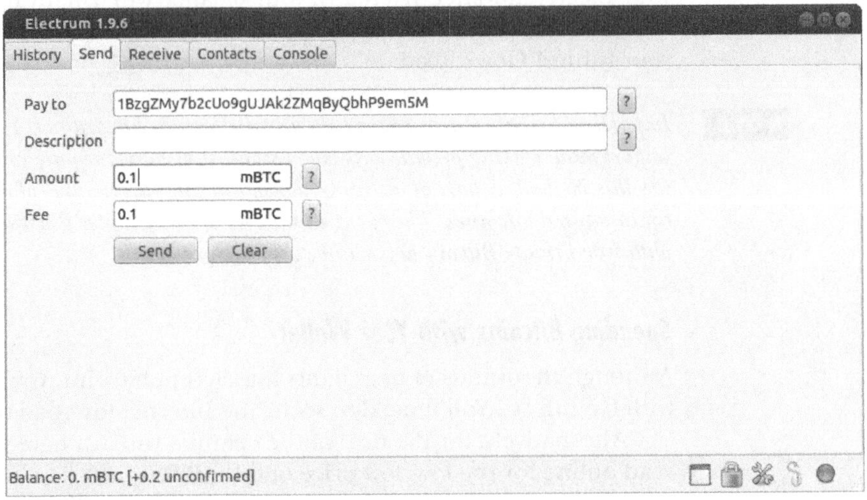

Figure 2-8: Sending bitcoins through Electrum

When you click **Send**, Electrum asks for your password and then confirms that the transaction has been transmitted. Almost immediately, you should see your fortune on the website. Welcome to the future! You've just made your first Bitcoin transaction!

Electrum's History section shows you the transactions you've made in the past. Transactions that display the word *pending* are not yet recorded on the Bitcoin public ledger (which typically occurs about 10 minutes after a transaction is sent).

If you're not interested in your fortune but want to practice sending bitcoins, you'll be pleased to know that many charities and nonprofit organizations now accept bitcoins. Some provide food for the homeless, defend online privacy rights, and support open source software (including Bitcoin). By searching online, you'll find numerous nonprofit organizations that have posted a Bitcoin address. We recommend giving your free millibitcoins to Sean's Outpost, a charity that feeds the homeless in Pensacola, Florida (its donation Bitcoin address can be found on its website, *http://seansoutpost.com/*). Unlike with the fortune-telling website, you might not receive a response from the website when you donate. But rest assured that the recipients have accepted your bitcoins if Electrum's History section displays the word *confirmed*. (Sometimes the confirmation status is indicated by a small dial icon or more than one confirmation is given for the transaction.)

You might be wondering how and where Electrum got a Bitcoin address. The answer is your Bitcoin wallet program.

Bitcoin Addresses Generated by Your Bitcoin Wallet Program

When you run a Bitcoin wallet program, it can generate a new Bitcoin address for you offline. No communication with the Bitcoin network is necessary, an unusual feature that surprises many people. With other addresses or numbers, for example, when you create a new email address, you must first find out whether the address is being used by someone else. The same is true when get a new phone number or when you open an account at a bank. However, when you want a new Bitcoin address, one is chosen at random from all of the possible Bitcoin addresses. What are the odds that a Bitcoin address randomly generated for you will be the same as one generated by someone else? We'll use an analogy: Consider all the grains of sand on Earth—from all the beaches and deserts. When you choose a single grain at random to be yours and another person chooses a grain of sand at random to be his, the odds that both of you would choose the same grain of sand would be over a trillion times more likely than the odds that you both generate the same Bitcoin address.[6]

While you can create Bitcoin addresses offline, you must be online to see how much money is in your addresses or to send money to others. That's because these additional actions require you to access the public ledger of Bitcoin, which we'll discuss next.

The Blockchain

All Bitcoin transactions are recorded into the *blockchain*. Throughout the remainder of this book, we'll refer to the Bitcoin ledger as the blockchain. The reason for its name is that new transactions are appended to the ledger in large chunks, or *blocks*. Whenever a new Bitcoin transaction is broadcast to the network, computers on the network add it to a growing pool of other new transactions. Then, about every 10 minutes, the transactions in that pool are bundled into a block and added to the blockchain (see Figure 2-9). To function properly, all Bitcoin wallet programs need access to an up-to-date copy of the blockchain, and every time a block is added, the wallet programs copy and add the block to their own blockchain.

---

6. Odds of a trillion times more likely are still a dramatic understatement. The possible value of Bitcoin addresses is 2^{160} ($\sim 10^{48}$), and the number of grains of sand on Earth is approximately 10^{19}.

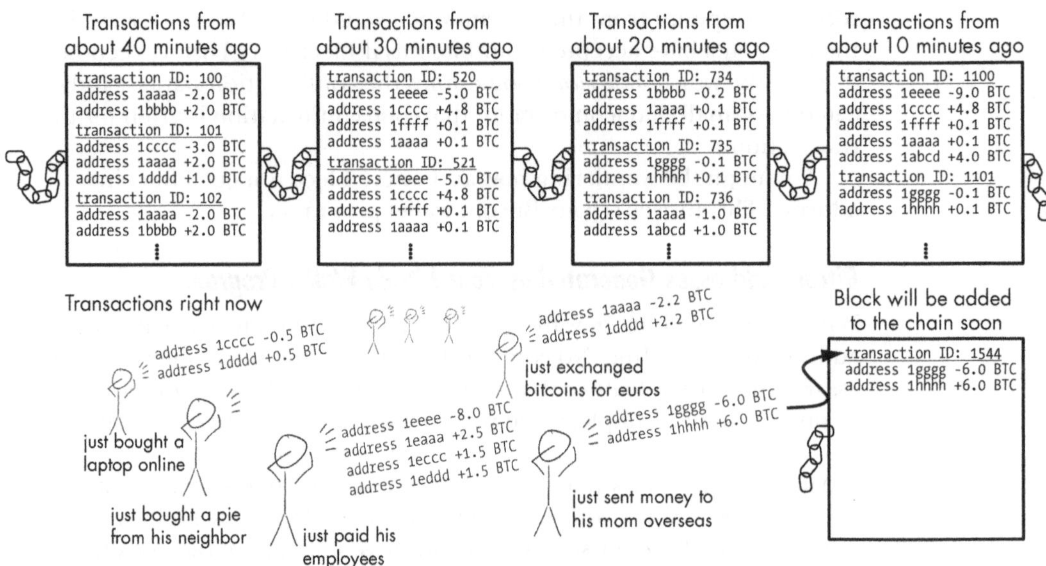

Figure 2-9: Bitcoin transactions are grouped into blocks that are added to the blockchain every 10 minutes.

The thousands of computers on the Bitcoin network that collect transactions and add them to the blockchain are called *miners*. We'll explain miners and the details of what they do later in the chapter. For now, keep in mind that anyone can be a miner (including you) by running open source Bitcoin-mining software on a computer that is connected to the Bitcoin network. At any given moment, tens of thousands of miners are connected to the Bitcoin network. All volunteer their computers for the purpose of adding new transactions to the blockchain (we'll explain why they do this in a moment).

Every block added to the blockchain is added by a *single* miner on the network. Then everyone else on the Bitcoin network follows suit and updates their own copy of the blockchain (this includes other miners and Bitcoin wallet programs). Why does only one miner add a block, and how is it decided which of the thousands of miners it is? This is where Bitcoin gets interesting—and a little technical.

Let's first consider why anyone would want to update the blockchain. Certainly, if you wanted to complete transactions, your Bitcoin wallet program would need the latest copy of the blockchain. However, you might not want to send or receive bitcoins for months, so why bother updating your copy of the blockchain in the meantime? For the Bitcoin system to work, many people need to keep up-to-date copies of the blockchain. The reason is that if only one person had the latest copy, she could manipulate the number of bitcoins people had on record. Therefore, good will alone isn't sufficient to keep the system running. But the lure of a reward is always an attraction.

The Blockchain Lottery

As an incentive for users to update the blockchain as frequently as possible, Bitcoin uses a lottery-based reward system. Many people become miners and try to be the *first* to add a block to the blockchain. Then, based on some probability, a winner is chosen and gets to add a block.

What is the purpose of using a lottery like this to run Bitcoin? Well, let's imagine Crowley wants to buy a $10,000 car from Clarice. (You'll learn more about our friend Crowley the Crocodile in the comic in Chapter 5.) Using traditional currency, two people engaging in this transaction would probably go to a bank and have the money transferred between their bank accounts (or use a cashier's check, which is analogous to this; see Figure 2-10).

Figure 2-10: Crowley sending $10,000 to Clarice through a traditional bank

They would do this at a bank because they need a trusted third party (a "banker") that manages a "money ledger" and moves the money on the ledger from one person's account to another. The banker's job is to make an announcement that Crowley and Clarice can trust; that is, to affirm that the ledger has been updated correctly. (The banker may or may not be sporting a monocle, wearing a top hat, and smoking a cigar.)

With Bitcoin, we also need a person to adjust a ledger, which in this case means adjusting the blockchain by adding a block to it. It turns out anyone can fill this role, as long as he is not connected with either party in the transaction, because that could lead to a conflict of interest. Picking a person randomly through a lottery helps accomplish this. So with Bitcoin, a lottery picks a random miner, who then announces to the network that certain Bitcoin transactions are valid (see Figure 2-11).

Of course, there's always a small chance this miner *does* know one of the persons involved in a recent transaction. This is why blocks are arranged in a chain: In roughly 10 minutes, when the next lottery winner is announced, this winner also confirms, as part of her announcement, that she agrees with all the transactions of the previous lottery winner (see Figure 2-12).

Figure 2-11: A random person running Bitcoin-mining software is chosen to confirm Bitcoin transactions.

In the process, each winner in the Bitcoin-mining lottery receives a reward, which is a certain amount of bitcoins. The reward includes all of the transaction fees for the transactions in that block, which motivates miners to collect as many transactions into a block as possible, increasing their reward. To be eligible for the reward from the next block, which is added 10 minutes later, a miner needs to have the latest copy of the blockchain to participate in the next round. This process is done automatically by open source Bitcoin-mining software that runs on computers controlled by the people involved in mining. Because of this incentive structure, thousands of miners constantly help process the transactions of Bitcoin users, making sure that the blockchain is always up-to-date.

The reward lottery is run by the community; no central authority exists to choose a winner. We'll skip the technical details for now (they're covered in Chapter 8) and just say that miners generate random numbers continuously, until they find a winning one. This takes about ten minutes. The community then verifies (also through cryptography) that the number found by the individual miner is the winner, and the miner adds a new block to the blockchain and collects the reward. When this happens, the phrase commonly used is that a miner has *found a block.*

Figure 2-12: With Bitcoin, each lottery winner confirms not only her own block of transactions, but also all the preceding blocks (that she considers to be valid).

Blockchain Forking

The lottery system works as expected most of the time. But occasionally two miners find a block at the same time, and the blockchain becomes *forked*, resulting in two different branches (see Figure 2-13).

Consider the following scenario as an example: Imagine that Crowley and Satoshi are miners and find the winning number within seconds of each other. If they are located far apart on the Bitcoin network (say, on opposite sides of Earth), one part of the network will identify Crowley as the winner and another part will identify Satoshi as the winner. In this case, Crowley and Satoshi will each add a block to the blockchain (each thinking that he is the winning miner for that round). The problem occurs when one part of the network copies Crowley's block and the other copies Satoshi's. As a result, now two blockchains disagree!

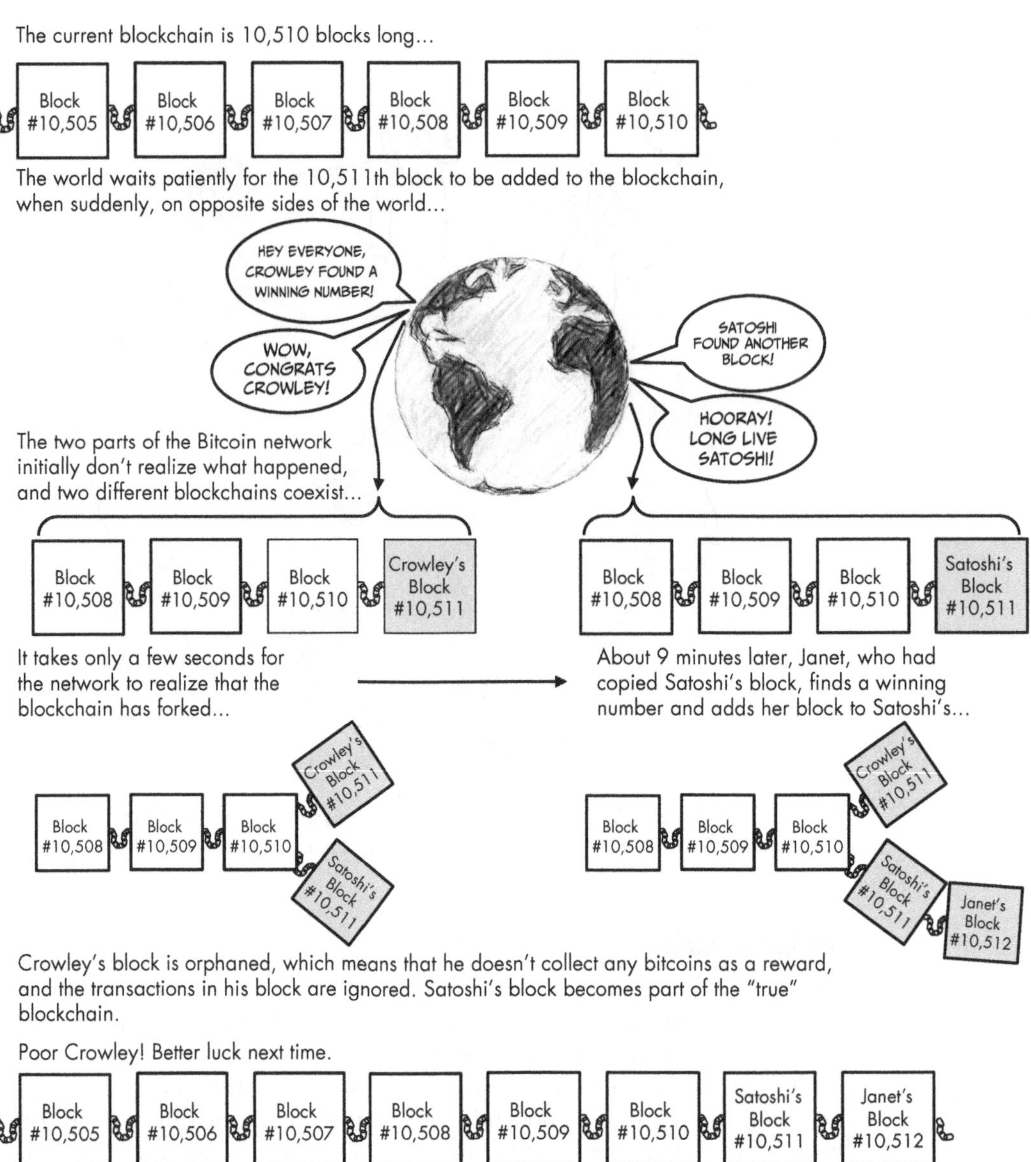
The current blockchain is 10,510 blocks long...
Block #10,505
Block #10,506
Block #10,507
Block #10,508
Block #10,509
Block #10,510
The world waits patiently for the 10,511th block to be added to the blockchain, when suddenly, on opposite sides of the world...
HEY EVERYONE, CROWLEY FOUND A WINNING NUMBER!
WOW, CONGRATS CROWLEY!
SATOSHI FOUND ANOTHER BLOCK!
HOORAY! LONG LIVE SATOSHI!
The two parts of the Bitcoin network initially don't realize what happened, and two different blockchains coexist...
Block #10,508
Block #10,509
Block #10,510
Crowley's Block #10,511
Block #10,508
Block #10,509
Block #10,510
Satoshi's Block #10,511
It takes only a few seconds for the network to realize that the blockchain has forked...
About 9 minutes later, Janet, who had copied Satoshi's block, finds a winning number and adds her block to Satoshi's...
Block #10,508
Block #10,509
Block #10,510
Crowley's Block #10,511
Satoshi's Block #10,511
Block #10,508
Block #10,509
Block #10,510
Crowley's Block #10,511
Satoshi's Block #10,511
Janet's Block #10,512
Crowley's block is orphaned, which means that he doesn't collect any bitcoins as a reward, and the transactions in his block are ignored. Satoshi's block becomes part of the "true" blockchain.
Poor Crowley! Better luck next time.
Block #10,505
Block #10,506
Block #10,507
Block #10,508
Block #10,509
Block #10,510
Satoshi's Block #10,511
Janet's Block #10,512

Figure 2-13: Bitcoin miners Crowley and Satoshi find a block at the same time, creating two copies of the blockchain. The resolution to the forked blockchain occurs when Satoshi's version of the blockchain adds another block before Crowley's, and Satoshi receives the reward.

Recall that your Bitcoin wallet program needs an up-to-date copy of the blockchain to function, but it doesn't know how to resolve a forked blockchain. Miners and Bitcoin wallet programs must decide which of the two versions of the blockchain to use. Forking is resolved by waiting to see which of the two branches adds yet another block first, which will happen about 10 minutes later. Then the longer branch will be considered the *true* blockchain, and the shorter branch will be ignored, or *orphaned*, by the entire Bitcoin network.

For most users, the process of forking and ignoring orphaned blocks goes completely unnoticed and has no negative impact on the use of Bitcoin. In our example, only the losing miner, Crowley, experiences a considerable impact because only one of the two miners involved can receive the reward. The losing miner is undoubtedly disappointed, but miners expect this to happen from time to time, so it comes as no surprise when it does.

Transaction Confirmations, Double Spending, and Irreversibility

A *transaction confirmation* is a common concept in Bitcoin. Some online merchants that accept bitcoins may require one or more transaction confirmations before delivering their good or service. Every transaction exists in some block on the blockchain. The blocks behind it are older, and the blocks ahead of it are newer. The position of a block relative to the tip of the blockchain is known as the *block depth.* The most recently added block has a depth of 1, the block behind it has a depth of 2, and so on. The number of confirmations a transaction has is equal to the depth of its block. So a transaction that has not been added to the blockchain (yet) has zero confirmations; it has one confirmation when it is added in a new block; it has two confirmations when a block is added ahead of it; and so on. The concept is simple enough, but why do merchants require transaction confirmations?

For low-value transactions, such as buying a cup of coffee, merchants normally forgo the transaction confirmation. You just send your bitcoins, grab your coffee, and go on your way. In general, Bitcoin transactions are irreversible, and merchants know within a few seconds after you click Send that you've paid for your drink (or whatever you're buying). However, if a merchant sells a high-priced item, such as a car, it becomes critical to consider transaction confirmations.

A malicious user with very significant computational resources (think of a James Bond–style supervillain) can try to *double spend* his bitcoins, which is essentially an attempt to trick the receiver into accepting bitcoins that were simultaneously sent to someone else as well (the "someone else" could be another Bitcoin address controlled by the supervillain). When miners on the Bitcoin network detect two transactions that spent the same bitcoins (but were sent to different addresses), they usually accept whichever one they received first and ignore the second. More important, it's impossible for both transactions to be added to a block because one contradicts the other. The supervillain's intent is for the merchant to ship the car but have the transaction be ignored and not added to the blockchain.

Fortunately, this devious scheme is usually unsuccessful because many merchants use special monitoring software and can recognize when two conflicting Bitcoin transactions are broadcast at the same time (at which point the supervillain may be kicked out of the car dealership). An even simpler solution for merchants to prevent this kind of payment fraud is to wait 10 minutes until the transaction has at least one confirmation before agreeing to ship the car. However, if a supervillain possesses truly extraordinary resources, such as many millions of dollars of computer hardware, he can attempt to make the Bitcoin network orphan the newest block in the blockchain, resulting in a single transaction confirmation being ignored. To cope with this remote possibility, merchants who sell high-end goods typically wait until a transaction has two confirmations before handing over the keys to the buyer. In general, the higher the value of the item being transacted, the more confirmations a merchant can demand before considering the transaction to be settled. The cost for a malicious villain to double spend those bitcoins rises exponentially with each confirmation.

Now that you know the basic function and concepts of the Bitcoin blockchain, you'll learn about mining bitcoins, which is perhaps the most mysterious aspect of Bitcoin.

Mining Bitcoins

Bitcoin mining is the competitive process of collecting transactions and adding them to the blockchain in the form of blocks. Why is it called mining? The term is derived from how bitcoins are initially distributed. Although the total supply of bitcoins is capped at 21 million, this total is reached slowly over time. In the beginning, the initial supply of bitcoins was zero. Bitcoin miners receive a reward for processing other people's transactions; each reward is a small sum of *newly minted* bitcoins that increases the total supply in circulation. In this sense, Bitcoin mining is similar to gold mining: Earth has a fixed amount of gold, and miners slowly dig it out over time.

As mentioned earlier, miners must find a certain winning number by generating numbers at random repeatedly to win these newly minted bitcoins. Because fast computers can generate these random numbers more rapidly, this creates an incentive for miners to use increasingly powerful computers to mine bitcoins. In the very early stages of Bitcoin, personal computers were commonly used to generate random numbers, but soon people started building special-purpose computers designed solely for Bitcoin mining. Today, mining bitcoins requires significant capital, expertise, and access to inexpensive electricity. In fact, the evolution of Bitcoin mining resembles the way gold mining has changed over times. At one time unearthing gold could be done by a person panning in a riverbed, but now excavation is performed by large companies with expensive drills.

The mining reward for finding a block has two components: The first part is transaction fees. When you send bitcoins to someone, a small amount of additional bitcoins is added as a transaction fee.[7] Transaction fees are typically a few cents and are part of the reward that miners receive when they win the lottery and add a new block to the blockchain. Because a block is a collection of hundreds or thousands of transactions, the miner's reward is the sum of all the transaction fees in that new block. The second component of the reward is a certain number of newly minted bitcoins.

The number of newly minted bitcoins that is provided as a reward diminishes gradually over time. The first 210,000 blocks—which based

7. Strictly speaking, this transaction fee is voluntary, but miners may ignore transactions that have no attached fees.

on a 10-minute spacing took about 4 years to mine—provided every winning miner with 50 newly minted bitcoins per block in addition to the transaction fees. The next 210,000 blocks (blocks (210,001 through 420,000) reward miners with only 25 newly minted bitcoins per block. Thereafter, the reward drops to 12.5, then 6.725, and so on. Because this mining process is the *only* source of new bitcoins, it is the reason no more than 21 million bitcoins will ever be in circulation.

Although every four years the number of newly minted bitcoins rewarded per block halves, the transaction fees per block will continue to grow as the Bitcoin user base grows. Eventually, the user transaction fees will be greater than the reward of newly minted bitcoins. At that point, the Bitcoin network will be sustained entirely through transaction fees.

The Complexity of the Bitcoin System

Most of us are used to using centralized payment services (e.g., PayPal, credit cards). We place our trust in the companies that run those services and don't need to know how the payment system works. But Bitcoin doesn't have a company to trust; instead, we can examine the system to decide whether or not we trust it.

If you investigated the system major credit card companies use to facilitate payments, you might be surprised by how complicated it is. Because we don't normally think about how digital payment systems work, it is not unusual that the Bitcoin system is befuddling and complicated to most. After reading this chapter, you should have a fairly good idea of how the entire system works. In later chapters, we'll delve further into certain details, such as the specific hardware and programs that Bitcoin miners use; however, the overall explanation of the Bitcoin system will not change from how it is described in this chapter. From this point on, we can focus on acquiring bitcoins and thinking about how they'll impact our global economy!

FOR THE MOST PART, WORKING WITH BITCOIN WALLETS IS PRETTY FOOLPROOF. HOWEVER, THERE IS ONE SCENARIO YOU NEED TO KNOW ABOUT THAT CAN CAUSE YOU TO LOSE ALL YOUR MONEY...

DO NOT DO THIS:

STEP 1

YAY! I HAVE CREATED MY FIRST BITCOIN WALLET!

STEP 2

AHH! THERE'S MY BITCOIN ADDRESS! LET ME WRITE DOWN MY ADDRESS AND PRIVATE KEY!

STEP 3

STEP 4

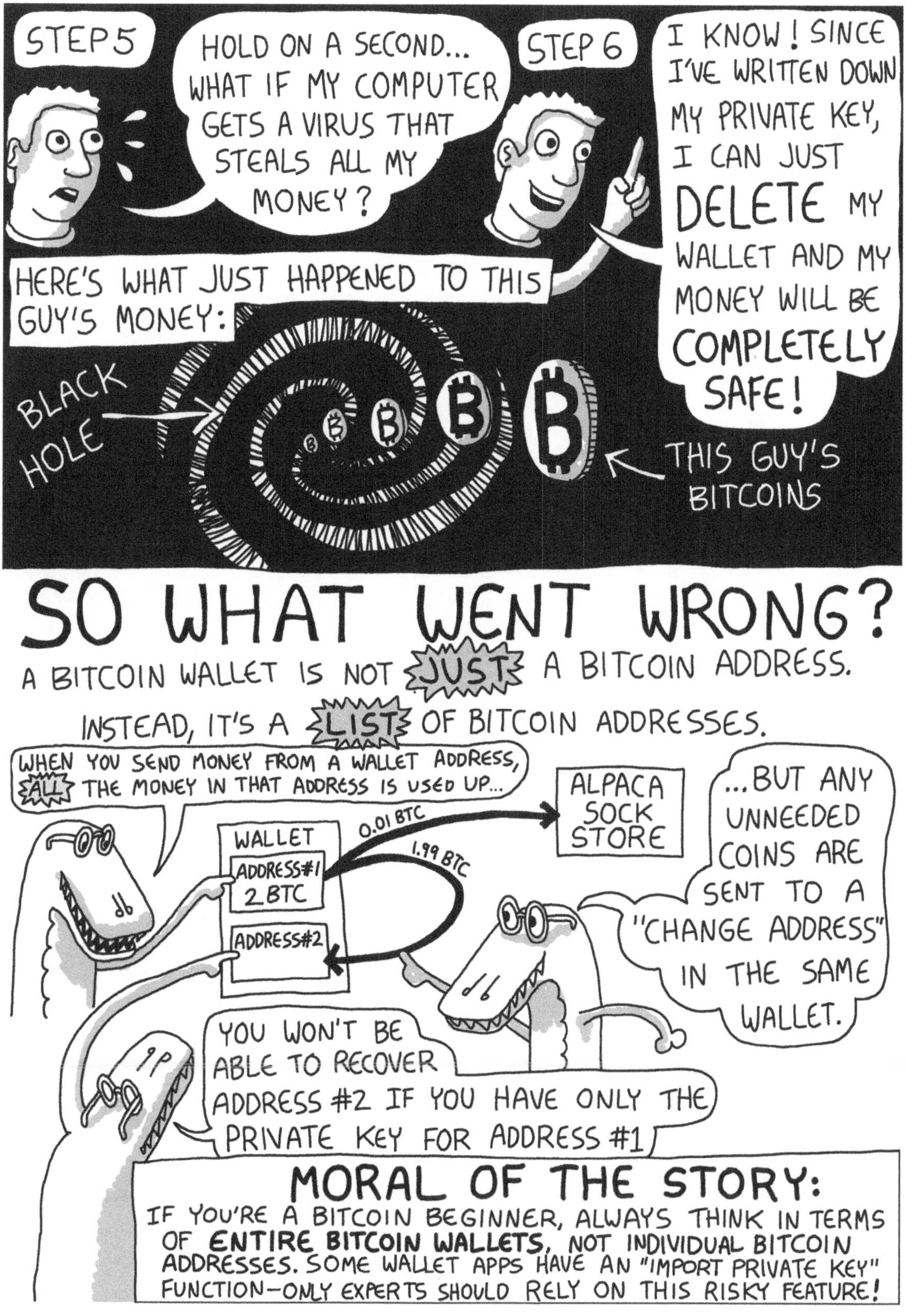

STEP 5

HOLD ON A SECOND... WHAT IF MY COMPUTER GETS A VIRUS THAT STEALS ALL MY MONEY?

STEP 6

I KNOW! SINCE I'VE WRITTEN DOWN MY PRIVATE KEY, I CAN JUST **DELETE** MY WALLET AND MY MONEY WILL BE **COMPLETELY SAFE!**

HERE'S WHAT JUST HAPPENED TO THIS GUY'S MONEY:

BLACK HOLE

THIS GUY'S BITCOINS

SO WHAT WENT WRONG?

A BITCOIN WALLET IS NOT **JUST** A BITCOIN ADDRESS.

INSTEAD, IT'S A **LIST** OF BITCOIN ADDRESSES.

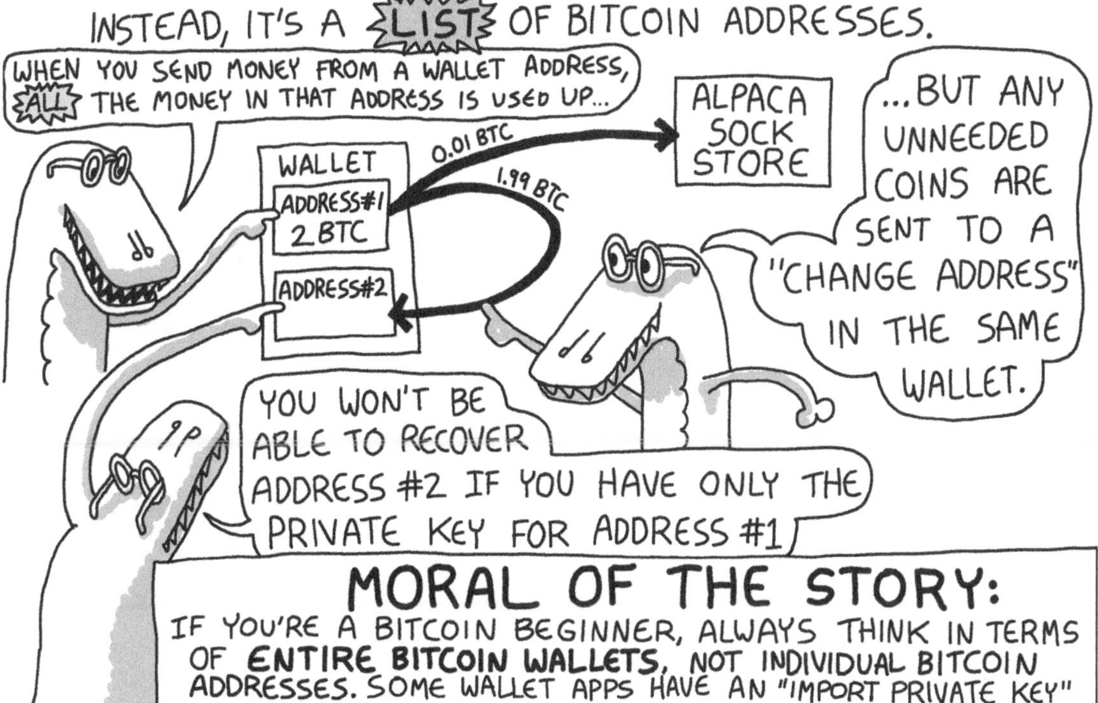

MORAL OF THE STORY:

IF YOU'RE A BITCOIN BEGINNER, ALWAYS THINK IN TERMS OF **ENTIRE BITCOIN WALLETS**, NOT INDIVIDUAL BITCOIN ADDRESSES. SOME WALLET APPS HAVE AN "IMPORT PRIVATE KEY" FUNCTION—ONLY EXPERTS SHOULD RELY ON THIS RISKY FEATURE!

3

STORING YOUR BITCOINS SAFELY, SECURELY, AND CONVENIENTLY

Unfortunately, nothing can be protected against loss with 100 percent certainty, but when done correctly, bitcoins can be stored *extremely* safely and securely, perhaps more so than any other financial asset. Stored incorrectly, however, bitcoins are vulnerable to loss due to technical failures (e.g., a computer or hard drive failure) or everyday disasters, and they can be an easy target for thieves as well. So before you purchase a significant amount of bitcoins, you need to learn how to—and how *not* to—store them.

In this chapter, we'll explain various methods of storing bitcoins and comment on their appropriateness for different use cases. Some storage methods are more secure than others but are less convenient. Once you are comfortable with the methods and concepts discussed in this chapter, you'll be prepared to handle bitcoins in any quantity.

1880
SAVINGS
SPENDING CASH
1980
SAVINGS
ATM
SPENDING CASH
MAX HEADROOM
2020
SAVINGS ON DEDICATED BITCOIN PC
SPENDING CASH

Storing Your Private Key(s)

Where *are* your bitcoins stored? It's a surprisingly tricky question. You must know that (1) the *amount* of bitcoins in your account is recorded on the blockchain, and (2) to *access* those bitcoins, you need to use a private key. The blockchain may be stored in a different location than your private key, and because both are necessary to use your bitcoins, it would seem at first that it is difficult to say exactly *where* your bitcoins are stored. But millions of identical copies of the blockchain are distributed all over the world, and because no disaster will ever erase every copy of the blockchain, you don't need to worry about how and where it is stored. Instead, you should focus on your private key. You (and only you) know your private key, so wherever you store this key is *where your bitcoins are*. Consequently, storing your bitcoins really means storing your private key. If you use a Bitcoin wallet, which is a collection of addresses and private keys, your bitcoins are stored wherever you store that collection (usually on a computer, phone, or portable USB drive in a *wallet file*).

The remainder of this chapter explains the challenge of storing your private key (or collection of private keys) in a way that prevents accidental loss and theft. Bitcoin allows you to *be your own bank*. But being your own bank comes with great responsibility and requires you to take serious security precautions. Alternatively, you can trust a third-party service provider to be your Bitcoin bank, in which case you won't need to worry about security directly; instead, you'll need to trust your service provider to keep your bitcoins safe. Fortunately, storing bitcoins securely is easy, even for beginners (see "Paper Wallets" on page 39).

Hot Storage vs. Cold Storage

Bitcoin storage methods are often distinguished by whether they are hot or cold, depending on whether or not the private keys are stored on Internet-connected devices. *Hot storage* refers to private keys that are stored on an online device or computer. *Cold storage* refers to private keys that are not accessible via the Internet. For example, if you use an offline computer to generate a Bitcoin address and its corresponding private key, any bitcoins sent to that address are in cold storage. But how can others send you bitcoins if your address was generated on an offline computer? Well, you share it with them! You can safely copy your public Bitcoin address and post it on a website (or email it to all your friends). However, the private key exists only on the offline computer where it was generated and remains confidential.

Because sending bitcoins requires a private key and an Internet connection, hot wallets are more convenient to use, but cold storage methods are more secure and better suited for long-term bitcoin storage. Note that a hot wallet cannot become cold by going offline.[1] Once a private key has been exposed to the Internet, it is unsafe to assume that it will provide the same protection as one that was never exposed.

---

1. Bitcoin wallets are perfect thermal insulators.

Sometimes, companies may advertise that they store their clients' Bitcoin funds in cold storage as a security feature but will simultaneously claim that those funds can be conveniently moved to a hot wallet automatically. This is a red flag. If any company states that it has an *automated process* for transferring funds from cold to hot wallets, most likely *none* of its funds are stored in cold storage. Cold storage requires a person to physically access an offline computer and *manually* authorize a Bitcoin transaction. You'll learn how to do this in "Storing Large Amounts of Bitcoins" on page 38.

Personal vs. Hosted Wallets

Many companies offer Bitcoin wallet services and programs to help you store your bitcoins. To the uninitiated, it isn't always clear whether these companies offer a personal wallet or a hosted wallet. With a *personal wallet*, you and only you know the private keys. The company that created the software does not control your bitcoins. Alternatively, with a *hosted wallet*, a third party knows your private keys and doesn't reveal them to you, but the company will send, receive, and store bitcoins on your behalf (not unlike a traditional bank, which stores your cash in a vault and won't give you the keys to open it). Some companies also offer *software as a service*. In this case, they host the wallet software on their servers but not the private keys. Users can log in, send and receive bitcoins, and monitor Bitcoin transactions using their own private keys (which the company never receives). We refer to such services as *online personal wallets* because the private keys are not hosted.

With both wallet types, the user interfaces may look and function in similar ways, but the ramifications of using one kind of wallet versus the other are quite different. In particular, the question of who is liable if bitcoins are stolen may be determined by who had access to the private keys. If you're in doubt, ask whether you have access to the private keys.

NOTE *The liability distinction can become blurred if multiple private keys are used to control the same bitcoins. A few online services require two private keys to spend the same bitcoins, one held by the company and the other by the customer. Assigning liability can be trickier in these cases (although as you'll see later in "Fragmented Private Keys and Multi-Signature Addresses" on page 41, using multiple private keys to store bitcoins is typically a good idea).*

The benefits of using a hosted wallet are that it is user-friendly and you don't have to worry *directly* about Bitcoin storage security. However, the hosting company must be both *trustworthy* and *competent* in that it will not maliciously run away with your bitcoins or let thieves steal them. Another detail to consider is that government or law enforcement officials can ask a hosting company to hand over your bitcoins. The company might oblige this demand, even if you would have disputed the request.

Although hosted wallets may be a popular choice for many future Bitcoin users due to their user-friendliness, we'll focus on personal wallets. Even if you decide to use a hosted wallet and let someone else manage the safety and security details, this chapter will help you make an informed decision when you're choosing hosted wallet service providers.

Safety, Security, and Convenience

Consider three major factors when you're comparing storage methods:

1. Safety (preventing the accidental loss of bitcoins)
2. Security (preventing the theft of bitcoins)
3. Convenience (ability to easily and quickly spend your bitcoins)

These factors can sometimes conflict with each other. Methods that make it convenient for *you* to spend your bitcoins are probably inadvertently making it easier for a *thief* to spend them as well. Similarly, making many copies of your private key and giving them to friends and family for safekeeping is a good strategy to prevent accidental loss; however, this strategy also makes it more likely that your private key will fall into the wrong hands. Combining safety, security, and convenience into one storage method is an area of constant innovation, and some newer methods have demonstrated an excellent balance of all three (see "Special Mention: The Bitcoin Hardware Wallet" on page 42).

Most people use two storage methods: one for storing small amounts of bitcoins conveniently but less securely and another for storing large amounts less conveniently but very securely. As Crowley the Crocodile illustrates in the comic at the start of this chapter, this is similar to having a small amount of cash in your pocket but keeping most of your money in a traditional bank account.

In the following sections, we've grouped storage approaches into two categories:

- Methods for small amounts of bitcoins that are convenient, easy to use, and *reasonably* safe
- Methods for long-term storage of large amounts of bitcoins that are extremely safe and secure (but not as convenient)

Storing Small Amounts of Bitcoins

Many easy-to-use methods for storing bitcoins are handy, but they all share one fundamental weakness: A sufficiently sophisticated attacker could potentially breach the layers of security and access your bitcoins from a remote location. However, this situation is not that different from the same event happening with traditional online banking. A hacker in a remote location, whether just on the other side of town or in another country, could drain your bank account by stealing your identity and deciphering your login credentials. For example, if you access your online bank account using a laptop, a malicious program could monitor your keyboard presses (i.e., a *keylogger*) and steal your password. Banks remedy this weakness by implementing strict daily withdrawal limits or other measures that mitigate the impact of fraudulent access. With Bitcoin, the best mitigation strategy is to store the majority of your funds in cold storage, which cannot be accessed remotely, and to use the more convenient methods for daily spending only.

Three reliable and easy-to-use methods for sending and receiving small amounts of bitcoins are described in the following subsections:

- Online hosted wallet services
- Online personal wallet services
- Personal hot wallet

Online Hosted Wallet Services

As discussed briefly earlier in this chapter, online hosted wallet services are popular because they tend to be easy to use, and users don't typically need to know about Bitcoin's inner workings. No software installation is required; users just sign up and log in to their wallet via a website using a web browser. Online hosted wallets seem familiar because they work like most traditional financial services. For example, when you open a bank account, the service handles your money on your behalf and manages all transfers, deposits, bill payments, and security measures. The same holds true of a hosted Bitcoin wallet: Although the bitcoins are yours, they are not directly in your possession (because you do not have access to the private keys). If the wallet service provider goes bankrupt, for example, you may lose your bitcoins.

Many providers hold bitcoins on behalf of hundreds or thousands of people and have invested in significant security measures. But it's difficult to know for sure whether the service provider is secure enough if it doesn't reveal the details of its storage methods. Be cautious; if you are able to access your hosted wallet using just a username and simple password, that is a warning sign that your provider might be vulnerable to online attacks (if you can access your bitcoins easily, so can a thief). Quality wallet service providers, such as the U.S.-based company Coinbase (which also offers convenient ways to buy bitcoins; see Chapter 4) require the use of two-factor authentication for users to access their bitcoins. Two-factor authentication requires the use of a phone, or another secondary device, in addition to a username and password.

Unfortunately, because the Bitcoin world is so new, no hosted wallet provider can claim a long track record of incident-free bitcoin storage.[2] For this reason, at this time we recommend that you do not trust any third parties with large amounts of bitcoins. Also, note that hosted wallets offer the least amount of privacy when you use bitcoins, because the provider knows who you are, the number of bitcoins you have, and all of your incoming and outgoing transactions.

---

2. Some services now offer insured deposits, which may reassure some users in countries with robust legal systems.

Online Personal Wallet Services

Online personal wallets, like the My Wallet service provided by Blockchain.info,[3] look and behave much like hosted wallets but with a key difference.[4] These wallet services provide you with the tools to send and receive bitcoins, but they don't know your private key. Instead, once the website loads locally on your device, (i.e., is no longer communicating with a distant web server), you generate your private keys from a password you type in. Whenever you send someone bitcoins, a signed transaction is sent to the web server, but your password (and hence your private keys) never leave your device. Fundamentally, this means these services cannot steal your funds. In addition, if the company goes bankrupt or otherwise disappears, you are only inconvenienced temporarily and none of your bitcoins are lost.

Although just as easy to use as hosted wallets, online personal wallets place a much greater responsibility on the user. Typically, you access these wallets online via a username and password, just as you would a hosted wallet, but if you forget your password, in this case you have no recourse. Because the service providers don't know your passwords, they cannot help you recover them.[5] If you use this method, be sure to write down your password in multiple secure places!

Online personal wallets often offer much greater privacy than hosted wallets, especially if they don't require any personally identifying information to register an account. But the service provider may keep track of usage patterns and other data that could subsequently be requested by law enforcement.

Personal Hot Wallet

Like the Electrum wallet discussed in Chapter 2, a personal hot wallet is a software program that runs on a device you own. Because no third party is needed to operate a personal hot wallet, using one maintains the spirit of decentralization that underpins Bitcoin. These programs give you complete control over your bitcoins without sacrificing convenience. However, an even greater responsibility is placed on you than if you use an online wallet service. Your private keys are saved on the same device that connects to the Internet and communicates with the Bitcoin network (the defining feature of a hot wallet); therefore, you need to be vigilant about protecting your device from malware, viruses, and other hacking attempts that could lead to theft.

---

3. Some Bitcoin companies have a tendency to name themselves using technical jargon from the Bitcoin lexicon, which can cause confusion. The company Blockchain.info and the public ledger known as the blockchain are completely different entities.

4. Pun intended.

5. Depending on how the online personal wallet service is implemented, passwords may be recoverable, but some other critical piece of information necessary for spending bitcoins would not be. If the company *can* recover all of the information necessary for you to spend your bitcoins, it is in fact operating as a hosted wallet, and you are entrusting that company with your money.

Is hacker theft likely to happen to you? To become a target of an attack, you would have to keep a large amount of bitcoins in your hot wallet and have advertised this information somehow. Both conditions are not recommended! Using a personal hot wallet is like carrying a traditional physical wallet; it's unlikely that you'll get mugged, but you shouldn't keep too much cash in your wallet or wave it around just in case.

As with a physical wallet, you can lose your hot wallet. If you are storing your private keys on your computer, keep in mind that your computer might be lost, stolen, or destroyed—and the bitcoins in your hot wallet might be worth more than the computer! Fortunately, unlike a physical wallet, you can back up your Bitcoin wallet. However, be mindful of *where* you store your backups. You may want to avoid using cloud storage, for example.

Many personal hot wallets are available (a full discussion of the different choices is provided in Chapter 9). Electrum (*http://electrum.org/*) and Multibit (*http://multibit.org/*) are recommended. Both are open source, have been in use for many years, are available on most platforms, and are *lightweight* (don't require significant computer resources). The original hot wallet, Bitcoin Core (formerly Bitcoin-Qt; *http://bitcoin.org/*), requires significant computer resources to run; therefore, casual users may opt not to use it.

Storing Large Amounts of Bitcoins

Cold storage methods, as described earlier, require physical access to information that is not accessible via the Internet. These five storage methods dramatically reduce the risk of theft:

- Paper wallets
- Encrypted paper wallets
- Offline transaction signing
- Fragmented private keys
- Multi-signature addresses

Instead of worrying about cyber-thieves, you only have to worry about local burglars (and only those who are Bitcoin-savvy). Most of these methods are suitable for safely storing large amounts of bitcoins for long periods of time. However, if you are storing a large Bitcoin fortune, consider having a security expert audit your storage method.

Note that you can safely experiment with any of these five methods using an online computer, as long as you use small amounts of bitcoins. Once you are comfortable with a particular method, you'll need either a dedicated offline computer (preferred) or at least a computer you can take offline temporarily.

When you're evaluating cold storage methods, it's handy to have the open source Bitcoin wallet generator at *http://bitaddress.org/*.

NOTE *You can download the entire website at* http://bitaddress.org/ *and run it on your computer after you disconnect from the Internet.*

When you first access the website, you'll be asked to move your cursor over a box of letters and numbers (or type letters) randomly to provide a source of randomness that the site uses to generate a Bitcoin address. The reason you need to do this that it is very challenging for computers to generate random numbers by chance because they follow strict instructions, making the results more predictable. For unimportant applications, such as playing Solitaire on your computer, a mediocre random number generator used to shuffle the virtual deck is no big deal, but for storing money, high-quality randomness is very important.

Paper Wallets

Using a paper wallet is perhaps one of the simplest and most popular cold storage methods. This involves generating a Bitcoin address and private key on an offline computer and then writing both down on a piece of paper but not saving a copy of the information on the computer itself. You can then store the piece of paper in a file cabinet, a personal safe, or in a safety deposit box at a bank. With the piece of paper safely locked away, you can continue sending bitcoins to the associated Bitcoin address for safekeeping. When you eventually decide to spend your saved bitcoins, you can use the *import private key* or *import paper wallet* function that most Bitcoin wallet programs include. At this point, your bitcoins will no longer be in cold storage.

If you want to spend only some of your saved bitcoins and keep the rest in a paper wallet, after importing your private key into a hot wallet, you should immediately store the remainder of your bitcoins in a *new* paper wallet (paper wallets are one-time use only). But be sure to prepare the new paper wallet ahead of time before importing bitcoins from the old paper wallet.

NOTE *Alternatively, you can spend a fraction of your paper wallet bitcoins by using a technique known as* offline transaction signing, *which is described in "Offline Transaction Signing" on page 40.*

Provided you keep the paper private key in a safe place, the paper wallet method is suitable for storing large amounts of bitcoins indefinitely. However, keep in mind such physical risks as flooding and fire. Also, do not scan, take photos of, or expose your paper private key to other methods of duplication, or you will compromise your paper wallet. Your bitcoins are only as safe as the least secure method by which you store your private keys. In particular, consider that some office photocopiers maintain records of every document they copy. The safest way to make a duplicate of your paper wallet, which is recommended, is to clearly handwrite a few extra copies and store those copies securely.

Encrypted Paper Wallets

The encrypted paper wallet method was invented to further improve the security of the paper wallet method. Essentially, instead of writing down the private key on a piece of paper, you write down an encrypted version of it.

The only way to decrypt your private key is with a password you choose, preventing thieves from accessing your private key and your bitcoins.

Hundreds of encryption schemes can be used for this purpose, but the most common scheme is *BIP38 encryption.*

NOTE *The Bitcoin developer community maintains a wish list of features called* Bitcoin Improvement Proposals (BIPs), *and this encryption standard is #38 on the list (features that have been implemented, such as this one, are still often referred to by their BIP numbers).*

To create a BIP38-encrypted paper wallet (go to *http://bitaddress.org/* and shake your mouse back and forth until you've generated enough random data and the Paper Wallet tab appears), you choose a passphrase and then generate a Bitcoin address with its associated encrypted private key. Your private key should start with the number 6, as opposed to a normal private key, which starts with the number 5.

NOTE *In computer science, passwords typically serve one of two functions: Either they are used to* authenticate *a user by asking the user to provide a password at the appropriate time, or they are used to* encrypt *data. For authentication, one can often get away with a short, word-length password (even though it is typically still a bad idea to do this). However, passwords used for data encryption must always be long: If they are shorter than 40 characters, they are often easy to crack. Hence, when passwords are used for this purpose, as we discuss in this section, it is a common convention to call them* passphrases *instead.*

But be forewarned: If you forget your passphrase, you'll permanently lose access to your bitcoins. Therefore, it's best to also write down your passphrase and store it in a different location than the paper wallet. As with ordinary paper wallets, make backup copies of the encrypted paper wallet to protect against flooding, fires, or theft. Always assume that your wallet is unsafe to ensure you are being vigilant about safety. If your encrypted paper wallet is stolen, use your duplicate copy to import your bitcoins into a hot wallet, and then store them in a new encrypted paper wallet. Even if a perpetrator eventually determines your passphrase, you will have moved your bitcoins by then.

Offline Transaction Signing

Offline transaction signing is the entry-level security method for Bitcoin businesses or serious users who regularly handle large amounts of bitcoins. This method requires two computers and is considerably more advanced than using paper wallets. One computer has a personal hot wallet that works just like Electrum, but the private keys are omitted. Therefore, when you click *send bitcoins*, you will be asked to perform an extra authorization step using a second computer, which contains the private keys and is not connected to the Internet. This second offline computer also has a Bitcoin wallet program installed and only functions to authorize, or *digitally sign*, the transaction. You use the offline computer to create a file that contains the digitally signed transaction, which you then copy to the online computer and broadcast to the Bitcoin network (see Figure 3-1).

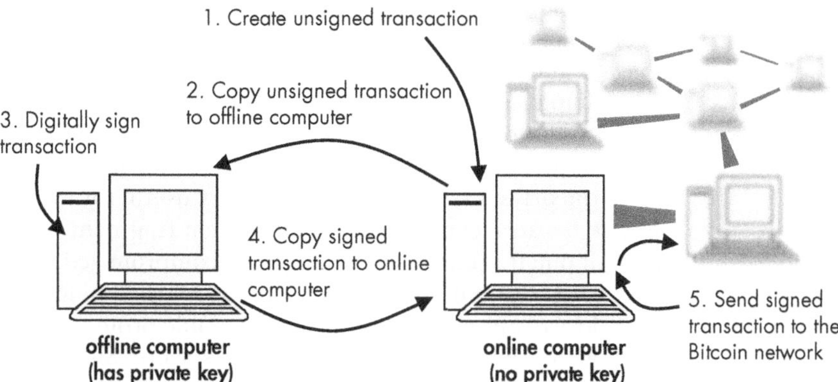

Figure 3-1: A schematic of how an offline and online computer work together to securely sign Bitcoin transactions without exposing a private key to the Internet

The online computer never ascertains the private keys. Offline transaction signing is similar to having a financial administrator with no signing authority write checks that then need to be signed by an authorized person before being mailed out. Although this method is very secure and can be used to store fairly large amounts of bitcoins, making many transactions per day can be a cumbersome process. One potential risk is losing the private keys stored on your offline computer; therefore, you should make backups of those private keys for reliable, long-term storage. Another risk is that your private keys may be compromised if your offline computer is stolen or seized.

An advantage of offline transaction signing instead of just importing keys from paper wallets is that a cold-to-hot storage transition never happens. Your bitcoins are always in cold storage, even when you spend from the address where they are stored.

You can use the Electrum offline transaction-signing feature, provided you have two computers. Another highly recommended wallet for offline transaction signing is the Armory Bitcoin Client (*http://bitcoinarmory.com/*), which is open source and designed with maximum security in mind. Armory offers many advanced security features, and if you are serious about highly secure Bitcoin storage and are an advanced Bitcoin user, you should certainly explore this option.

Fragmented Private Keys and Multi-Signature Addresses

Fragmented private keys and multi-signature addresses involve splitting into pieces the information required to spend bitcoins and storing them in disparate geographic locations. Both techniques achieve extremely high levels of Bitcoin storage security and safety. As enterprise-level Bitcoin security strategies, they are (or should be) implemented by large Bitcoin businesses (major currency exchanges, hedge funds with Bitcoin assets, etc.). Let's look at each strategy in turn.

Fragmented Private Keys

Using a cryptographic trick known as *secret sharing*, a Bitcoin private key can be divided into many fragments, and only a certain number are required to reconstruct the key. This is sometimes referred to as an "m *of* n" *private key*, where *m* and *n* stand for the necessary and available number of fragments. For example, a private key might be split into five fragments, but any three can be used to reconstruct the key, making a "3 of 5" private key. None of the individual pieces on their own reveal any meaningful information about the private key. This strategy is very useful for highly secure Bitcoin storage because companies can store each fragment in a separate, safe place; if one fragment gets damaged or compromised, the bitcoins will still be safe. In addition, other fragments can be used to move the bitcoins to a new address. Several different cryptographic protocols are used for secret sharing, but the most popular is Shamir's Secret Sharing method, for which organizations can easily find open source implementations on the Web.

Multi-Signature Addresses

Using multi-signature addresses, or multiple private keys, as opposed to using a single private key in multiple pieces, also provides a similar level of highly secure storage. Bitcoins are stored in an address that requires more than one private key to use them. Companies can specify how many keys exist and the number required to spend the stored bitcoins; for example, if three keys are specified, any two keys could be sufficient to complete a transaction. For safekeeping, businesses can also distribute these keys to different people if the organizations don't want to entrust a single person with the authority to move bitcoins. For example, a Bitcoin bank can ensure that no single employee (even the CEO or president) is solely able to move customers' funds. Each employee at the Bitcoin bank can have his own private key, with all of the keys corresponding to the same Bitcoin address, but no single private key is sufficient to move the bitcoins. To authorize the transfer of bitcoins from the bank's Bitcoin address, multiple employees need to use their private keys to digitally sign the transaction. One main difference exists between multiple private keys and multiple fragments of a single private key: With multiple private keys, at no point does one person ever have complete control, whereas with multiple fragments of a single private key, the person who combines the pieces to construct the private key has complete control. Using multiple private keys is an extremely secure and responsible way to manage very large amounts of bitcoins.

Special Mention: The Bitcoin Hardware Wallet

The hardware wallet is a relatively new Bitcoin storage method. It is a small device that fits in your pocket and stores your private keys in such a way that no one can extract them from the device. The hardware wallet acts as the offline computer in the previously mentioned offline transaction-signing method, but it is more convenient because you can plug it into your online computer. Your bitcoins are never at risk, even if you have viruses on your online computer. When you click *send bitcoins* in your Bitcoin wallet software on the online computer, you then need to confirm the transaction on the hardware device—usually by pressing a button. The hardware wallet uses the internally stored private keys to sign a transaction, which is then sent to the online computer.

This method is almost as convenient as using the personal hot wallet, but it is more secure because it is impossible for your private keys to be exposed to the Internet. Your bitcoins on the device will always be in cold storage. One downside to this method is that you need to purchase a piece of hardware, as opposed to just downloading a free open source program. Another disadvantage of using your hardware wallet is that you can lose it, which might result in lost bitcoins (although some hardware wallets provide ways to back up your bitcoins). Although the hardware wallet is an excellent combination of convenience and security, you might not want to rely on one to store your bitcoins for decades, because no data is yet available on the lifetime or durability of such devices.

TREZOR

One brand of hardware wallet that has received a lot of attention is Trezor (*http://www.bitcointrezor.com/*). We find the Trezor hardware wallet to be an excellent, relatively easy-to-use use device, but because Trezor devices are new, there is still the possibility that a bug or security flaw is yet to be discovered (as is true, in principle, of Bitcoin itself).

Created by SatoshiLabs, the Trezor (see Figure 3-2) is a small device that "stores your bitcoins" (that is, it stores your private keys). When you want to spend your bitcoins, you use a USB cable to plug the Trezor into a laptop. It doesn't have to be your own laptop; you can use a complete stranger's laptop and still safely spend your bitcoins. This is, perhaps, the defining feature of the Trezor: It doesn't require you to trust the laptop that you plug it into. This is helpful if you're traveling and don't have your own laptop with you: You can use any computer at your destination. Since most bitcoins are stolen by exploiting security holes in smartphones and laptops, using the Trezor dramatically cuts down on the risk of Bitcoin theft. So how does it work?

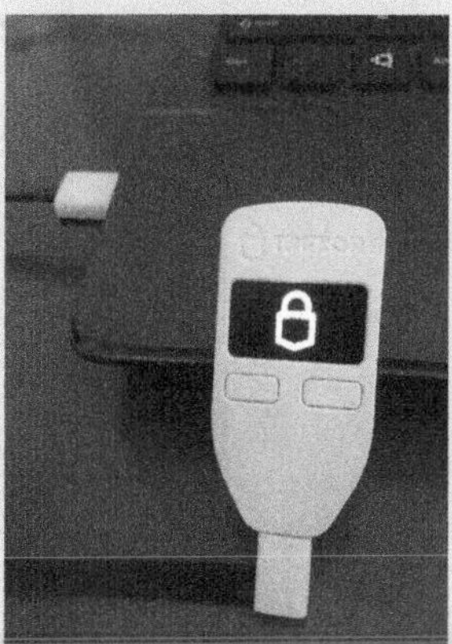

Figure 3-2: The Trezor device

(continued)

Smartphones and laptops are also devices that can store private keys, but unlike the Trezor, they treat those keys like any other data, i.e., as information that can be viewed, copied, or modified. Viruses on a laptop can search for the private key data, copy them, and broadcast them to a remote server, leading to stolen bitcoins. The Trezor, on the other hand, never allows the private key data to be viewed or copied by you or a virus. Instead, when you want to spend bitcoins, it uses its internal private keys to sign a transaction that it then gives you. The Trezor is like a paranoid chef who will never reveal his secret recipe but will cook for you anytime you want.

Configuring the Trezor is slightly laborious (it may take 5–10 minutes for beginners), but this does not need to be done more than once.

1. Plug the Trezor into your laptop.
2. Visit *https://mytrezor.com/*. Install the necessary plugins so that your laptop knows how to communicate with the Trezor. You may need to restart your browser to continue once the plugins are installed.
3. Navigate to *https://mytrezor.com/* again. The website will recognize that your Trezor has not been configured yet and will ask you to give your device a unique name. Enter a name and click **Continue**.
4. Enter a new PIN using your laptop.
5. Enter the PIN again to verify you did not make a mistake in the previous step.
6. The Trezor device will now display a recovery seed so that you can recover your bitcoins in case you lose your device. This is the *only* time that the Trezor will ever reveal (indirectly) its private keys (they are derived from the seed). Once the configuration process is done, the private keys can never again be viewed or accessed. Write down the recovery seed on a piece of paper (or two), and store it in a safe place.
7. Congratulations, you are ready to use your Trezor! If you have bitcoins stored elsewhere, you can send them to your Trezor by clicking Account ▸ Receive to find a receiving Bitcoin address.

Operating the Trezor is much simpler:

1. Plug the Trezor into a laptop.
2. Open a Bitcoin wallet program on the laptop that is configured to work with the Trezor (or visit *https://mytrezor.com/*, a website created by SatoshiLabs designed specifically for Trezor users).
3. On the laptop, choose how many bitcoins you want to spend and where you want to send them. Click **Send**.

4. The Trezor will ask you to enter your PIN. (This is to prevent someone from being able to steal your Trezor and spend your bitcoins.) Enter your PIN using the laptop.
5. The Trezor will display the transaction details. Press the corresponding button on the Trezor to confirm (or the other button to deny) the transaction. The Trezor will now create a signed Bitcoin transaction and send it to the laptop.
6. The laptop automatically broadcasts the transaction to the Bitcoin network. Your bitcoins have been sent!

These steps take only a minute to carry out and are quite convenient for tasks like online shopping (the Trezor was not designed, however, to be used at a point-of-sale terminal like the cash register at a coffee shop).

The Trezor also supports advanced features, such as the use of passwords (in addition to the PIN) and hierarchical deterministic wallets for multiple accounts. These features are more than we can cover in this little box, but you are encouraged to check out the Trezor website (*http://www.bitcointrezor.com/*) for more details. At the time of this writing, the Trezor is selling for about $120, but you can pay only with bitcoins.

Special Mention: The Bitcoin Brain Wallet

Using the brain wallet to store bitcoins is a unique and somewhat mind-blowing technique. In this method, you store bitcoins entirely in your brain by *memorizing your private key*. We should note in advance that this storage method is impractical in several respects and recommended only for Bitcoin/cryptography experts. Because nothing tangible exists to steal or seize, you can use this method to store your bitcoins when you don't have control over your physical environment (e.g., living in a dorm room, crossing through security checkpoints, etc.). However, you must create a long, unforgettable passphrase that you can commit to memory, especially if you will be storing large amounts of bitcoins. Then you feed the passphrase into a computer program (running on an offline computer) that accepts any text as input and outputs a private key and Bitcoin address. In the following example, the passphrase is short and easy to guess, so your stored bitcoins would be at risk.

```
passphrase: "bitcoin for the befuddled" <--- way too short
private key: 5JS1PoX1e7b48VnBtaeYohJvoe8NTGBTdBa9KELJR9UjoeL9ukx
bitcoin adddress: 1EjtJ53dXFT7cmP5ETiQuyc9fPy96FEPBh
```

However, the following passphrase is sufficiently complex.

```
passphrase: "crowley likes beaches, lisp programming, ravioli and sasquatches
conradbarski chriswilmer nostarchpress"
private key: 5Ke7Unhs9Ghc4UmhVZXptjPZiVFn48fnN1xGeoctsKrHdpdJtAD
bitcoin address: 1FqwT4844gvjP6GCELW5NaR1gMCQKRcaSP
```

After generating your passphrase on an offline computer, you *ignore* the private key and copy only the Bitcoin address. You do not want to store the private key anywhere, even on an offline computer. You'll need the private key when you want to move your bitcoins, and at that point you can *re-create* it from your memorized passphrase (and import it into a Bitcoin wallet, like Electrum, or use it for offline transaction signing). By not storing the private key anywhere, you prevent others from stealing it from you, either physically or digitally. You can write down your passphrase and keep it hidden in a safe place, of course, but then it wouldn't strictly be a *brain* wallet (however, it can be a good idea).

Brain wallets are useful for reasonably long-term storage (a few years) of significant amounts of bitcoins, but they are not convenient for day-to-day transactions. Also, storing large amounts of bitcoins in a brain wallet for decades could be risky, because you might forget the password. Additionally, people are inherently deficient at choosing passphrases that computers cannot guess, and increasingly powerful computers might be capable of guessing every possible passphrase that a human could generate. For very long-term storage of large quantities of bitcoins, it is safest to use a randomly generated private key (with a high-quality source of randomness).

Choosing the Storage Method That's Right for You

The best storage route to take is to start small and choose an easy storage method that you're comfortable with (see Figure 3-2). Keep in mind that *human error* while using a complicated Bitcoin storage scheme is a real risk factor. Once you're more comfortable with how Bitcoin works, you can gradually increase the amount of bitcoins you own and the level of security you use.

Although no system is 100 percent secure, you can store your bitcoins more securely than gold or traditional currencies. Storing bitcoins might *seem* less secure than having cash in a traditional bank account, but the reason might be simply that many people feel less comfortable with unfamiliar technology. Someday we might look back and think it should have been obvious that a decentralized currency that is impossible to counterfeit and is built on cryptographic principles is more secure than traditional currencies.

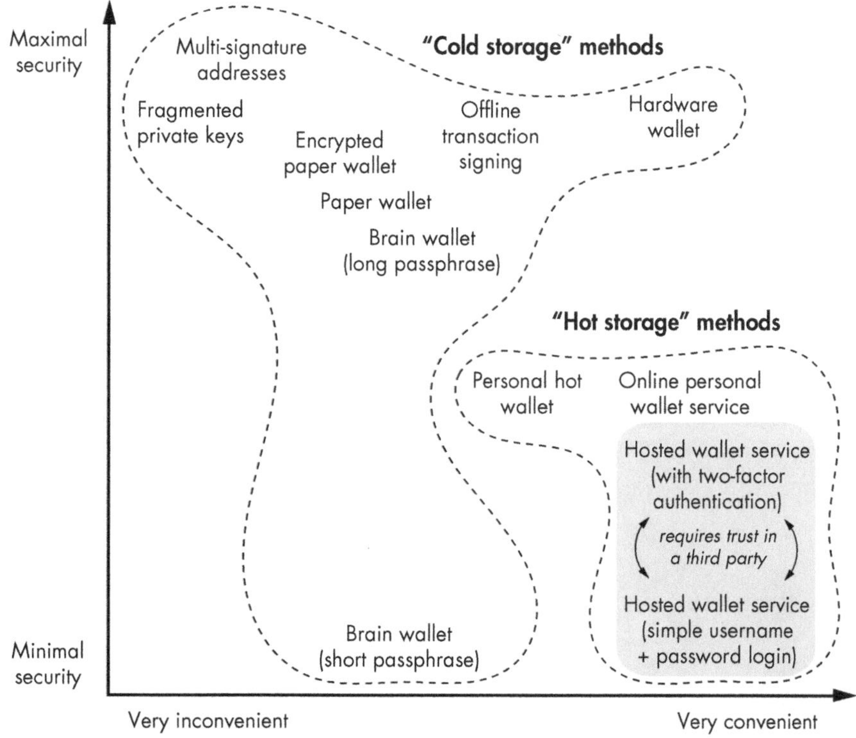

Figure 3-3: A summary of Bitcoin storage methods. These strategies span the spectrum from low security (but convenient) to high security (but inconvenient). This chart is not comprehensive because new methods are constantly being developed. For example, one of the best methods on this chart, the hardware wallet, was not possible until 2014, five years after the start of Bitcoin.

4

BUYING BITCOINS

Buying bitcoins is essentially just like buying any other kind of currency. Think about the various ways in which you typically exchange US dollars for Japanese yen or Mexican pesos. For small amounts of money, you could probably find a friend to exchange a few dollars for the currency you want. For moderate amounts, you can visit a currency exchange shop, like those at most international airports, which is convenient but charges high fees. If you want to exchange thousands of dollars or you are a currency day trader and don't want to pay high fees, you need to register an account at a major currency exchange. All of this is true for bitcoins as well, except that the infrastructure is not yet as well developed as it is for traditional currencies (right now, an airport currency exchange shop probably couldn't tell you the difference between a bitcoin and a banana).

The bottom line is that you have many different ways to buy bitcoins, even today: You can buy them locally, from your friends or those in your area; you can buy them from middlemen, both online and in brick-and-mortar stores; or you can buy them from major Bitcoin currency exchanges. It's important to remember that whenever you buy bitcoins, you are buying them from *someone who has them already* (exchange services merely facilitate this transfer); bitcoins are not sold directly from a Bitcoin company. Therefore, no individual sets the price of a bitcoin; the price is decided collectively by those who buy and sell them every day (i.e., by the free market).

Why Not Just Mine Bitcoins?

Although you can obtain bitcoins by mining them, it is not easy (or free) to do so. Unless you plan to quit your day job and become a full-time Bitcoin miner (see Chapter 8), it's not practical to obtain significant amounts of Bitcoin through mining. Bitcoin mining requires highly specialized computer hardware, cheap electricity, and a high degree of patience.

Ways to Buy Bitcoins

Broadly speaking, you can buy bitcoins in three main ways:

- **The easy way:** Through middleman companies

- **The efficient way:** Through currency exchanges

- **The fun and futuristic way:** Through person-to-person purchases

Middleman companies make money helping people buy bitcoins easily, with a minimum of fuss. These companies usually have decent customer service and shield you from needing to understand all the complexities of currency trading. However, like all middlemen, they charge a fee for this convenience.

A more efficient way is to buy bitcoins directly from a *Bitcoin exchange.* Exchanges directly connect people buying and selling bitcoins using a sophisticated currency exchange system. These exchanges are somewhat advanced and can be intimidating for a beginner. However, exchanges are where most large Bitcoin purchases and sales happen. For this reason, exchanges usually offer the best prices for purchasing bitcoins. Also, by purchasing directly from an exchange, you minimize the number of parties involved in a large purchase, which decreases the risk of a problematic transaction. For large Bitcoin purchases ($5,000 or more), *always* deal directly with an exchange. Using an exchange is also a good choice for smaller purchases, as long as you have the time and inclination to learn the ins and outs of how a currency exchange works.

Simply buying bitcoins directly from folks in your area, *person-to-person,* is the most fun because you get to meet others interested in this new currency. Of course, trading money directly with strangers might make some people uncomfortable. But most bitcoiners believe that person-to-person purchases are most likely the wave of the future. Some hope for a more decentralized world in which large corporations become obsolete as technology makes it more practical and convenient for people to interact directly. Perhaps someday face-to-face exchanges will become the most efficient, cheapest, and fastest way to buy bitcoins.

Buying Bitcoins the Easy Way

At this time, the easiest way to buy bitcoins is through an established Bitcoin middleman, more accurately called a *Bitcoin exchange intermediary.* Exchange intermediaries consist of companies that have already registered their own accounts on one or more Bitcoin exchanges and will buy or sell bitcoins on your behalf. Typically, exchange intermediaries offer to sell bitcoins only at the market price; you can't set your own price. Additionally, these companies may only convert currency in one direction. For instance, during the 2013 Bitcoin price run-up, many folks new to the Bitcoin community wanted to purchase bitcoins quickly. Not surprisingly, many businesses that traded bitcoins for dollars, but not necessarily dollars for bitcoins, quickly appeared to fill this need.

There are also clear benefits to using a middleman, however. The paperwork involved is minimal, and many services offer to get you bitcoins in mere minutes (as opposed to days or weeks). The fees typically range from 1 to 10 percent, but the service and customer support are often better than with exchanges.

NOTE *Bitcoin intermediaries are roughly analogous to PayPal, which acts as a middleman to help you make Internet purchases using your bank account. If you've used PayPal, you'll find that using an exchange intermediary is a very similar experience.*

Table 4-1 lists some popular exchange intermediaries. You should try to choose a company that charges the lowest fees and offers the best user experience. Be sure to check online for reviews of these services and try to find out if they have a good reputation in the Bitcoin community before making your decision. Many of these services operate only in limited geographical regions, so some might not be available to you.

Table 4-1: Popular Bitcoin Exchange Intermediaries

Company name	Services offered*	Location	Established
Bitcoiniacs	Buying or selling bitcoins at market price; brick-and-mortar Bitcoin store	Kelowna, Canada	2013
BTCquick	Buying bitcoins using a credit card	Denver, CO	2013
Circle	Buying and selling bitcoins via bank or credit card.	Boston, MA	2013
Coinbase	Buying and selling bitcoins at market price; Bitcoin wallet hosting	San Francisco, CA	2012

* Only a partial description of services

WARNING *Unfortunately, many times in the past fraudulent and poorly run companies have been involved in the buying and selling of Bitcoin. Undeniably, in the future this may be true of any of the companies we mention in this chapter. It is your own responsibility to properly vet specific companies before trusting them with your money.*

Before we walk you through the exact steps involved in buying bitcoins from one of these companies (see "Buying Bitcoins with Coinbase" on page 58), we first need to discuss a couple of technical concepts. One concept you absolutely need to understand is two-factor authentication, which is a way to do online transactions (as well as a framework for thinking about such transactions) that can greatly reduce your risk of getting hacked and/or robbed. Another concept we need to discuss is the difference between reversible and irreversible financial transactions. Understanding this difference helps explain why long waiting periods are often involved when acquiring bitcoins from service companies.

Authentication Factors

Since the dawn of digital technology, many methods have been conceived for computer users to prove their identities: passwords, iris scans, key fobs, face recognition, and several others. However, all of these security measures can be defeated. If you enjoy science fiction movies, you're familiar with the myriad ways this can be done.

However, you can overcome these weaknesses by organizing the many authentication methods into three main categories and then choosing two to use. This is known as *two-factor authentication.* The three categories are as follows:

- **Something you know:** Your password, your first pet's name, your signature, and so on
- **Something you own:** A key fob, your smartphone, and so on
- **Something you are:** Your fingerprint, your face, your eyes, your voice, and so on

It turns out most of the weaknesses in each of these categories are very different. That means that if you pick two authentication methods in two different categories, it will be far more difficult for a hacker to break into your account. This is what we mean when we say two-factor identification. We will discuss an example of this in practice shortly.

The Hassle of Converting Dollars (or Other Currencies) into Bitcoins

One common criticism of bitcoins is that it can be such a hassle to obtain them. Typically, you'll wait several days before you can buy bitcoins with your dollars through an exchange intermediary. People are often mystified by the fact that they can buy items on Amazon in 10 seconds but that it takes many days to buy bitcoins, no matter where people try to buy them.

Reversible Transactions

The reason, surprisingly, is that the world economy as it currently exists is built around contracts and reversible transactions. Transfers of financial value between two parties usually involve very similar steps, whether we're dealing with a credit card payment, check deposit, bank wire, stock purchase, or mortgage loan. Any financial asset that is typically tracked in a financial ledger (which nowadays includes most things besides paper cash) are handled in this way. The steps are as follows:

1. **One of the parties, or both parties together, draft a legally-binding contract.** Sometimes this contract is written out formally (such as when you initiate a mortgage loan) and sometimes it is made implicitly based on previously agreed-upon terms. For instance, when you enter your credit card information into Amazon, you are bound by a contract you signed ahead of time with your credit card issuer, a contract that stated that you would honor the debt incurred by using your credit card in this way.
2. **The terms of the contract are broadcast to all affected parties.** If you initiate a bank wire, your bank, as well as the bank receiving the funds, will be notified about the bank wire request. Similarly, someone selling decorative soaps on Amazon would be notified that you used your Visa card to purchase a bottle of raspberry hand soap. At this point, there is usually still some leeway for the parties to still opt out of the contract, in a time period which may be called a *settlement period* (or a *hold* or *rescission period*, depending on the type of asset and the exact circumstances involved.)
3. **The purchased assets are delivered and financial records are updated.** After a period of time, once the banks have updated their ledgers, the balance from the bank wire shows up in the recipient's bank account. Similarly, your raspberry hand soap is handed off to the post office for delivery.

The crucial step in this process is that the information entered in the bookkeeping ledgers by your bank (or at E-Trade, the mortgage company, or the soap seller) is really meaningless in terms of determining who "owns" an asset—these ledgers have no legal bearing. The only way to know whether you own the money in your bank account, the money in your Paypal account, or a share of Google at E-Trade is to look at the original contracts. If somebody contacts your bank and says, "Actually, all the money in Bob's account belongs to me because Bob and I signed this contract that proves this is the case" and this person can go through the many legal hurdles required to prove that that money indeed belongs to her, Bob's money will not be safe at that bank. It does not matter whether the bank's internal ledgers say he is entitled to that money.

The bottom line is that because legal contracts almost always remain open to dispute and because ledgers maintained by banks, mortgage companies, E-Trade, Amazon, etc., are all subject to the legal system, it is reasonable to argue that our traditional financial system is based upon financial transactions that are *reversible*. Unless there are statutes of limitation that supersede the original contracts years into the future, the settlement period we mentioned in step two is indefinite.

This is true in theory and in practice. All of the following types of transactions can be (and frequently are) reversed by at least one person involved in the transaction days after the fact (and usually also weeks or months after the fact):

- Bank wires
- Credit card transactions
- Mortgage loan contracts
- Stock purchases
- Check deposits

For some of these transactions, the only party that can reverse the purchase may be the larger, more powerful entity involved in the transaction. For instance, you may not be able to change your mind about the share of Google you bought a day ago, but you wouldn't be surprised to learn that E-Trade makes you wait 10 business days before pulling that share out of your E-Trade account and will be more than happy to take that share away from you if the bank wire you used to fund that share is reversed by your bank after the fact.

Irreversible Transactions

However, there are some types of financial transactions that are completely irreversible. The most common transaction of this type is a transfer of physical, paper money. If the ATM machine goes crazy one day and spits out $10,000 in cash that you don't actually own and you decide to bury that money in the woods that evening, no legal contract, action by the bank, or action by the government will ever be able to recover that cash; if you decide not to tell them where you buried this money, it is not directly reachable by the legal system.[1]

Bitcoins have this same property, which is why people sometimes call it *digital cash*. If you give somebody bitcoins using a standard Bitcoin transaction, nothing you can do or say can ever reverse that transaction. Such a transaction is enforced using pure mathematics and is not a party to any legal contract, in itself.

1. Of course they might be able to seize another ten thousand dollars you own from another source, but that would not constitute a "reversal" of the original transaction for the sake of this discussion.

Combining Reversible and Irreversible Assets

Now we can finally understand why it is often a hassle to buy bitcoins. When you buy an irreversible asset using a reversible asset it leads to something call an *impedance mismatch*: While it is possible to build efficient financial systems that involve reversible transactions (our modern financial system) and those that involve irreversible transactions (as is currently found in the world of cryptocurrencies), it is difficult to exchange assets between these two categories.

This is why banks have such strict cash withdrawal limits at ATMs and why it can take several days to buy a bitcoin. In both cases, the institution has no way of reversing the irreversible transaction if something goes wrong and needs to take extra precautions that the reversible half of the transaction has a high probability of completing successfully before agreeing to the transaction, especially if large amounts of money are involved.

NOTE *If you are sent raspberry hand soap by mail via an Amazon purchase, this is arguably also an irreversible transaction. However, such products, if obtained fraudulently, are hard to sell to another party (unlike Bitcoin). This is another reason why an online seller of soaps is less at risk of fraud than a company selling bitcoins.*

Why Irreversible Transactions Are Arguably Superior

Many people, when they hear that Bitcoin transactions are irreversible, will have the following thought: "I kind of like the fact that I can reverse a credit card transaction if someone sells me a deficient product." However, it is still straightforward to perform reversible transactions with Bitcoin. Many systems exist for doing this, usually using a feature in Bitcoin called *multi-signature transactions*, which we will discuss in some detail in later chapters.

It is true that currently, with standard Bitcoin transactions, the protections a buyer has when buying something off of the Internet are not as strong as those built into the credit card system. This is a weakness of Bitcoin and something the Bitcoin community needs to strive to resolve. But the fact is that both reversible and irreversible transactions are useful depending on the circumstances. For instance, if you are selling a bicycle to a stranger for $100, you probably wouldn't want a potentially reversible asset in exchange, such as a personal check. Instead, you would say to the stranger, "cash only please" (or maybe "Bitcoin or cash only please" after you finish this book).

Therefore, because Bitcoin allows for reversible transactions wile your Visa credit card will never allow for a strictly irreversible transaction, one can argue that irreversible financial instruments are superior: They are a more basic building block on top of which more complicated forms of transactions can be built, including reversible financial transactions with enforcement via traditional contracts, if desired.

In conclusion, we believe it can be a bit unfair to criticize the design of Bitcoin for the fact that bitcoins are hard to purchase with a credit card or bank wire. Part of this difficulty is caused by the design of the traditional financial system itself.

Buying Bitcoins with Coinbase

In the United States, the most popular Bitcoin exchange intermediary by far is Coinbase. Let's walk through the steps of buying bitcoins using Coinbase. As with all of the methods of buying bitcoins that we will discuss, it is prudent to start small; buy only modest amounts of bitcoins until you are comfortable with the process.

NOTE *If you decide to use another middleman instead of Coinbase, the steps involved are roughly the same, even if some of the details are different.*

Step 1: Registering at Coinbase

To register at Coinbase, go to *http://coinbase.com/*, and choose **Sign Up**. Then enter your email address and choose a password (Figure 4-1).

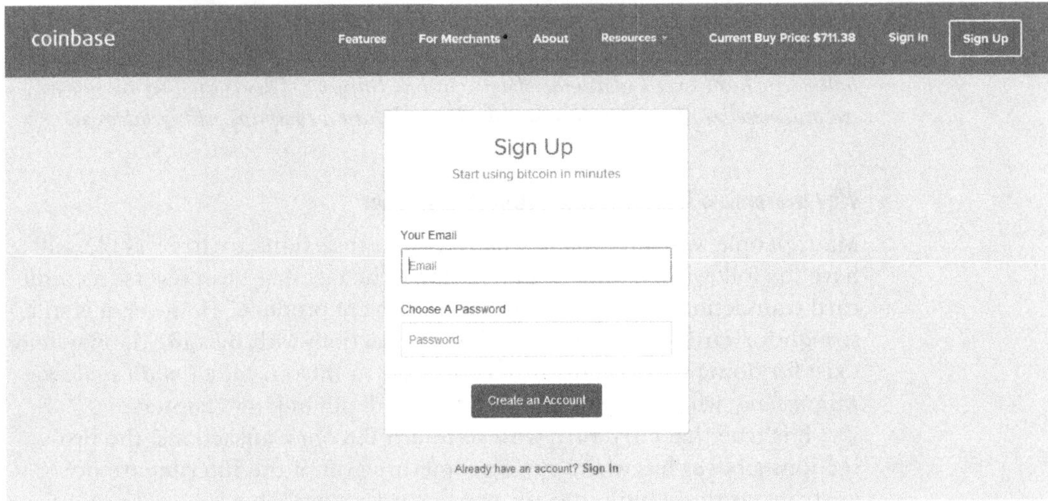

Figure 4-1: Sign Up screen for Coinbase

Click **Create an Account**. At this point, Coinbase will send an email to your account to have the address verified.

Step 2: Setting Up Two-Factor Identification

The easiest way to set up a second authentication method is to run an app on your iPhone or Android phone that proves you own a phone with a specific phone number. Coinbase lets you do this. Once set up, your two-factor authentication for your Coinbase account will be:

1. **Something you know:** Your Coinbase password
2. **Something you own:** Your smartphone

Currently, Coinbase uses an app called Authy that you can install on your phone from the iTunes App Store or Google Play Store. After installing this app on your phone, configure it by following the instructions, which require you to enter your phone number and verify your email address again.

Now you're ready to use Authy to link your phone to your Coinbase account. After logging into Coinbase, go to Account Settings and verify your phone (Figure 4-2).

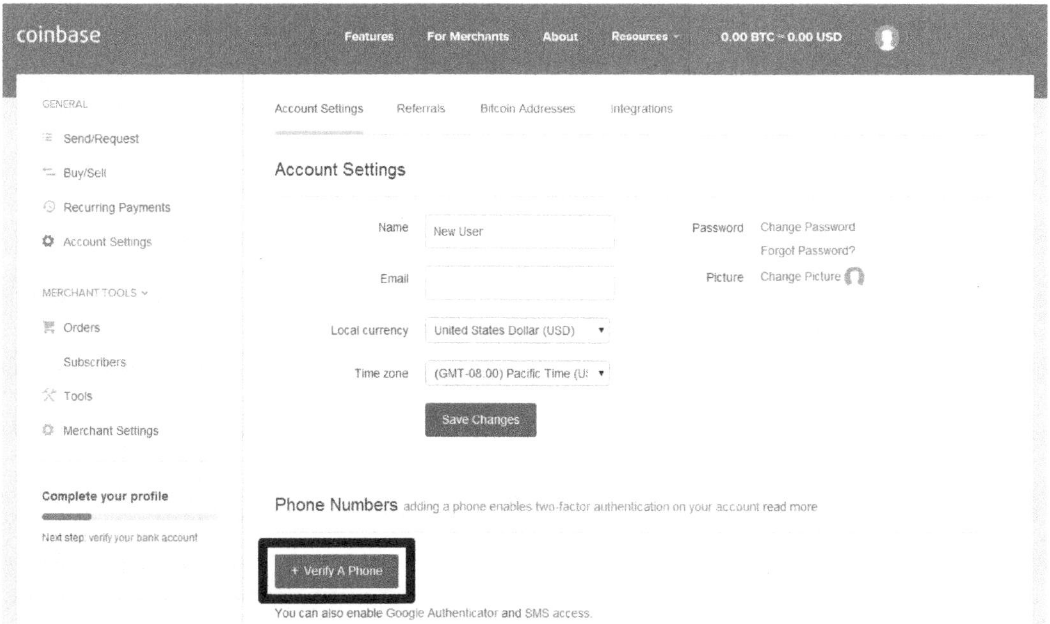

Figure 4-2: Account Settings screen for Coinbase

Click **Verify A Phone** and enter your phone number. Authy will detect that you're trying to link to Coinbase and display a Coinbase option (Figure 4-3).

Figure 4-3: The Authy app detects your use of Coinbase.

Choose **Coinbase in Authy** to display a code, which Coinbase will ask for as the next step. Enter the code to verify your phone.

Now, if others try to access your Coinbase account, they'll need to not only know the Coinbase password but also have access to your smartphone.

Step 3: Linking Your Bank Account to Coinbase

To purchase bitcoins in Coinbase, you need to link your Coinbase account to a bank account. Log into Coinbase, choose **Buy/Sell**, and then choose

Payment Methods. Click **Add Bank Account** and provide your bank account information (Figure 4-4).

Most likely, you'll have to wait several days before your bank account is fully verified. Then you'll be ready to continue with step 4 of the instructions.

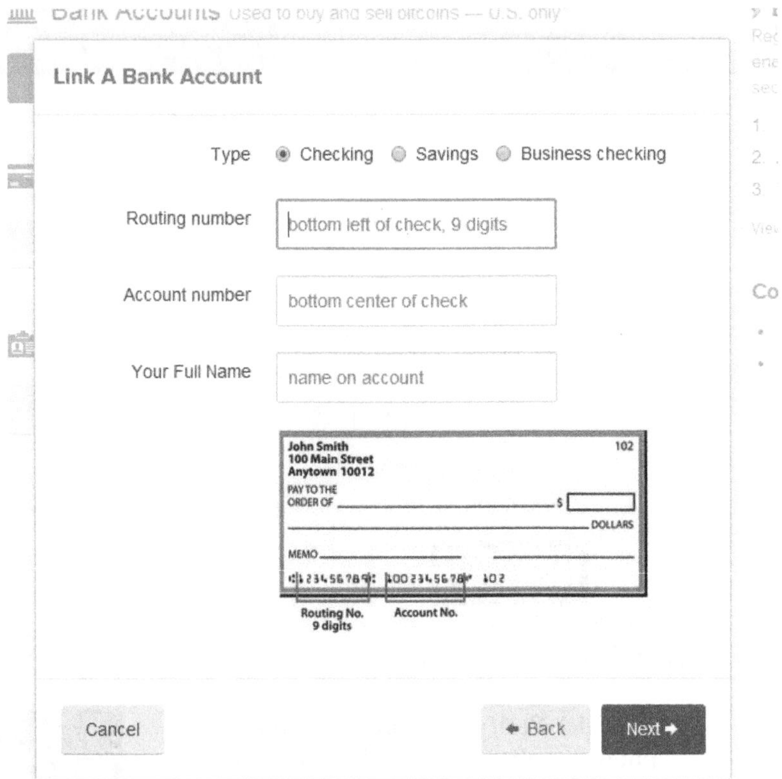

Figure 4-4: Screen for entering bank account information on Coinbase

Step 4: Buying Bitcoins on Coinbase

With your bank account confirmed, you can place your first Bitcoin order. Figure 4-5 shows the screen you'll see when you click Buy/Sell.

This screen is self-explanatory: You simply type in the number of bitcoins you want to buy and then click **Buy Bitcoin**. After confirming your purchase, Coinbase will transfer the dollar equivalent of these bitcoins from your bank account. After waiting a few more days, you should have your first bitcoins!

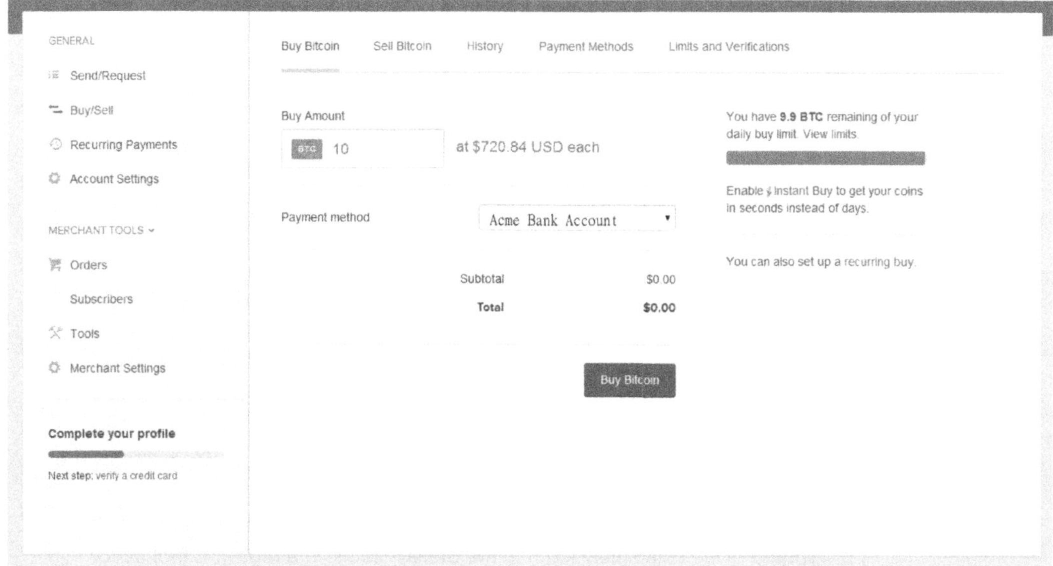

Figure 4-5: The Buy Bitcoin screen on Coinbase

Step 5: Protecting Your Shiny New Bitcoins

When your bitcoins are available, Coinbase will notify you via email that your bitcoins are in your Coinbase wallet. But because your Coinbase wallet is managed by Coinbase, if Coinbase ever crashes, gets hacked, or goes bankrupt, your funds could be at risk. Consequently, you should take some extra steps to protect the bitcoins you've bought.

Although Coinbase might be a trustworthy company and has a marginal chance of going bankrupt, why take even the slightest chance of losing your bitcoins? By simply transferring your coins from your Coinbase wallet into your own self-managed wallet, you can make sure the risk of loss from a third-party company are zero percent.

NOTE *Be sure to read Chapter 3 to learn about personal wallets and safe Bitcoin storage.*

In the past, bitcoins stored in wallets managed by Bitcoin middlemen and Bitcoin exchanges have been lost. Nowadays, the risk of this happening is much lower due to the maturation of the financial Bitcoin ecosystem. Nonetheless, it's always smart to store your bitcoins on these sites only for the absolute minimum amount of time possible. Bitcoin makes it extremely easy to manage your own money. Take advantage of this ability and don't trust the management of your money to an exchange intermediary.

BITCOIN ATMS: THE ULTIMATE BITCOIN MIDDLEMEN?

As previously stated, one of the annoyances of purchasing bitcoins at this time is that buying them can be a bit cumbersome due to traditional financial instruments, like credit cards and bank wires, being reversible. But the most obvious irreversible financial instrument is the almighty dollar bill. If a person hands you a dollar bill, that person can't reverse that transaction (short of being charged with physical assault).

Consequently, an ATM-like Bitcoin-buying device would make it extremely convenient to simply buy bitcoins using paper dollars. Such a machine could let you purchase bitcoins very quickly, because both currencies involved would be irreversible. The convenience of an ATM that charges comparable fees to Coinbase's could potentially make it the ultimate Bitcoin middleman. And, indeed, some Bitcoin ATMs have been built and have proven very popular. The first was set up in a coffee shop in Vancouver, Canada.

However, it is impossible to know whether such ATMs will ever be widespread or be completely legal in the United States. The reason is that dollar bills and bitcoins share more than just irreversibility. They also both allow for a certain amount of anonymity. For this reason, a Bitcoin ATM would indirectly be a fantastic tool for anonymizing money for money laundering and other nefarious purposes. And, unfortunately, many countries will not hesitate to ban anything that can aid a criminal, even if it would be tremendously beneficial to law-abiding citizens. Therefore, it's difficult to predict how commonplace Bitcoin ATMs will be in the future.

Buying Bitcoins the Efficient Way

The most efficient way to buy bitcoins is directly from a currency exchange. This requires a bit more time and has a steeper learning curve than using a middleman, but it is a somewhat safer and more cost-effective way to buy a large amount of bitcoins.

NOTE *Using a Bitcoin exchange is similar to using a brokerage account (like E-Trade or Ameritrade). If you've done any online equity trading, most of the information in this section should be familiar.*

At a *currency exchange*, you can deposit money in one currency and offer to exchange it for another currency at a rate that you choose. For example, you could offer to exchange $1 for 100 bitcoins, but you might find few takers. Other users who already own bitcoins might be equally generous and offer to trade their bitcoins for $100 million. Neither party is likely to have its offer satisfied. However, by raising your *bid* and other users lowering their *ask*, you will eventually meet in the middle and an exchange will take place. At popular exchanges, at any given moment, thousands of bids and asks are submitted for a wide range of offered rates. But the official rate is usually a number in between the highest bid and the lowest ask.

NOTE *The more users involved in the offering, the closer the bid and ask rates tend to be. But it's theoretically possible for the highest bid to be $200/BTC and the lowest ask to be $300/BTC, in which case it is difficult to say what the real exchange rate.*

Many Bitcoin currency exchanges are available to choose from, so which one should you register with? The currency exchanges make their money by charging a small fee for every trade (usually less than 0.5 percent), so basing your choice on the fee structure is one possibility. However, more important than fee structure are security, regulatory compliance, and trade volume. Many Bitcoin exchanges have been running successfully without issue for years, but some exchanges have been hacked (i.e., robbed) in the past or pressured by government authorities into shutting down for not obeying financial regulations. Trade volume is also an important factor to consider when choosing an exchange. The larger the trade volume, the more likely you are to get a fair price for your bitcoins, and the more bitcoins you are able to buy and sell per day. A small currency exchange that trades only 10 bitcoins per day on average will not be able to fill your bid orders quickly if you are trying to buy 100 bitcoins. Large trade volume is also indicative of the trust in and security of the currency exchange.

Of the three factors to consider when choosing an exchange, only trade volume information is easy to find. Table 4-2 lists exchanges that have reasonably high volume. In lieu of concrete information about a currency exchange's security practices and regulatory compliance, it is advisable for beginners to do business only with exchanges that have been operating for several years. The reason is that presumably, any issues with security or regulatory compliance have already been resolved or the exchange wouldn't exist. This statement may seem unfair to new exchanges, because they might even offer better security than older do exchanges. But when it comes to matters of money, being cautious is justifiable.

Table 4-2: Bitcoin Exchanges with Reasonable Volume

Exchange name	Currency pairs offered	Physical location	Established
ANXBTC	AUD/BTC, CAD/BTC, CHF/BTC, EUR/BTC, GBP/BTC, HKD/BTC, JPY/ BTC, NZD/BTC, SGD/BTC, USD/BTC	Hong Kong, China	2011
Bitstamp	USD/BTC	Bank in Slovenia, HQ in UK	2012
BTC China	CNY/BTC	China	2011
BTC-E	EUR/BTC, RUR/BTC, USD/BTC	Ukraine*	2010
CampBX	USD/BTC	Atlanta, Georgia, USA	2011
Cavirtex	CAD/BTC	Canada	2011
Kraken	EUR/BTC	San Francisco, California, USA	2012

* It is not exactly clear which country BTC-E is located in, because this company maintains a certain level of anonymity. If you're thinking to yourself, "Why would I send my money to a company if I don't even know what country it's located in?" then we think you're asking a very sensible question.

The country in which you live and the currency you want to exchange for bitcoins are also factors in choosing an exchange. Some exchanges facilitate only USD to BTC operations, whereas others offer multiple *currency pairs*.

You might notice that some Bitcoin currency exchanges offer currency pairs you have not heard of—for example, LTC, FTC, TRC, PPC, XPM, and so on. These other digital currencies—called *alternative coins* or *altcoins*—were created after, and largely inspired by, Bitcoin. To learn more about such digital currencies, check out "The Strange World of Altcoins" on page 181.

Many exchanges also have *different* BTC/USD exchange rates! This means you can sell bitcoins at a higher price on one exchange and buy them for a lower price on the other exchange. So this is free money, right? Well, yes and no. If the price difference is substantial and you are the first person to notice it, then indeed you have an opportunity to make some free money. However, you do need to keep in mind the amount of work it takes to transfer non-Bitcoin money in and out of exchanges; your time and effort aren't free. But more than likely, others will have noticed this difference before you and will have seized the free money opportunity, which is known as taking advantage of *arbitrage*. Any remaining difference in price between exchanges reflects the costs, due to trading fees and transfer fees (and other factors beyond the scope of this book), of moving money from one exchange to another. If one Bitcoin exchange rate is substantially different from all the others, it may indicate an underlying problem and probably should be avoided.

Additionally, it is important to remember that a currency exchange is not a bank. You should not leave significant amounts of money, whether fiat currency or bitcoins, sitting your exchange account. After purchasing bitcoins, transfer them to your personal Bitcoin wallet for safekeeping.

Buying Bitcoins from a Currency Exchange

Currently, no clear front-runner exists among the Bitcoin currency exchanges. Therefore, the following are general steps that you should apply to any Bitcoin exchange.

Step 1: Setting Up an Account and Linking to Your Bank Account

The first steps when buying bitcoins on an exchange are identical to the steps you used with Coinbase: Go to the exchange's website, create an account, and then connect it to your bank account. Some exchanges cannot be directly linked to your bank account and instead require you to send money via a bank wire or another method.

Step 2: Transferring US Dollars to Your Exchange Account

Bitcoin exchanges are different from exchange intermediaries in that they don't transfer the dollar equivalent from your bank account. On these sites you first need to transfer just dollars to your exchange account before you can turn them into bitcoins.

Step 3: Placing an Order to Buy Bitcoins

Once you've funded your exchange account with bitcoins, you can participate in the exchange market by placing an order for bitcoins. Usually, an exchange site will let you enter two types of orders: market orders and limit orders. Let's explore the properties of each order type so you can determine which is right for you.

Market Orders

By placing a *market order*, you specify that you want to buy bitcoins immediately at the best price currently available. The advantage of market orders is that they are executed quickly, so you won't have to wait for your bitcoins. Closing an order quickly is valuable if you have reason to believe the price will soon increase.

However, market orders have several important shortcomings. First, because you're specifying that you'll take *any* price to obtain your bitcoins quickly, there is always a rare chance the Bitcoin price might exhibit a momentary spike, forcing you to pay a much higher price than expected.

Second, if a commodity (any commodity, in fact) is traded at a low volume, it usually will also have a *large spread*, which is a large gap between the current best buy price and best sell price. Traders commonly make a guess as to the fair value of a commodity by taking the average of the buy and sell prices. If a commodity has a large spread, the price you'll pay at a market buy price will be significantly higher than the theoretical true price. Therefore, you should use market orders only for commodities that are traded at a high volume, which would have a small spread. For the most part, bitcoins have a relatively high volume at the large exchanges. So you might be satisfied paying this small premium for your bitcoins in exchange for getting your coins immediately.

Another more nebulous risk with market orders is that they make it possible for your order to be manipulated if another person learns about your order ahead of time, even if only by milliseconds. An outside person, a person inside the exchange company, or even the actual company that knows about your order in advance could buy some coins before your order is processed and then resell them to you at a slightly inflated price.

NOTE *Surely you've heard about the recent high-frequency trading shenanigans on Wall Street, some of which involved similar tricks with market orders.*

Limit Orders

To buy bitcoins with a *limit order*, you specify that you don't want to pay more than *X* dollars for each bitcoin and that you're willing to wait until you can get this price. Typically, you'll name a price lower than the current market price for bitcoins; then you'll wait for the price to drop to your price target. The risk with a limit order is that if the price of bitcoins keeps rising nonstop after your order is placed, your order will never execute. However, usually enough small market fluctuations occur in the Bitcoin markets that most limit orders with a limit close to a recent trade price will be successful.

Despite the extra time involved in obtaining your coins and despite the fact that your order may never be executed, a limit order has more advantages than a market order. For this reason, if you can wait to get your bitcoins, it's best to always use limit orders.

One advantage of using limit orders is that you won't be surprised by an unexpectedly high purchase price because you're the one who gets to decide on the ceiling for the price. Another advantage is that you can get a decent price, even if the trading volume on the exchange is low (with a large spread). Still another advantage is that other parties have more difficulty manipulating limit orders.

One final advantage is that limit orders are considered *market-making orders* by the operators of the exchanges. In essence, this means limit orders narrow the spread of a commodity by putting a new price on the table, whereas market orders widen the spread by eliminating prices. Although most current Bitcoin exchanges charge identical fees for market and limit orders, in other financial markets, limit orders often are available at a discount due to the benefits they offer the exchange operators. Therefore, in the future it is likely that Bitcoin exchanges will offer special discounts for limit orders on bitcoins as well.

Buying Bitcoins the Fun and Futuristic Way

As stated earlier, the fun and futuristic way to buy bitcoins is *person to person*. Today, it is relatively easy to find other bitcoiners online who live in your vicinity and meet them to buy bitcoins for cash. It can be fun to meet other people with whom you share an interest in bitcoins. Of course, some risk is always a possibility when performing financial transactions with strangers, so person-to-person transactions aren't for everyone. But we're currently seeing a major renaissance in person-to-person transactions in many fields.

Recently created businesses—such as Airbnb (a service that helps people privately rent out rooms), RelayRides (a service that lets you rent out your car), and Moxie Jean (a site for reselling children's clothes)—have proven that in our modern world most people are actually rather trustworthy. Additionally, if a good online rating system is available to mitigate cheating, you can perform financial transactions with strangers with relative safety.

These facts drive home one of the central lessons of the Bitcoin revolution: Technology can help society become more decentralized and less reliant on traditional, top-down companies and governments to perform many useful tasks. For this reason, person-to-person Bitcoin transactions are likely the future and might one day be faster, safer, and more cost-effective than any other Bitcoin-buying method.

Step 1: Finding Someone to Buy From

Your first step when finding a Bitcoin seller might be to simply ask your friends and family if they want to exchange bitcoins with you. Perhaps your uncle, niece, or cousin's best friend has a large amount of bitcoins. Also, by searching local Bitcoin listings, such as the listings maintained by LocalBitcoins.com, you can find people in your area who might be willing to meet up to exchange bitcoins. Other popular local listing sites, like Craigslist, sometimes list people who want to exchange bitcoins for dollars or vice versa.

When you're dealing with strangers, it's always best to find out whether they've previously engaged in successful Bitcoin transactions. LocalBitcoins.com also has a rating system that can help you determine this information. If no information about the sellers is available, purchase only a small amount from them the first time.

Step 2: Deciding on a Meeting Place

Any public place should be fine for a Bitcoin transaction; the most popular choice is usually a coffee shop. Keep in mind that you'll be carrying cash, so make sure you park your car in a public area if you're driving.

If you are performing a large transaction and want more safety, several additional options may be available to you. Some banks are more than happy to lend you a conference room for a business transaction, so be sure to ask. (They might charge a fee for this.)

NOTE *For very large Bitcoin transactions, you can't rely on an informal process. Instead, you'd be smart to get legal representation, write up a formal contract describing the transaction, and perform the trade in a law firm's office.*

Step 3: Handing Over the Money and Getting Your Bitcoins

You are at the coffee shop and are face-to-face with the seller. What happens next? Well, it depends on whether you want to use a Bitcoin escrow service as part of the transaction. We'll explain how escrow works shortly, but let's assume you're *not* using an escrow service for this transaction (most person-to-person transactions are done without escrow).

A Face-to-Face Bitcoin Purchase Without Escrow

By convention, the person who posted the online ad is paid first. Because most Bitcoin ads are for selling bitcoins, you (the buyer) will hand an envelope containing your dollars (or other fiat money) to the seller first. (Typically, people who place ads have established a long transaction history on LocalBitcoins.com, so it's only fair they get their payment first.)

The Bitcoin seller should then send the agreed-upon number of bitcoins to the public Bitcoin address in your Bitcoin wallet. Be sure to ask the seller to include a reasonable transaction fee in the transaction (currently, 0.0001btc is a reasonable fee). Within a few seconds, you should receive notification on your smartphone or laptop (connected to the Internet) that the money has been sent to your wallet.

For small transactions, you can now consider the exchange complete! However, for larger transactions, ask the seller to wait for additional confirmations in the blockchain. The first transaction confirmation should arrive in approximately 10 minutes and reliably guarantee that the money was transferred correctly. However, for very large transactions, you may want to wait for up to six confirmations just to be safe.

NOTE *Some wallet apps on your computer may not show the number of confirmations by default. In this case, try hovering your mouse over the transaction in question. Likely a pop-up hint will appear that will give you this information.*

Problems During Person-to-Person Transactions

Most transactions are straightforward and successful, especially if the seller has an established history of legitimate transactions. However, in the rare cases that problems arise, two types of complications tend to occur.

One is getting robbed on your way to the coffee shop: This happens when the seller has set up a meeting simply as a ruse for a convenient robbery. To avoid this scenario, be cautious if a seller asks for too many details about your appearance or the type of car you drive. These questions should raise a red flag.

The other dangerous scenario plays out as follows:

- You: "Okay, here's the envelope with my $500."
- Fraudulent Seller: "Okay, I just sent the bitcoins to your address. We're done!"
- You: "Hold on a second; I didn't get a notification that the money arrived."
- Fraudulent Seller: "I sent it properly. You're a beginner and don't know what you're doing. Now you're going to have to wait an hour for the money to show up because blah blah blah. I can't wait here all day; it's your fault you messed this up. Gotta run." (The fraudulent seller then tries to hurry out the door with your envelope.)

Again, this type of scenario rarely happens and is of course outright theft. You can avoid it by dealing only with sellers who have a solid reputation. You can also avoid it by relying on a Bitcoin escrow service, as discussed next.

A Face-to-Face Bitcoin Purchase with Escrow

One of the benefits of Bitcoin is that the Bitcoin blockchain has a built-in scripting language that allows you to use some convenient and secure techniques that are impossible with other types of money. One such technique is a *multi-signature transaction*, which gives you additional safety when performing Bitcoin transactions with another person. A multi-signature transaction requires multiple people to agree to a payment before it can be completed. In finance-speak, this allows you to set up a Bitcoin escrow service. An *escrow service* is a third party that holds on to an amount of money and makes sure the transaction goes smoothly before releasing the cash. However, a multi-signature transaction is more elegant than a traditional escrow service. Theoretically, a conventional escrow service can abscond with the money, but this is impossible with a multi-signature transaction.

This is because the third party does not actually have full control of the money—it is merely an arbitrator that can only make a binary decision as to whether or not the buyer or seller deserves the funds. Also, because multi-signature transactions are baked in to the Bitcoin system, they are very inexpensive to use, if not free.

NOTE *Even though multi-signature transactions are technically a slightly separate concept from escrow services, we'll still use the term* escrow service *for the remainder of this discussion.*

Currently, the most popular way to set up a Bitcoin escrow service is to use Bitrated (*http://bitrated.com/*), which is free at this time (although you need to choose an independent arbitrator, some of whom charge fees).

In addition, be aware that LocalBitcoins.com offers a similar escrow service, although it does *not* use Bitcoin's multi-signature feature. Therefore, you would need to trust the LocalBitcoins.com website with your money. Also, it is more expensive than using Bitrated.

NOTE *It's also technically feasible to set up a similar escrow system without an arbitrator. Instead of requiring the arbitrator to side with the buyer or seller to process the transaction, the buyer and seller can commit to a multi-signature transaction where they have to agree with each other. However, the money simply ends up in a black hole if a dispute transpires between the parties involved. The benefits of using this system are saving the expense and avoiding the complexity of dealing with an arbitrator. But this type of escrow is less popular because of said black hole.*

Because most person-to-person transactions are completed without a Bitcoin escrow service, you'll need to make sure the seller agrees if you intend to use this service. Not everyone is familiar with this concept yet. If you and the seller agree to use the service, your face-to-face transaction should go as follows:

1. The Bitcoin seller sends the bitcoins to the escrow service.
2. As the buyer, you verify that the bitcoins are in the escrow account as promised.
3. You hand the seller your envelope of dollars (or other fiat currency).
4. The seller signs off on the escrow, and you get your bitcoins.

As a result, at no time can the seller abscond with your dollars without sending bitcoins.

Satoshi Square

If meeting with strangers one-on-one makes you uncomfortable, you may be interested in going to a *Satoshi Square* event. Several major cities, such as New York, San Francisco, Boston, Toronto, and Vancouver, have had regular *live Bitcoin exchanges* where large groups of people meet in public spaces to buy and sell bitcoins. These meetups are also called *buttonwood exchanges*, named after the buttonwood tree under which the original Wall Street traders supposedly traded in the 1700s.

Still Don't See a Buying Option That Works for You?

If none of the options discussed in this chapter meet your needs for acquiring bitcoins, you have another alternative to acquire bitcoins that is probably better than any other: Sell something to bitcoiners for bitcoins! Die-hard bitcoiners dream that someday they'll be able to relinquish all fiat currencies. Someday, we can imagine, you won't need to buy bitcoins with other money, because bitcoins will *be* the money.

CHAPTER 5: Lost at Sea

A CRYPTOGRAPHIC ADVENTURE

A WHILE AGO, CROWLEY THE CRYPTOGRAPHER WAS ON A CRYPTOGRAPY CRUISE TO LEARN ALL THE LATEST ADVANCES IN THE FIELD.
HEY CROWLEY, HAVE YOU HEARD ABOUT THE 2 P.M. LECTURE? SOMEONE IS DEMOING A REAL WWII ENIGMA MACHINE!
WOW! THAT'S SO COOL!
HEY GUYS, I'LL BE RIGHT BACK... GOTTA REFRESH MY DRINK.
OF COURSE, SEE YOU LATER!

EXCUSE ME, SIR...
TAP! TAP!
...YOU AREN'T BY ANY CHANCE CROWLEY THE FAMOUS CRYPTOGRAPHER?
HMM... WELL, YEAH... AND YOU ARE... ??
I PREFER TO STAY ANONYMOUS...
MIND IF I CALL YOU "BAGHEAD" THEN?
I'D RATHER YOU DIDN'T...
WOULD "DR. NO" WORK FOR YOU?
UM, NO...
ALRIGHT, THEN HOW ABOUT "DEEP THROAT"?
IF YOU HAVE TO CALL ME SOMETHING, CALL ME...
SATOSHI!

SO DR. CROWLEY, I'D LIKE TO TELL YOU ABOUT A NEW TYPE OF MONEY I INVENTED CALLED BITCOINS!
A NEW TYPE OF MONEY?! OK, WHY DON'T YOU TELL ME HOW THIS SO-CALLED "MONEY" IS SUPPOSED TO WORK...
SURE! BUT FIRST I HAVE TO EXPLAIN HOW BANKS ARE CREATED WITH BITCOIN...
MEANWHILE...
...NOW WE HAVE ENCODED THE MESSAGE *"YOUR MOMMA SMELLS LIKE SAUERKRAUT"* ON A REAL WWII ENIGMA MACHINE!
IT JUST SO HAPPENS, I WAS ALSO ABLE TO BORROW A REAL WWII GERMAN SHORT-WAVE RADIO FOR THIS PRESENTATION! NOW WE CAN TRULY SEE HOW THE FULL PROCESS USED TO WORK!

ELSEWHERE...
KAPITÄN... AFTER THESE MANY YEARS, WE HAVE FINALLY RECEIVED AN OFFICIAL, ENCODED MESSAGE FROM A SHIP AT 27°NW AND 30 NAUTICAL MILES!
REALLY? WHAT DOES IT SAY?
MEANWHILE, ON THE SHIP...
...AND SO HERE YOU CAN SEE I HAVE 40 BITCOINS IN THIS ACCOUNT...
I'M AFRAID THEY HAVE INSULTED YOUR MOTHER!
BANG!
TAKE THAT, YOU SCHWEINEHUND!

IN THE CHAOS THAT FOLLOWED, THERE WASN'T ENOUGH TIME TO MAN THE LIFE RAFTS. CRYPTOGRAPHERS EVERYWHERE JUMPED IN PANIC AND CLUNG TO ANY DEBRIS THEY COULD FIND.
LUCKILY, CROWLEY WAS ABLE TO USE HIS PHD DISSERTATION AS A FLOATATION DEVICE...

SPLASH!
TWO DAYS HE SPENT FLOATING IN THE OCEAN...
WHEN FINALLY...

ALL CROWLEY COULD DO WAS DRAG HIMSELF ONTO THE SHORE.
HE SLEPT ALL DAY AND NIGHT IN THAT SAME SPOT.
THE NEXT MORNING, CROWLEY FINALLY HAD ENOUGH ENERGY TO EXPLORE THE ISLAND. HOWEVER, IT TOOK HIM ONLY A FEW MINUTES. THERE WAS NOTHING THERE EXCEPT A FEW PALM TREES (WITH DATES AND COCONUTS) AS WELL AS MANY BIRDS. THEIR PRESENCE SUGGESTED THAT OTHER LAND COULD BE NEARBY.
WITH HIS STRONG CROCODILE JAW, CROWLEY EASILY PUNCTURED THE COCONUTS AND DRANK THE DELICIOUS COCONUT MILK!

OTHERWISE, ALL CROWLEY HAD WAS THE PAPER FROM HIS PHD DISSERTATION, THE PENCILS FROM HIS BREAST POCKET, AND HIS LUCKY DIE.
HMM... I GUESS I'M JUST GONNA HAVE TO WAIT HERE AND HOPE A RESCUE TEAM FINDS ME...
AND SO, HE BEGAN TO WAIT.
AFTER A WEEK, HE DECIDED HE WOULD LEARN HOW TO JUGGLE PENCILS...
AFTER TWO MONTHS, HE WAS A MASTER PENCIL JUGGLER.
THE NEXT FOUR MONTHS HE SPENT PLAYING YAHTZEE AGAINST HIMSELF.

THEN, ALL OF A SUDDEN, CROWLEY HAD AN IDEA...
HEY... WITH THIS PAPER, MY PENCILS, AND MY DIE, I HAVE EVERYTHING I NEED TO TRY OUT SOME OF THE IDEAS THAT "SATOSHI" GUY WAS TELLING ME ABOUT!
AND SO CROWLEY GOT TO WORK WITH THE CALCULATIONS.
AFTER MANY MONTHS OF WORK, HE HAD ACCOMPLISHED HIS GOAL: HE HAD CREATED HIMSELF A BANK ACCOUNT!
PUBLIC ADDRESS
1LdzhAhiV6vmypkRH
FZCeLvAoSgPxe7RPj
PRIVATE ADDRESS
5K8DMnKeQ2KmB2482
wTYLq2746wQKrQ4Ni
dbsRmUe3AabMB

WHAT CROWLEY DID (CREATING HIS OWN BANK ACCOUNT) WAS AN AMAZING FEAT!

JUST THINK ABOUT IT: IF YOU WANTED TO CREATE A BANK ACCOUNT WITH A TRADITIONAL CURRENCY (SUCH AS DOLLARS), WHAT WOULD YOU DO? GO TO A BANK, OF COURSE!

BUT WITH BITCOINS, WE DON'T NEED NO STINKIN' BANKS! (NOR DO WE NEED PAYPAL™, OR STRIPE™, OR MASTERCARD™, OR EVEN A SOVEREIGN GOVERNMENT™...)

ANYBODY CAN BE THEIR OWN BANK AND CAN CREATE BANK ACCOUNTS AT WILL. ALL YOU NEED IS A SOURCE OF RANDOM NUMBERS (LIKE A DIE) AND SOME CALCULATIONS. AND, WITH A COMPUTER, THE CALCULATIONS TO CREATE SUCH A BANK ACCOUNT TAKE ONLY A FRACTION OF A SECOND.

AT ITS HEART, A BITCOIN BANK ACCOUNT IS NOTHING MORE THAN TWO ADDRESSES: A PUBLIC ADDRESS AND A PRIVATE ADDRESS. IF YOU WANT SOMEONE TO SEND YOU MONEY, YOU GIVE THEM YOUR PUBLIC ADDRESS. TO ACCESS THAT MONEY, AND THEN YOU USE THE PRIVATE ADDRESS.

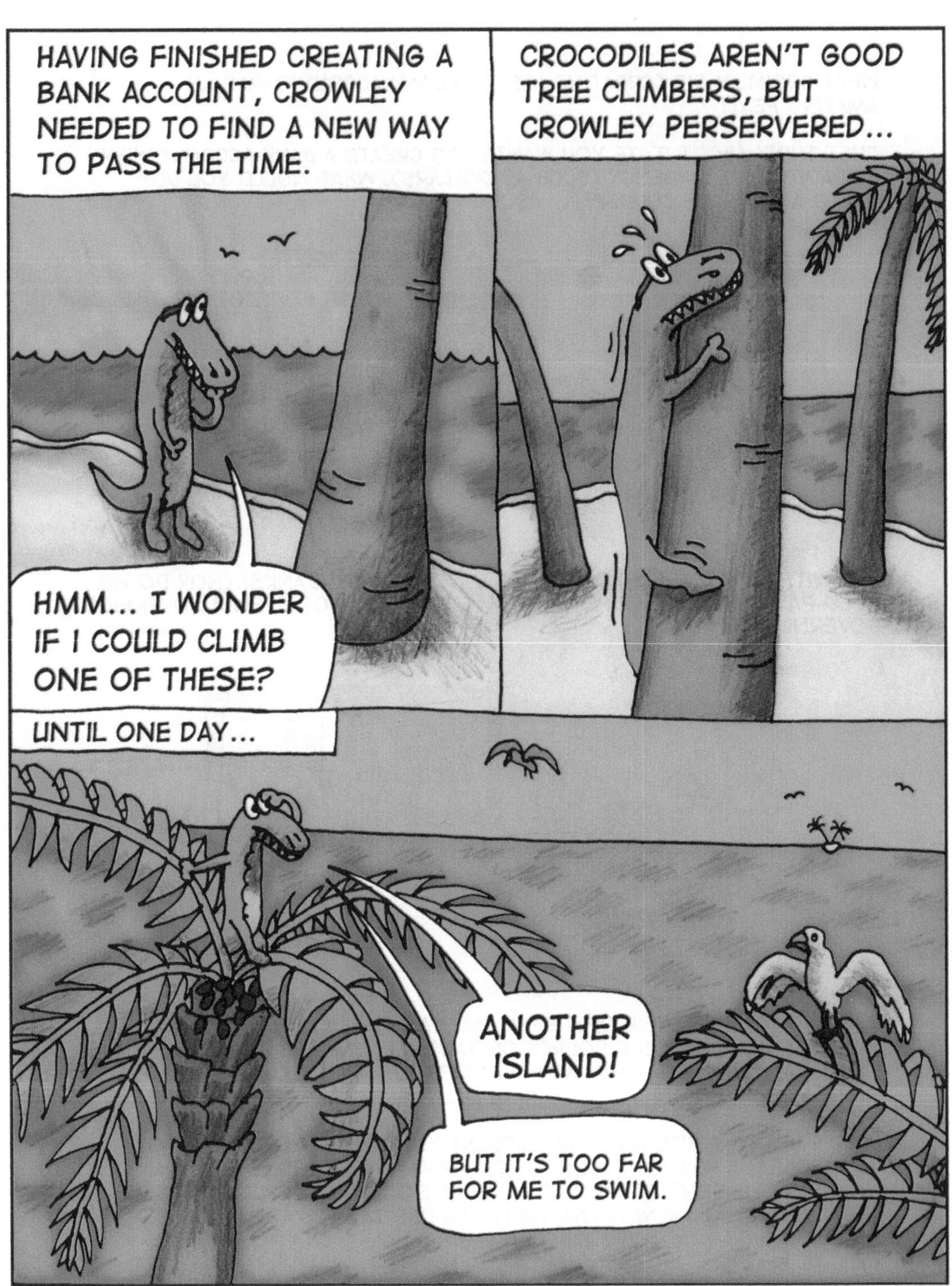
HAVING FINISHED CREATING A BANK ACCOUNT, CROWLEY NEEDED TO FIND A NEW WAY TO PASS THE TIME.
HMM... I WONDER IF I COULD CLIMB ONE OF THESE?
CROCODILES AREN'T GOOD TREE CLIMBERS, BUT CROWLEY PERSERVERED...
UNTIL ONE DAY...
ANOTHER ISLAND!
BUT IT'S TOO FAR FOR ME TO SWIM.

HOWEVER, CROWLEY SAW A RED PARROT THAT HAD JUST FLOWN FROM THE OTHER ISLAND.
HMM... MAYBE I COULD ATTACH A NOTE TO THIS BIRD...
GOTCHA!
HELP! I'M TRAPPED ON AN ISLAND!
I'M A CASTAWAY FROM A CRUISE SHIP. IF YOU
HIS NOTE PLEASE
E HELP!
SINCERELY,
CROWLEY, THE CROCO
CRYPTOGRAPHER
MY BITCOIN ADDRESS
1LdZhAhiV6vmypkRHFZCeLvAoSgPxe7RP
AND JUST FOR FUN, BECAUSE HE WAS SO PROUD OF HIS WORK, HE PUT HIS BITCOIN ADDRESS AT THE BOTTOM OF THE LETTER.

THE NEXT DAY...
THE BIRD HAS A NEW NOTE!
HI CROWLEY, THIS IS SATOSHI! I, TOO, AM TRAPPED ON AN ISLAND! I CAN SEE YOUR ISLAND HAS DATE PALMS ON IT... COULD YOU SEND ME SOME DATES? I HEARD YOU HAVE A PHOTOGRAPHIC MEMORY, SO YOU'LL REMEMBER I SHOWED YOU THAT MY BITCOIN ACCOUNT WITH THE PUBLIC ADDRESS 17QGqFshx9NfXh5TrfMkn1m34bWr2hL1AY HAD 40 BITCOINS IN IT. I JUST SENT YOU ONE OF THOSE IN PAYMENT FOR THE DATES!
-SATOSHI

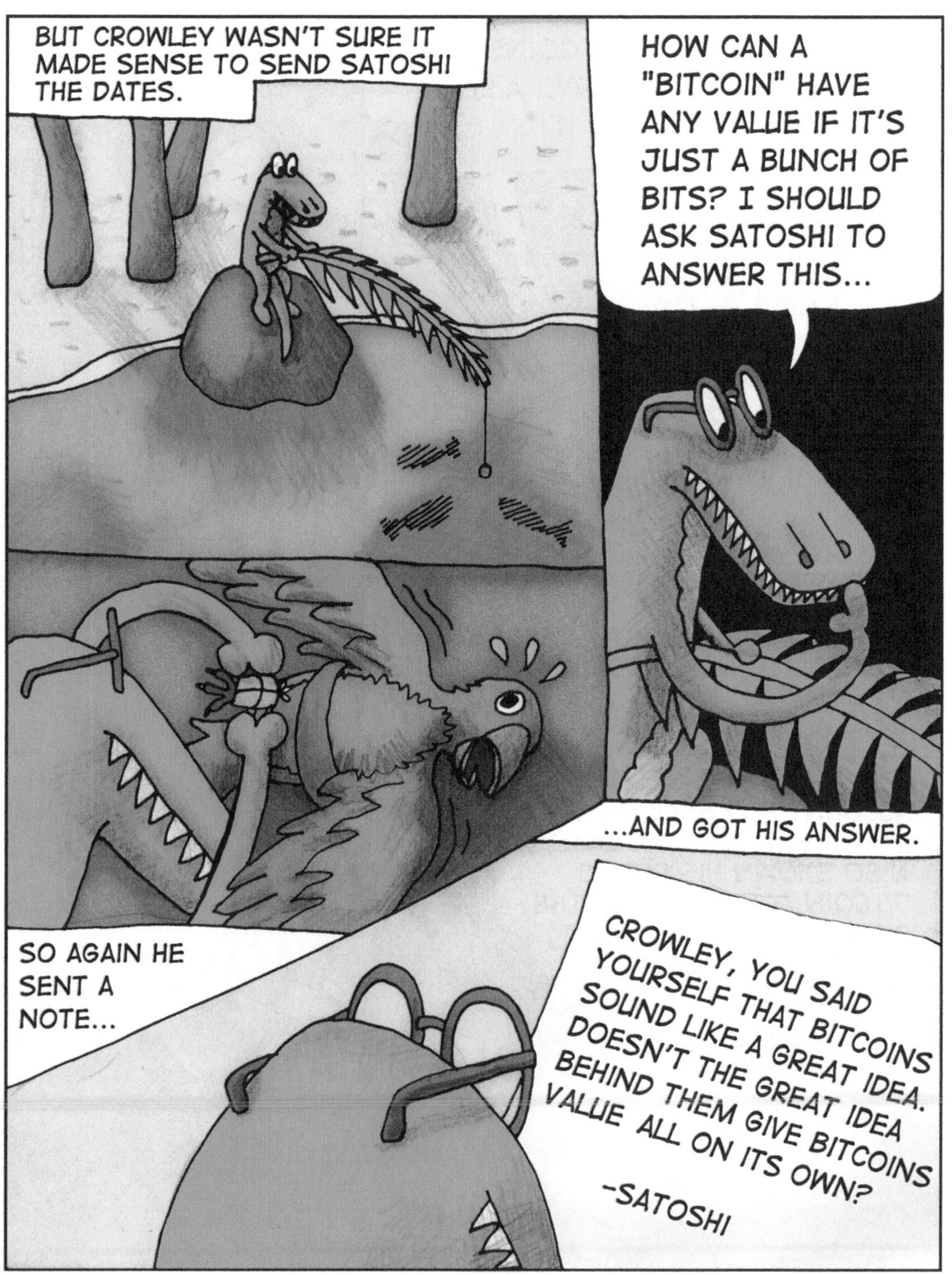
BUT CROWLEY WASN'T SURE IT MADE SENSE TO SEND SATOSHI THE DATES.
HOW CAN A "BITCOIN" HAVE ANY VALUE IF IT'S JUST A BUNCH OF BITS? I SHOULD ASK SATOSHI TO ANSWER THIS...
SO AGAIN HE SENT A NOTE...
...AND GOT HIS ANSWER.
CROWLEY, YOU SAID YOURSELF THAT BITCOINS SOUND LIKE A GREAT IDEA. DOESN'T THE GREAT IDEA BEHIND THEM GIVE BITCOINS VALUE ALL ON ITS OWN?
-SATOSHI

HMM... I SUPPOSE BITCOINS ARE A GOOD IDEA AND DESERVE A LEAP OF FAITH. OK, I'LL DO IT!*
*THESE DAYS YOU NO LONGER NEED FAITH TO ACCEPT BITCOINS. THE REASON IS THAT PEOPLE NOWADAYS ARE HAPPY TO GIVE YOU COLD, HARD DOLLARS FOR THEM.
BUT WAIT A SECOND...
IT'S TRUE I KNOW SATOSHI'S ACCOUNT HAD ENOUGH MONEY IN IT... BUT HE'S PROBABLY ALSO SHOWN HIS PUBLIC BITCOIN ADDRESS, AND THE BITCOINS IN HIS ACCOUNT, TO OTHER PEOPLE, AS WELL...
ARGH... THIS PERSON COULD BE A SATOSHI IMPER-SONATOR!

HOW DO I KNOW YOU'RE REALLY SATOSHI!?
HERE'S HOW YOU KNOW I'M SATOSHI... I TOOK THIS SENTENCE:
"I, Satoshi, hereby send 1 bitcoin to Crowley's bitcoin account at address 1LdZhahiV6vmypkRHFZCeLvAoSgPxe7RPj"
AND THEN I ENCODED IT WITH THE PRIVATE KEY FOR MY ACCOUNT TO GET THE FOLLOWING:
HOiD8Jtav271iZGDP1znkUFXzZRvVX
dFFHthGaTg50OrEpFvy8OW3kqOWHyi
UmbOVNiZSeieL8ZyhmX12/GBR0E=
YOU CAN USE MY PUBLIC KEY TO PROVE THAT ONLY SATOSHI COULD HAVE DONE THAT!

As you can see, Satoshi was able to sign a message with his own private key and thus prove to Crowley that he (Satoshi) owned a certain Bitcoin address. To understand how this is possible, you need to learn about a weird asymmetry that mathematicians discovered a long time ago:

1. It's very easy to figure out if a large number has factors (i.e., that it isn't a prime number).
2. It can be very, very hard to figure out what those factors are.

Now, most regular people would expect that these two ideas would be equally hard to figure out: After all, it seems like there's no way to know whether factors exist without actually *finding* those factors. But as it turns out, mathematicians came up with some strange algorithms that can solve problem #1 without needing to solve problem #2 (one popular algorithm is called the *Miller-Rabin primality test*).

So why does this little asymmetry matter? Actually, almost every modern technology you can think of was invented by some clever person who noticed a seemingly inconsequential asymmetry:

- Antibiotics exploit tiny asymmetries in bacterial versus animal cell metabolism.

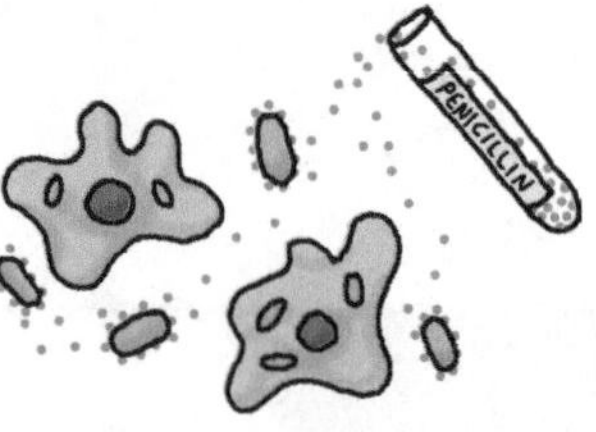

- A steam engine exploits small pressure differences between steam and water mixed with air.

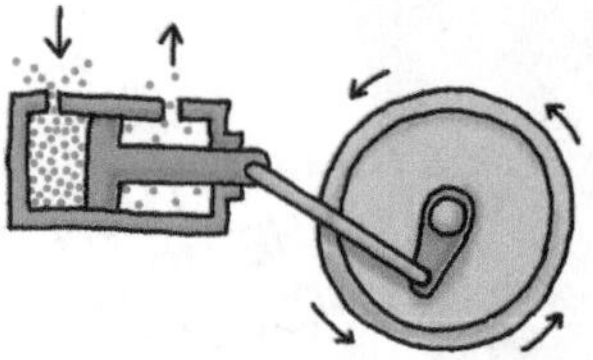

- Computer chips work due to tiny differences between two impure variants of silicon, called p-type and n-type silicon.

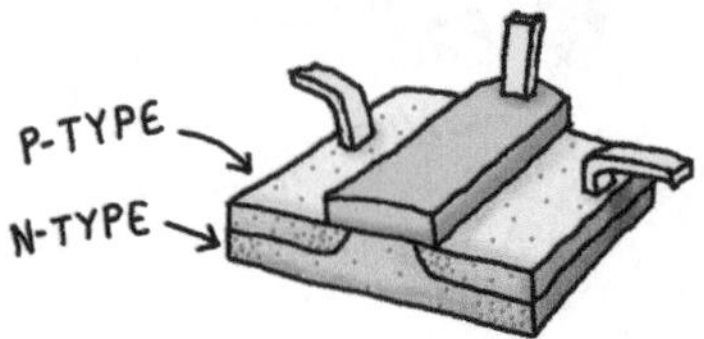

Heck, cosmologists tell us that the only reason our galaxy exists at all is due to tiny asymmetries in the amount of matter and antimatter that were created by the Big Bang, leaving a surplus of matter that went on to create everything we see!

Anyway, some smart guys in the 1970s looked at this asymmetry in number factoring and noticed that if they multiplied two large prime numbers (which are very easy to find, given #1), it was virtually impossible to figure out what the original numbers were (because of #2)!

Most modern cryptography is based on this little fact: It turns out that using such prime numbers, you can create a private/public cryptographic key pair (we cover this cryptography in detail in Chapter 7), which is exactly what private and public Bitcoin addresses are!

Why does this matter? Well, it turns out that if you have such a pair of keys, you can do a couple of almost magical tasks with them:

1. If a person has a public key, they can create a message that only the owner of the private key can read. (This is called *public key encryption.*)
2. If a person has the private key, they can create a message that cannot be forged, because any person can use the public key to verify the authenticity of this message. (This is called a *digital signature.*)

In our example, Satoshi signed a message with his private key in this way while promising 1 bitcoin to Crowley.

As you saw, this is Satoshi's public key:

```
17QGqFshx9NfXh5TrfMkn1m34bWr2hL1AY
```

Here is the message promising the bitcoin to go to Crowley's Bitcoin address:

```
I, Satoshi, hereby send 1 bitcoin to Crowley's Bitcoin account at address
1LdZhahiV6vmypkRHFZCeLvAoSgPxe7RPj.
```

Here is the signature, created with the fancy-pants cryptography we've been discussing:

```
HoiD8JtaV271iZGDP1znkUFxzZRvVXdFFHthGaTg50Or
EpFvy8OW3kqOwHyiUmbOVNiZSeieL8ZyhmXl2/GBROE=
```

At this point, you should be asking one very important question: Can we actually prove that this is a valid, signed message? Why yes, we can do so very easily! Just follow these steps:

1. Go to *http://brainwallet.org/#verify* (or one of many other sites like it).
2. Enter the message and the signature.
3. Click **Verify Message**.
4. You can now see that the message was signed by Satoshi, the owner of Bitcoin address `17QGqFshx9NfXh5TrfMkn1m34bWr2hL1AY`!

CROWLEY COULD SEE THE TRUTH IN THIS, BUT SOMETHING STILL NAGGED AT HIM THAT NIGHT...
WAIT! WHAT IF THERE'S ANOTHER GUY ON ANOTHER ISLAND AND SATOSHI IS TELLING BOTH OF US HE SENT THE BITCOIN FROM HIS ACCOUNT?
THE NEXT DAY...
WHAT IN THE...
3.1 bitcoins sent from
1Gc3Z7VBSPzACi5dZcETFPCnoc3XGkcYyA to
1KhajdjTt5bCiYGcf3F728nXjwRONKd8e
0.2 bitcoins sent from
1LzJvmDxjnukziGxCSmcbAzwukyj7MpEtA to
1HkUxk7GdrpMtkpBGL6wqbRPXr9PgE3WDp
102.2 bitcoins sent from
1GGpb4nwA6wgj13D3yvdSp4ny8Z7QmoXnB to
1NQNst4w2ktyRoh6CnBNB4g4SrJwnBL3VQ
0.001 bitcoins sent from
1LUGVUnHJv2sZ98EVwKog2wKThwa5P5ZtC to
1AmdtJ16nhB9Rhqhaiv6UQh3goypB7K3nR
1022.22 bitcoins sent from
1FrPhoMDrKAmp4uBPMGuwFRuc3dtpZXXVz to
1LNqyrYyH6S4MydKSY2vUR8kYo4tARfQRR
0.0023 bitcoins sent from
IT'S A GIANT LEDGER OF FINANCIAL TRANSACTIONS!

"DEAR CROWLEY, YOU'RE WORRIED THAT I MIGHT HAVE DOUBLE SPENT THAT BITCOIN."
"THE ONLY WAY TO BE SURE I DIDN'T DO THIS IS TO READ THROUGH THIS LEDGER THAT HAS A RECORD OF EVERY BITCOIN EVER SPENT. YOU WILL SEE IT CLEARLY ACCOUNTS FOR THE 1 BITCOIN I SENT TO YOU. BUT, OF COURSE, YOU STILL CAN'T BE 100% SURE I DIDN'T FALSIFY SOME ENTRIES...
SATOSHI
OTHERS
CROWLEY
OTHERS
...BUT IT TURNS OUT THERE ARE MANY OTHER CRYPTOGRAPHERS TRAPPED ON ISLANDS RIGHT NOW. IF YOU ATTACH NOTES TO SOME OF THE *OTHER* BIRDS ON YOUR ISLAND, YOU CAN ASK FOR OTHER, INDEPENDENT COPIES OF THE LEDGER TO MAKE SURE IT'S GENUINE!"

SO CROWLEY SPENT A DAY CATCHING ALL THE BIRDS ON THE ISLAND AND ATTACHING NOTES TO THEM.
SQUAK!
SQUAK!
WOW! THIS PERSON ALSO WANTS TO BUY SOME DATES.
HI, MY NAME IS LISA! HERE'S MY VERSION OF THE LEDGER. ALSO, I SENT YOU 2 BTC FOR SOME DATES!

CROWLEY GOT SIX COPIES OF THE LEDGER FROM ALL THE ISLANDS. NOW HE HAD TO MAKE SURE THEY ALL MATCHED.
HEY, WAIT A SECOND... THIS ISN'T RIGHT!
ONLY TWO OF THEM SAY THAT SATOSHI SENT ME MONEY... AND THE OTHER FOUR SAY THAT LISA SENT ME MONEY, INSTEAD.
SO CROWLEY WROTE TO SATOSHI...
"CROWLEY, YOU CAN'T TRUST LISA: SHE'S A SCAMMER TRYING TO STEAL FROM YOU! FOUR OF THE BIRDS PROBABLY WENT TO THE SAME ISLAND... ***HER ISLAND!*** SHE IS PRETENDING TO BE FOUR SEPARATE PEOPLE IN ORDER TO TRICK YOU INTO ACCEPTING A FORGED LEDGER!"

SINCE BITCOIN IS A PEER-TO-PEER TECHNOLOGY, MAKING SURE YOU GET AN ACCURATE COPY OF THE GLOBAL LEDGER IS VERY DIFFICULT: ANY ONE OF THE PEERS YOU CONNECT TO MIGHT TRY TO SWINDLE YOU... AND SOME OF THEM MIGHT EVEN BE IN CAHOOTS WITH EACH OTHER.
TRANSACTIONS
TO GUARD AGAINST THIS, SPECIAL BITCOIN USERS CALLED ***MINERS*** HAVE BEEN ARRANGING THE NUMBERS FROM THE TRANSACTION LEDGER INTO CROSSWORD PUZZLES.* EACH FINISHED CROSSWORD IS CALLED A ***BLOCK***. THE ENTIRE LEDGER IS ARRANGED IN A CHAIN OF SUCH BLOCKS CALLED A ***BLOCKCHAIN***.

WAIT A SECOND...
EUREKA! I HAVE CREATED ANOTHER ELEGANT CROSSWORD PUZZLE FOR THE LATEST TRANSACTIONS. NOW I CAN ADD IT TO THE CHAIN!
*MINERS DON'T REALLY CREATE CROSSWORD PUZZLES, BUT YOU'LL HAVE A GOOD CONCEPTUAL UNDERSTANDING IF YOU THINK OF THE BLOCKCHAIN THAT WAY.

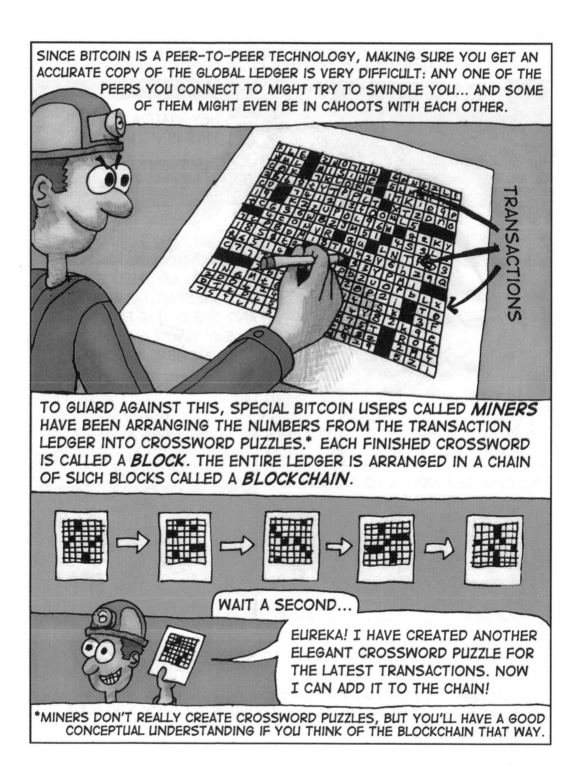

WHY WOULD YOU WANT TO ARRANGE THE LEDGER ENTRIES INTO A CROSSWORD PUZZLE? BECAUSE A CROSSWORD PUZZLE REQUIRES A LOT OF TRIAL AND ERROR TO GENERATE AND ITS SHAPE IS HIGHLY DEPENDENT ON EVERY ENTRY.

HMM... IF I PUT THE NUMBER 58723984523 ACROSS, I NEED TO PUT 06244443255 DOWN, BUT THEN I CAN'T PUT ANYTHING NEXT TO IT... DARN, I'M STUCK...

IT MIGHT TAKE A DAY FOR ONE MINER TO FIND A SOLUTION. BUT BECAUSE MAKING THIS CROSSWORD PUZZLE IS A HAPHAZARD PROCESS, USUALLY ONE OF THE MANY MINERS WILL GET LUCKY AND FIND A SOLUTION IN MERE MINUTES.

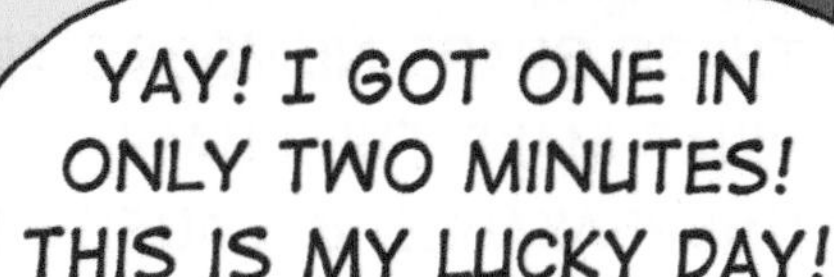

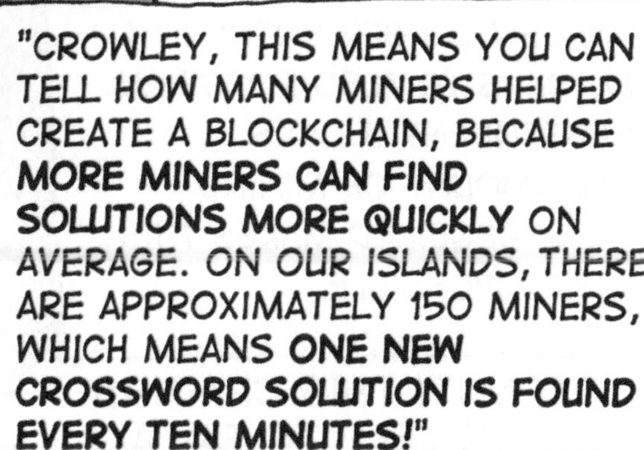

AS AN EXTRA PRECAUTION AGAINST FORGERY, MINERS ADD AN EXTRA NUMBER TO EACH CROSSWORD THAT ENCODES THE "SHAPE" OF THE PREVIOUS BLOCK.

SHAPE#

SHAPE#

SHAPE#

(COMPUTER GEEKS KNOW THIS **"SHAPE NUMBER"** AS THE **HASH** OF THE PREVIOUS BLOCK.)

THESE SHAPE NUMBERS ARE WHAT MAKE THE CHAIN UNBREAKABLE. BECAUSE OF THEM, THE ONLY WAY TO FORGE A LEDGER ENTRY IN A BLOCK IS TO ALSO FORGE ALL SUBSEQUENT BLOCKS. THE AMOUNT OF MINING WORK REQUIRED MAKES THIS NIGH IMPOSSIBLE.

DARN IT! THIS CHAIN IS IMPOSSIBLE TO BREAK!

SO WHY DO MINERS DO ALL THE WORK REQUIRED TO CREATE THESE CROSSWORD PUZZLE BLOCKS? VERY SIMPLE: MINERS ARE ALLOWED TO ADD AN EXTRA ENTRY TO A NEW BLOCK THAT DEPOSITS 25 FREE BITCOINS* INTO THEIR OWN ACCOUNT! THESE 25 "MINED" BITCOINS ARE CREATED OUT OF THIN AIR AND ARE A MINER'S REWARD.

IN THE EARLY DAYS, IT WAS EASY TO EARN COINS BY MINING.

WOO-HOO! NOW MY KIDS CAN GO TO COLLEGE!

BUT NOWADAYS, THE COMPETITION IS FIERCE, AND IT'S UNLIKELY YOU'LL "STRIKE IT RICH" AS A MINER ANYMORE.

CLACK!

YOU MINE 25 COINS
AND WHADAYA GET,
ANOTHER DAY OLDER
AND DEEPER IN DEBT...

CRACK!

A BLOCKCHAIN GANG, AKA A MINING POOL

*25 BITCOINS AS OF TODAY: THE NUMBER OF COINS DECREASES OVER TIME.

HOLY COW, THAT WAS ONE EPIC LETTER! I'M GOING TO SLEEP ON THIS A BIT AND COME UP WITH A PLAN IN THE MORNING!
YAWN!
WHEN CROWLEY WOKE UP IN THE MORNING, HE KNEW EXACTLY WHAT TO DO...
THANKS FOR SENDING ME THE LEDGER, DEAR BITCOIN-USING STRANGER... BUT THIS TIME, WOULD YOU MIND SENDING ME A COPY OF THE FULL BLOCKCHAIN INSTEAD?

SOON THEREAFTER, CROWLEY HAD SIX COPIES OF THE BLOCKCHAIN SENT TO HIM. NEXT, HE HAD TO ANALYZE THEM AND MAKE SURE NO ONE CHEATED IN CREATING CORRECT CROSSWORD PUZZLES.
A WHILE LATER...
OK, THERE ARE NO ERRORS IN ANY OF THE BLOCKS IN THESE SIX BLOCKCHAINS...
BUT, AS BEFORE, ONLY FOUR OF THEM HAVE LISA'S TRANSACTION IN WHICH SHE SUPPOSEDLY SENT ME 2 BITCOINS. THOSE BLOCKCHAINS HAVE ***TWO CROSSWORD PUZZLES AFTER*** THE ONE THAT INCLUDES LISA'S TRANSACTION.

ON THE OTHER HAND, ONLY TWO OF THE BLOCKCHAINS HAVE SATOSHI'S PAYMENT.
HOWEVER, THOSE BLOCKCHAINS HAVE ***TWENTY BLOCKS*** AFTER THE ONE IN DISPUTE, MANY MORE THAN IN THE OTHER VERSION OF THE BLOCKCHAIN. SO EVEN THOUGH I GOT FEWER COPIES OF THAT VERSION OF THE BLOCKCHAIN FROM PEERS, WE KNOW THAT ***FAR MORE MINERS IN THE BITCOIN NETWORK PARTICIPATED IN CREATING THAT VERSION***. THEREFORE, WE CAN BE SURE THAT IT IS THE MORE TRUTHFUL VERSION OF THE LEDGER. THIS MEANS LISA IS A SCAMMER WHO CREATED A FORGED VERSION OF THE BLOCKCHAIN!

CROWLEY WAS FINALLY CONVINCED THAT SATOSHI HAD INDEED SENT HIM 1 BITCOIN WITHOUT ANY DOUBT! WITH FULL CONFIDENCE, CROWLEY COULD FINALLY SEND HIM SOME DATES IN EXCHANGE!

AND WITH THAT, SATOSHI, CROWLEY, AND THE OTHER CRYPTOGRAPHERS HAD CREATED A NEW CURRENCY THAT WAS COMPLETELY DECENTRALIZED AND SECURE AND COULD BE DIRECTLY SENT AS PURE DIGITAL INFORMATION BETWEEN ANY TWO PEOPLE ON A NETWORK.

THE END...

...OR IS IT?
DARN... I'M STILL STUCK ON THIS ISLAND... BUT AT LEAST I HAVE SOME MONEY NOW.
HMM... I WONDER IF ANYONE COULD SELL ME SOME BANANAS?
LOOKS LIKE MY ORDER HAS ARRIVED!
GREAT! LOOKS LIKE I ALSO HAVE ANOTHER ORDER FOR DATES FOR 1.5 BTC!
AND THIS WOMAN KNOWS A GUY ON ANOTHER ISLAND SELLING STRAW HAMMOCKS FOR 4 BTC.
I AM CERTAINLY TIRED OF SLEEPING ON SAND... I WONDER IF HE COULD MAKE ME A DELUXE HAMMOCK WITH CUP HOLDERS?

MANY YEARS LATER...
HMM... I'M REALLY GETTING THE HANG OF THESE COCONUT MOJITOS... WOAH! IS SOMETHING OUT THERE?
HOLY COW!

AFTER ALL THESE 50 YEARS, FINALLY ***A SHIP!***
ERM... I MEAN HOVERCRAFT? OR MAYBE AN EKRANOPLAN... PERHAPS?
SPLASH!
SPLASH!
HI THERE, OLD-TIMER... HAH! YOU LOOK LIKE YOU'VE NEVER SEEN A LEVITATING YACHT BEFORE!
ACTUALLY, I HAVEN'T SEEN ANYTHING FROM THE OUTSIDE WORLD IN OVER FIFTY YEARS! I'VE BEEN WAITING TO BE RESCUED FOR ALL THIS TIME...
SPLISH!
SPLASH!
NO PROBLEM, DUDE. TELL YOU WHAT... I'LL BE BACK HERE IN A MONTH, AND THEN I'LL BE HAPPY TO TAKE YOU TO THE MAINLAND.

A MONTH?! WHY CAN'T YOU JUST TAKE ME NOW?
I'D REALLY LOVE TO, BUT THIS YACHT IS A RENTAL AND I'M HEADING TO THE ANTARCTIC BASIN FOR MUTANT JELLYFISH SEASON. IF I PLAY MY CARDS RIGHT, I COULD EARN UP TO 0.0001 BITCOINS DOWN THERE THIS MONTH!
WHAA??... UHM, OK... WELL, HOW 'BOUT I JUST PAY YOU A HUNDRED TIMES THAT MUCH RIGHT NOW... WOULD THAT WORK?
WELL YEAH, OF COURSE. WOWZER! YOU MUST BE RIDICULOUSLY RICH. WHAT, DO YOU OWN A WHOLE BITCOIN, OR SOMETHING?
I CAN TELL YOU ABOUT IT ALONG THE WAY... BUT FIRST I'D LIKE YOU TO HELP ME STOP BY A NEIGHBORING ISLAND SO I CAN LOOK IN ON AN OLD FRIEND...

AND SO CROWLEY AND THE YOUNGSTER TOOK A DRIVE IN THE HOVER YACHT OVER TO SATOSHI'S ISLAND...
?
NOTHING! THERE'S NOTHING HERE!
I *KNOW* THIS WAS THE PLACE THE BIRDS WERE FLYING TO... HOW CAN THIS BE?
WAIT! I SEE SOMETHING BEHIND THAT ROCK OVER THERE...
OH, NEVER MIND. IT'S JUST A PAPER BAG.
THE END

6

WHY BITCOIN IS A BIG DEAL

There is no question that Bitcoin is a novel technology, and certainly the idea of a universal stateless currency is audacious. However, many doubt that Bitcoin will make a lasting impact on the world's economies. Indeed, you may be wondering: Is Bitcoin a world-altering technology or merely a technological gimmick? In this chapter, we'll discuss both sides of this question. Because reviewing the past is often the first step in understanding the future, let's start by briefly delving into the history of Bitcoin and digital currencies in general.

> The root problem with conventional currency is all the trust that's required to make it work. The central bank must be trusted not to debase the currency, but the history of fiat currencies is full of breaches of that trust. Banks must be trusted to hold our money and transfer it electronically, but they lend it out in waves of credit bubbles with barely a fraction in reserve. We have to trust them with our privacy, trust them not to let identity thieves drain our accounts.
> —Satoshi Nakamoto, first post on the P2Pfoundation forum about Bitcoin, February 11, 2009

> I think that the Internet is going to be one of the major forces for reducing the role of government. The one thing that's missing, but that will soon be developed, is a reliable e-cash. A method whereby, on the Internet, you can transfer funds from A to B, without A knowing B or B knowing A.
> —Milton Friedman, American economist and Nobel laureate, 1999 interview conducted by the National Taxpayers Union Foundation

> Are you kidding?! In the future, when people look back at the early days of Bitcoin, they'll say, "It was so obvious that the ability to move money anywhere, instantly, at near-zero cost would be a huge success." Bitcoin is to money what the Internet was to communication.
> —Adam Draper, founder and CEO of Boost, Curt Hopkins's "Venture Capitalists Take a Chance on the 'Bitcoin Revolution,'" *The Daily Dot*, March 19, 2013

> Stay away. Bitcoin is a mirage. It's a method of transmitting money. […] A check is a way of transmitting money, too. Are checks worth a whole lot of money just because they can transmit money? Are money orders? [...] The idea that it has some huge intrinsic value is just a joke in my view.
> —Warren Buffett, chair and CEO of Berkshire Hathaway, CNBC's *Squawk Box*, March 14, 2014

A Brief History of Digital Currencies

The birth of the Internet led many, including economist Milton Friedman, to assume that the invention of some sort of digital money would soon follow. Arguments in favor of digital money were numerous. One obvious benefit realized early on was that it might help prevent counterfeiting:

> The advent of high-quality color copiers threatens the security of paper money. The demands of guarding it make paper money expensive. The hassles of handling it (such as vending machines) make paper money undesirable. The use of credit cards and ATM

cards is becoming increasingly popular, but those systems lack adequate privacy or security against fraud, resulting in a demand for efficient electronic-money systems to prevent fraud and also to protect user privacy.
—Jörg Kienzle and Adrian Perrig in "Digital Money: A divine gift or Satan's malicious tool?" (1996)[1]

However, the creation of a secure digital money system must overcome many obstacles that might not be readily apparent. For example, anything stored in digital form can be copied and duplicated infinitely—so how can you prevent users from duplicating their money? Also, the money must be stored in a secure form that can't be easily stolen or tampered with but can be backed up in the event of hardware failure.

Initially, these and other obstacles were tackled by people like David Chaum, one of the early pioneers of digital money. Chaum studied problems in cryptography while completing his PhD at the University of California, Berkeley, and was particularly interested in ways people could transfer money digitally and anonymously. He went on to create DigiCash in 1992, a company whose mission was to establish a digital, anonymous cash system (called *e-cash*). The system used a concept called blind signatures to guarantee the anonymity of its users, but a central company or bank was needed to ensure that each unit of ecash wasn't spent twice. Chaum's was not the only digital money company. By the mid-1990s, several private companies were developing electronic cash systems, mainly hoping to facilitate online purchases in the then nascent Internet. In addition to DigiCash, others—including First Virtual Holdings, Cybercash, and even a division of Microsoft—were significantly invested in developing digital money solutions. At the time, the use of credit cards to make payments via the Internet was rare, and these efforts were seen as critical to enabling e-commerce.

But almost all attempts to create digital money had the same Achilles' heel: A trusted middleman was needed to keep track of everyone's transactions. Unfortunately, many companies like DigiCash had much difficulty garnering that kind of trust from consumers and banks (whose cooperation they also needed). The reluctance was understandable: If a company operating a digital money system collapsed due to a catastrophic event, the value of the currency units could vanish overnight.

Obviously, it's precarious for an entire currency to have a fragile single point of failure. Even the *perception* of such a point of failure can ruin its prospects as a meaningful currency. In the 1990s, the existential threat to digital currency companies was that a government agency might force them to close. Digital currencies were such recent inventions that the regulations to manage them were absent or ambiguous. Consequently, digital currency companies did not have a good idea of what the government would or would not consider acceptable.

DigiCash was challenged by many obstacles when it tried to meet various national regulatory requirements. In particular, regulators would

---

1. This work is available at *http://users.ece.cmu.edu/~adrian/projects/memoire1/memoire1.html.*

not allow the e-cash anonymity feature to remain; mechanisms needed to be built in to allow law enforcement to trace the movement of money to prevent money laundering, which undermined one of the primary advantages of e-cash. These impediments, combined with slow adoption, forced DigiCash to declare bankruptcy in 1998. Other companies faced even worse fates. Gold & Silver Reserve Inc., which maintained a gold-backed digital currency called e-gold, was shut down. Its proprietors were indicted by the US Department of Justice for violating money-laundering regulations.

Ultimately, the regulatory burdens and lack of consumer demand for digital money led companies to abandon the concept. By the late 1990s, Visa and MasterCard had worked out the technical details of secure online credit card payments. With their already large market share, credit cards became the preferred method for consumers to make online purchases. Hence, many of the posited benefits of a stand-alone digital currency were never realized.

For a decade after the fall of DigiCash, it seemed clear that the idea of a purely digital currency was untenable due to the need for a trusted central party, which in turn was prone to failure (whether due to financial or legal problems).

The Dawn of Bitcoin

In 2008, a design was finally released for a practical digital currency that did not rely on the brittle dependency of a centralized third party: Satoshi published his white paper on Bitcoin.

The key factor distinguishing Bitcoin from its predecessors was that Bitcoin was not a company (or a product of a company) but merely a set of rules, a *protocol*, that dictated how digital transactions should be handled by a network of computers. Anybody could read the rules and follow them, but no individual could "own" or change them.[2] Because Bitcoin had no central point of failure, it didn't need a government's permission to exist: There was no Bitcoin company to shut down or central organizer to incarcerate. Essentially, the Bitcoin protocol was just the clever use of mathematics to transmit value between people.

In the 1990s, many digital cash companies were playing a game of legalistic chess with governments, trying to make moves to carve out a legal niche for their products without running afoul of anti–money laundering laws. However, without exception, they all lost at this game. For good or ill, Bitcoin "solved" this problem by simply upending the chessboard: In a system without a central mediator, it wasn't possible to charge a specific person with money laundering.

2. Yuri Takhteyev, a researcher at the University of Toronto, compared Bitcoin to hockey: "Hockey is just a collection of rules that describe a particular sport. Nobody owns the rules of hockey, and if anybody wants to change the rules, they can do so as long as they don't mind playing by themselves. It is possible for the rules of hockey to change, but only if everyone agrees to the new rules. Bitcoin is the same way." (*http://www.research.utoronto.ca/what-is-bitcoin/*)

Additionally, with Bitcoin, no single party could simply decide to shut down the system. As long as there was one person in the world who continued to run Bitcoin-mining software, the whole system would keep running. This represented a clear break from past digital currencies, and so a buzz surrounding the technology began building as soon as the first Bitcoin client became available in 2009.

Given the past history of money-laundering charges against digital currency providers, it is perhaps not surprising that Satoshi decided to remain anonymous. Even though he had no control over the operation of the Bitcoin network by design, a risk would always be present that someone could charge him (falsely) with "operating Bitcoin." Cleverly, he sidestepped this risk by declining to reveal his identity.

Bitcoin's First Four Years

Written under the pseudonym Satoshi Nakamoto and distributed on a cryptography mailing list in October 2008, a paper titled "Bitcoin: A peer-to-peer electronic cash system" was the first public mention of Bitcoin. This eight-page document outlined the basic design of Bitcoin but did not delve into any of the implementation details. In online discussions that followed, Satoshi claimed that he[3] had been working on Bitcoin's design since 2007. Shortly after publishing the paper, Satoshi released the first version of a program that implemented the idea, dubbed Bitcoin-Qt 0.1, and invited others to download and try running it. The first block in the blockchain, often referred to as the *genesis block*, was added by Satoshi on January 3, 2009. When he added the block to the blockchain, he inserted a short message, which all miners can do. In the genesis block, Satoshi wrote, "The Times 03/Jan/2009 Chancellor on brink of second bailout for banks." This was the January 3, 2009, headline on the front page of *The Times*, a British newspaper. By including this message in the genesis block, Satoshi proved that he couldn't have added it to the blockchain before that date. Some think that the message choice also revealed a bit about Satoshi's motivations for creating Bitcoin.

Because the code was open source, anyone could download, review, or modify it. Soon a small band of volunteers joined Satoshi in contributing new features and fixing bugs (however, the fundamental design never changed). Many cryptographers and programmers began to participate in Bitcoin's development, including notable computer scientists like Hal Finney, who were longtime contributors to digital currency research (among other topics).[4] Although Satoshi communicated frequently via forum posts and emails with early Bitcoin users and developers, he never revealed personal details about himself. One of the main contributors, Gavin Andresen, earned Satoshi's trust over time and gradually

---

3. We actually don't know whether Satoshi Nakamoto is a man, a woman, or a group of people.

4. Hal Finney developed a *reusable proof-of-work* system that overlaps significantly with Bitcoin's *proof-of-work* used in mining.

took control as the unofficial lead developer of the Bitcoin project. On December 12, 2010, Satoshi posted a comment about the latest update to the Bitcoin software (now v0.3.19):

> There's more work to do on DoS [denial of service], but I'm doing a quick build of what I have so far in case it's needed, before venturing into more complex ideas.

He was never heard from again.[5] To this day, nobody knows Satoshi's true identity, although countless people have published theories on who he might be, often naming either notable cryptographers or brilliant reclusive mathematicians. Not surprisingly, everyone who has been fingered as the inventor of Bitcoin has denied it.

In Bitcoin's first year, anyone could generate *several hundred* bitcoins a day by mining on an ordinary laptop computer. At that time, however, it wasn't obvious that bitcoins had any value. Even some of the early enthusiasts who appreciated Bitcoin as an important intellectual achievement didn't believe their bitcoins were worth keeping after being mined. Many deleted their wallets when they were done playing with the software. From 2009 to early 2010, it was not meaningful to speak of the "price" of a bitcoin. Nobody had traded anything of value for one (at least publicly), so Bitcoin remained a mere mathematical parlor trick.

But in early 2010, small-scale currency exchanges opened, and bitcoins began trading for less than a penny each. An important moment occurred on May 18, 2010, when a forum user, laszlo, offered to send 10,000 bitcoins to anyone who would order two large pizzas for him (see Figure 6-1). This is considered the first recorded exchange of goods for bitcoins. At the time, many felt that laszlo was getting the better end of the deal. But when bitcoins reached parity with the US dollar on February 9, 2011, the joke was on laszlo; he had spent what had become $10,000 worth of bitcoins on some pizzas.

Bitcoins continued to increase in value, and on April 3, 2013, a Porsche in Texas was sold for 300 bitcoins at the rate of about $130 per bitcoin. Less than a year later, another sports car, the 2014 Lamborghini Gallardo valued at a little over $200,000, was purchased for 216 bitcoins, corresponding to about $925 per bitcoin (Figure 6-1).

By the end of 2013, more than a hundred million dollar's worth of goods had been exchanged. Thousands of small merchants and a dozen or so major retailers and online businesses had begun accepting bitcoins as payment. The bitcoin exchange rate that year went as high as $1,000 per BTC, which was a 500,000-fold increase from when the pizzas were purchased in mid-2010. Major Bitcoin currency exchanges were seeing trading volumes of $500 million *per month*.

5. On March 6, 2014, a user account belonging to Satoshi Nakamoto posted on the P2Pfoundation forum to clarify that he was not *Dorian Satoshi Nakamoto*, a man who at the time was being harassed by journalists because they mistakenly believed he was the inventor of Bitcoin.

Although these Bitcoin adoption numbers were remarkable in their own right, Bitcoin also impacted the world at large in less quantifiable ways. Let's explore the influence Bitcoin has had next.

Figure 6-1: Photographs of the pizzas purchased by laszlo for 10,000 bitcoins in May 2010 (left) and the 2014 Lamborghini Gallardo purchased for 216 bitcoins in December 2013

Bitcoin's Early Impact

Although Bitcoin is still a very new technology, we can already point to several notable achievements, not only in computer science but also in economics and politics.

It Is the Largest Distributed Computing Project in History

Less than three years after its inception, Bitcoin had already eclipsed famous distributed computing projects, such as SETI@home, in terms of total computing power.[6] Two years later, that computing power had further grown by a thousand times. By April 2014, if you combined the strength of the world's top 500 supercomputers, the result would be a computer less than 0.05 percent as powerful as the Bitcoin network. This incredible growth, particularly in recent years, was made possible by the large-scale manufacturing of special-purpose computer chips designed solely for Bitcoin mining. In addition to the enormous increases in computing power, the very existence of factories producing hundreds of thousands of single-purpose Bitcoin-mining computer chips has been remarkable. (We'll discuss the potential negative environmental impact of Bitcoin mining later in this chapter.)

It Is a Massive Economic Experiment with Already Surprising Results

Prior to 2009, most people would have reasonably assumed that computer-generated tokens, which anyone could create with free software, could

6. These are only rough estimates; the computing power of supercomputers and such projects is often measured in the number of floating-point operations per second (FLOPs). Bitcoin doesn't use floating-point operations but rather purely integer-based operations, so assumptions need to be made about how to compare these two types of numeric calculation.

never have meaningful value. This assumption turned out to be dramatically false. Bitcoin's value grew by 1,000 percent each year for five consecutive years (from less than a penny each in 2009 to over $1,000 by the end of 2013). Within five years, the total value of all bitcoins in circulation was greater than the money supply of the national currencies of more than 100 countries.[7] The low fees and higher security associated with Bitcoin, compared to credit card–based payment systems, gave merchants good reasons to accept it. As of September 2014, at least 40,000 online retailers were accepting Bitcoin,[8] as well as over 5,400 brick-and-mortar stores.[9]

Although the long-term viability of Bitcoin as an economic tool is still in question, the fact that it has attained value at all has challenged many people's notions about the nature of money. Not surprisingly, economists have been paying attention to Bitcoin, and research is being published analyzing the economics of Bitcoin. More than 2,100 scholarly articles on the economics of Bitcoin had been written as of September 2014.[10]

It Has Prompted Serious Discussions Within Governments About the Role of Digital Currencies

Although some companies had dabbled in the issuance of digital currencies to their customers prior to Bitcoin (sometimes even currencies that exist only in a computer game), these actions didn't attract the attention of governments or large financial institutions, except for some law enforcement actions. Bitcoin, on the other hand, has stirred heated debates among politicians, regulators, and bankers. Several US Senate hearings have been dedicated to discussing the subject. Central banks in dozens of countries have issued statements or reports specifically in regard to Bitcoin, and so have major banks and financial institutions. In November 2013, for instance, the United States held congressional hearings on the regulation and the future of Bitcoin, and these received widespread publicity.

Bitcoin has drawn society's attention to the potential promises and perils of digital currencies in a largely digital world. Even if Bitcoin disappears, its creation has already influenced future legislation and policies toward digital currencies.

The Future Potential of Bitcoin

A quote that has been attributed at various times to several people, including Niels Bohr and Yogi Berra, is the maxim "Prediction is very difficult, especially about the future." Nonetheless, in a book about Bitcoin, we would be remiss if we didn't explore its potential in the future.

---

7. Here we are using *the narrow money stock*, also called the *M1*, of each country's national currency as a comparison.

8. As claimed on the BitPay home page in September 2014

9. As claimed on the CoinMap home page in September 2014

10. As indicated by a search of the Google Scholar article index in September 2014

First, we'll look at the existential risks for Bitcoin—situations that could cause bitcoins to become worthless. Second, we'll look at the two main roles that Bitcoin could play in a future world, either as a method of storing value or as a method of exchange. Third, we'll consider some quantitative assessments of a successful future economy built around Bitcoin.

What Are the Existential Risks to Bitcoin?

For Bitcoin to survive long term, it must have advantages over existing currencies, or its adoption rate will stall. Also, because it is a software technology, Bitcoin needs to instill confidence that its network cannot be destroyed by computer bugs or hacks. Additionally, Bitcoin won't survive if it can be extinguished by outside entities, such as governments or corporations. Finally, it won't survive if it is somehow replaced by another, possibly better form of money (perhaps another cryptocurrency). Let's look at each of these existential risks to Bitcoin in succession.

Does Bitcoin Have Advantages over Existing Currencies?

Many have argued that Bitcoin is just a fad, and after the fad is over, people will realize that Bitcoin has no advantages over paper money. As Paul Krugman has asserted in regard to Bitcoin, "So do we need a new form of money? . . . We have huge economic problems, but green pieces of paper are doing fine—and we should let them alone."[11]

However, a strong case can be made that Bitcoin *does* have significant advantages over traditional currency. An ideal currency has certain properties that make it as useful as possible. Those properties include portability, divisibility, durability, scarcity, and fungibility. Let's look at each property in turn:

- **Portability:** In a perfect world, money should be light, compact, and easily transported. By this measure, bitcoins easily trounce paper currency: Bitcoins weigh nothing, are stored effortlessly even in large quantities, and can be moved across the world within minutes. Of course, as part of a world financial system, electronic mechanisms are available for storing and transporting traditional currencies in digital form, improving the portability of those currencies as well. However, in terms of simplicity, cost, and speed of portability, Bitcoin has clear advantages at this time.
- **Divisibility:** Everyone knows the frustration of needing to pay someone a small dollar amount but only having a large bill and no change. This problem cannot exist with bitcoins since bitcoins are completely divisible to fractions of a penny. Because computers are efficient at crunching numbers, it's no surprise that they can handle the task of dividing Bitcoin amounts in any way necessary to make change.

11. Paul Krugman, "The Antisocial Network," *New York Times*, April 14, 2013, *http://www.nytimes.com/2013/04/15/opinion/krugman-the-antisocial-network.html*

- **Durability:** By design, every bitcoin is stored within the Bitcoin blockchain, a computer file that is stored on many thousands of computers across the world. As long as a person doesn't lose the private key that protects their money, that person's bitcoins are indestructible. On the other hand, the US Federal Reserve estimates the life span of a dollar bill at 5.9 years.[12]

  Of course, another aspect of durability is that the value of a bitcoin must be maintained into the future. Although the value of a bitcoin in the future is unpredictable and volatile day to day, it has generally increased from year to year. One can certainly argue, however, that durability of Bitcoin in terms of maintaining its value is not a certainty until the network of users grows much larger.
- **Scarcity:** The primary innovation of Bitcoin is the decentralized creation of scarcity for a digital asset, which is necessary for bitcoins to retain any monetary value. Therefore, like paper money, bitcoins can maintain a limited supply. However, with paper money you need to trust the government (i.e., the owner of the printing presses) to maintain this scarcity over time and hence prevent inflation.
- **Fungibility:** It's important for any dollar bill—or any bitcoin—to be equally valid for payment. If a recipient of money constantly needs to worry about whether they have received "good money" or "bad money," the utility of the currency is damaged. As you know, paper money can be traced physically by tracking the serial numbers on bills or electronically through tracing mechanisms built into our modern electronic payment system. Similarly, bitcoins are traceable by following coins through the public blockchain. Hence, neither traditional currency nor Bitcoin has a clear advantage in terms of fungibility.

With regard to some of the properties that determine the utility of currency, Bitcoin scores quite favorably, especially in term of portability and scarcity. Therefore, it is unlikely that Bitcoin will ever fail *solely* because it offers no advantages over traditional money.

Can Bitcoin Be Destroyed via Bugs or Hacks?

Another commonly proposed reason for which Bitcoin may be extinguished at some point is that it might have bugs and can be hacked. Clearly, if a hacker was able to obtain an arbitrary number of bitcoins from thin air or found a way to transfer bitcoins from other people's wallets at will, Bitcoin would quickly disappear into obscurity.

However, it is currently unlikely that such a bug exists. Many reputable security researchers have studied Bitcoin and have been impressed by the quality of its code. For instance, Dan Kaminsky, a respected security expert, wrote an article for *Business Insider* in April 2013 titled "I Tried Hacking Bitcoin and I Failed." In the article, he talks in glowing terms about Bitcoin's security model.

---

12. *http://www.federalreserve.gov/faqs/how-long-is-the-life-span-of-us-paper-money.htm*

However, the most important reason to believe that the Bitcoin system is unlikely to contain serious flaws is based on an economic argument: If anyone figured out how to hack the core network, they could become phenomenally rich. Such a person could potentially extract billions of dollars from the network before the value of the currency collapsed. The simple fact that no person has done this yet, despite the enticing incentives to do so, makes a strong case against the existence of any such flaws in the currency.

Can Bitcoin Be Destroyed by Governments or Corporations?

In the early days of the Internet, we became accustomed to the idea that we would connect to a central server (run by Google, Amazon, Yahoo!, etc.) using a web client in order to browse online. This model for using the Internet is commonly called a *client-server architecture.* However, since those days, many new Internet-based applications have started using a *peer-to-peer architecture.* In this decentralized model, a software application finds other "like-minded" peer applications on the Internet and connects with these peers to operate the application. Early applications that used this approach include BitTorrent (for movie downloading) and Gnutella (for music discovery/downloading). Bitcoin also uses a peer-to-peer network in its design.

Peer-to-peer systems have many advantages over traditional client-server systems, including improved durability and performance. Because of these advantages, it is likely that these systems will become increasingly ubiquitous.

One benefit of using peer-to-peer systems over traditional architectures is their indestructibility: As long as a peer-to-peer app user can find other peers to connect to, the network will continue to exist, and it can do so without any central point of failure. For this reason, it is extremely unlikely that a government or other entity could ever completely extinguish the Bitcoin network, no matter how powerful that entity is.

Of course, the government of a country could decide to declare the use of Bitcoin illegal, and such declarations could greatly impact the value and utility of Bitcoin. However, short of someone completely shutting down the Internet, Bitcoin will continue to exist despite any such declarations. Also, since Bitcoin is inherently global, there is a limit to the impact the laws of a single government can have on its value and utility. Draconian laws passed against Bitcoin in one country may merely shift its use and development (and associated jobs!) to other countries.

Can Bitcoin Be Supplanted by Another Cryptocurrency?

All of us had a front-row seat when Google appeared out of nowhere with its superior search engine technology and left a long list of defunct, and now almost forgotten, search engines in its wake. Does anyone remember the search engine powerhouses of Lycos or Altavista? Is it possible that Bitcoin will similarly fade into obscurity when some new, better cryptocurrency comes along?

Developers who contribute to the core Bitcoin protocol tend to be very conservative. Not only does no developer want to take the blame for introducing a bug into a multibillion-dollar system, but even if a more radical feature was added, the Bitcoin community would be unlikely to accept it. Arguably, this is exactly what you want to hear if you are one of the people who have, in aggregate, billions of dollars relying on a well-functioning Bitcoin network. It's in everyone's interest to be extremely careful in making any fundamental changes to the core Bitcoin system. Even so, this conservative approach heightens the danger that an upstart currency could emerge, à la Google, and eat Bitcoin's lunch.

Of course, we have no way of knowing what fantastic features a new currency would need such that it could supplant Bitcoin. However, three main reasons exist to believe that Bitcoin may be able survive the onslaught of newcomers: network effects, the nature of cryptocurrency volatility, and the recent development of cryptocurrency-pegging technology.

The network effect is the simple concept that people want to use a currency only if other people will accept it as payment. The more users a currency has, the more useful it is. This creates a natural barrier for the adoption of new currencies (and certainly has hindered the adoption of Bitcoin relative to traditional currencies in its first few years). Currently, Bitcoin has the largest adoption of any cryptocurrency, so newer ones would need to have easily distinguishable advantages over Bitcoin to overcome its network advantage. But how does volatility factor in?

From an economics standpoint, any asset that becomes newly available to an open market needs to first undergo a *price discovery process*. This was part of the reason for the Internet bubble in 2000: People simply didn't know the value of the stocks of eBay, Yahoo!, and other tech companies because similar companies had not existed in the past. Eventually, as people became more familiar with Internet-focused corporations, it became clearer how to reasonably assign a price to each company's stock.

Bitcoin has been undergoing a similar price discovery process, which is still in its very early stages: The price of a bitcoin has been swinging wildly up and down since the currency's inception. As more and more users have started to use it, however, the volatility has modestly decreased (i.e., the swings, in relative terms, have become less violent). If Bitcoin volatility continues to decrease, this trend may give Bitcoin a significant advantage over future cryptocurrencies: Because Bitcoin is guaranteed to be the *oldest* cryptocurrency, new currencies might be unable to catch up in this "volatility race," and Bitcoin will always remain less volatile than upstarts.

If Bitcoin maintains advantages in terms of network effects and volatility, it may make sense for new cryptocurrencies to use *pegging* to link themselves to the Bitcoin network instead of trying to replace the Bitcoin network entirely. Recently, two well-known cryptocurrency developers and entrepreneurs, Adam Back and Austin Hill, have suggested that the value of new cryptocurrencies could be directly linked one-to-one with the value of a bitcoin by using cryptography to allow coins to "jump" between blockchains using clever algorithms. If this idea succeeds, it may be possible to create cryptocurrencies with new technological advancements into *side chains* of Bitcoin. Side chains are separate blockchains with different rules that share the same pool of coins as Bitcoin, allowing the new currency to share the same volatility (or lack thereof, potentially) and network benefits as Bitcoin proper.

If the side chain idea (or a similar peg-based idea) is successful, future cryptocurrencies would benefit from Bitcoin's existence and even augment it rather than replace it. For these reasons, Bitcoin might never be entirely replaced by other cryptocurrencies. That being said, if a cryptocurrency is created that really is so much better than Bitcoin that we all switch, that wouldn't really be a bad outcome, would it?

Now that we've discussed the existential risks, let's explore what Bitcoin's future might look like.

What Role Might Bitcoin Play in the Future?

The two main uses of a currency are as a means of storing savings and as a payment mechanism. If we want to hypothesize about the future impact of Bitcoin, we need to compare and contrast these two roles of money and explore which role the currency can take on—because the role that Bitcoin plays can make a big difference in terms of the value of the Bitcoin economy, as well as the value of an individual bitcoin.

Using Bitcoin for Savings

Bitcoin potentially has much to offer as a mechanism for storing savings. The reason is that its total supply is precisely known. Also, if used properly, it cannot be easily seized or stolen. You might imagine that in the future, it could become a preferred vehicle for saving your wealth instead of cash, precious metals, or real estate.

In this role, Bitcoin's use may be most comparable to that of gold, currently the most popular decentralized medium for storing savings. If we could estimate how much wealth is currently saved in gold, it would indicate the scope of possibility for Bitcoin to be used in a similar way.

Can we estimate how much wealth is currently stored as gold? As this book goes to press, it is estimated that all the gold above ground (as opposed to gold yet to be mined) is valued at about $9 trillion. Roughly half that amount is used for jewelry, and the rest is in gold bars or coins, which are used simply as a store of value. Let's conservatively assume that everyone who possesses gold jewelry does so purely for its beauty, not as a form of savings. That leaves $4.5 trillion worth of gold used purely as a means of savings.

So if bitcoins were ever widely adopted for saving wealth, the Bitcoin economy would eat into the market share of a $4.5 trillion gold economy.

Another way to estimate the amount of money currently in savings is to look in aggregate at how much wealth exists in the world. Today, the average net worth of a person (combining all the billionaires with the destitute poor) is about $25,000. This value consists of savings held in cash *and* wealth held in other types of assets. Hence, the total wealth currently kept in savings worldwide is about 7 billion times that much, or approximately $175 trillion.

If Bitcoin were ever to become a popular store of value, it would represent some fraction of that $175 trillion. Even if only 1 percent of the world's wealth was stored in the form of bitcoins, the total value of the Bitcoin economy would be in the multitrillion-dollar range. Since we know that there will only ever be at most 21 million bitcoins in circulation, each bitcoin would need to be worth hundreds of thousands of dollars in order for Bitcoin to store 1 percent of the world's wealth.

Using Bitcoin as a Medium of Exchange

If Bitcoin becomes primarily used as a medium of exchange (i.e., a payment mechanism), people would keep only as many bitcoins on hand as they needed for purchases and would keep the bulk of their savings in other places. Currently, most people use traditional currencies this way. They spend US dollars (or euros, yen, etc.) to make purchases, but they save the majority of their wealth in bonds, stocks, mutual funds, or other assets that don't lose value due to steady inflation.

Because Bitcoin transaction fees are low, the payment network is not proprietary, no identity information is unnecessarily revealed, and the transaction security is based on modern cryptography, Bitcoin is potentially a superior medium of exchange compared to national currencies.

To estimate the impact Bitcoin might have if it were used widely as a payment mechanism, we need to estimate how much money (of any type) is currently in active circulation across the world for payment purposes. Specifically, we need answers to two key questions:

1. How many expenses does a person have to pay on a regular basis?
2. How long will it take a given bitcoin to be reused within the economy as it passes from person to person?

To answer question 1, we can use the fact that the current median yearly income of a person in the top-earning billion people in the world is roughly $15,000. Let's assume that from this income, $3,000 is put toward savings and that this person spends $1,000 a month.

To answer question 2, let's estimate that it currently takes about a month for a dollar to be respent. In other words, if you buy a hamburger at a restaurant today for $10, let's assume that it will take about a month before those same$10 are spent by the restaurant owner.

Using these assumptions, we can roughly estimate that approximately $1,200 needs to be in circulation per person at any moment. For 1 billion people, a total of $1.2 trillion worth of currency needs to be in circulation as a medium of exchange for the world economy to function.

If Bitcoin became a widely adopted medium of exchange, some part of this $1.2 trillion payment economy would be executed in bitcoins. Again, because of the hard limit of 21 million bitcoins, we know that if bitcoins were used for just 1 percent of the world's transactions, then each bitcoin would need to be worth tens of thousands to hundreds of thousands of dollars.

Clearly, Bitcoin has a long way to go in terms of adoption before it reaches these staggering numbers (if it ever does). We will always use many different assets as a form of savings (stocks will never go away, for example, no matter how popular Bitcoin gets), and we will use many different payment mechanisms. That being said, nothing stops Bitcoin from being used to some degree as *both* a medium of exchange and a form of savings, and the more widely it is used, the more useful and convenient it will be to its users.

In this section, we have discussed the potential value of Bitcoin under certain adoption scenarios, but we have little basis for predicting just how much it will be adopted. Depending on the adoption level we assume, we could forecast virtually any value of a future bitcoin, from hundreds of dollars to millions. Somewhat ridiculously, if we assume almost all of the world's savings are stored in Bitcoin, we can even imagine a billion-dollar bitcoin, because the amount of savings and assets in the world is so incredibly immense!

For this reason, it doesn't make sense to try to assign a precise estimate to the value of bitcoins in the future. The best we can do is suggest that Bitcoin has potential as a technology, and in the future it could be a big deal—that is, if it doesn't first fail in the many possible ways we've considered.

UNIT OF ACCOUNT

It's theoretically possible in the distant future that a currency like Bitcoin could be used to denominate the prices of goods as an international standard. Using Bitcoin as a *unit of account* is certainly an intriguing idea, and this purpose is commonly mentioned in economic texts as an important role of money, but it would have negligible economic impact on the future world economy. The reason is that using Bitcoin as a pricing standard, in itself, doesn't directly affect how many bitcoins or other goods are bought or sold, simply because you can "measure" items in Bitcoin without needing to own them.

The Dangers of Decentralized Digital Money

After discussing the many potential benefits of a currency like Bitcoin, we would be remiss if we didn't also examine the potential dangers of this technology. Here, we'll consider the ways that Bitcoin might be harmful to society if it is widely adopted. Even if the technology is sound, some ethical reasons might exist for opposing Bitcoin.

Bitcoin and Illegal Activity

Given the early and eager adoption of Bitcoin by illegal product marketplaces, such as the infamous Silk Road website that allowed customers to buy drugs and other illegal products via mail order, it has been argued that Bitcoin's privacy features enable criminals. Arguably, there's some truth to this debate: Just as water always seeks the lowest level, criminals will always seek tools that give them the most anonymity and protection against law enforcement.

However, in 2013, the US government successfully found and prosecuted the alleged creator of Silk Road and arrested alleged drug dealers selling products on the site. The swiftness with which Silk Road was dismantled seems to have been a strong deterrent for other marketplaces trying to adopt Silk Road's business model. For now at least, only limited evidence suggests that Bitcoin offers criminals any meaningful protection from the law.

Additionally, arguing that technologies that promote anonymity are somehow suspect from a purely moral perspective creates dangerous precedents. With the recent widespread use of public cameras, facial recognition technologies, social networking sites, and GPS-enabled cars, it is becoming more difficult for people to maintain their privacy each year. This erosion of privacy has its own downsides, compromising personal liberties.

For this reason, a counterargument can be made that encouraging and destigmatizing the use of privacy-enhancing technologies like Bitcoin may actually be *positive* for society. The idea that it's acceptable and normal to use tools that protect privacy is called *anonymity by default.* If you agree that valid reasons exist to remain anonymous in many situations and that anyone doing so doesn't "have something to hide," you will appreciate the privacy protections afforded by the Bitcoin currency.

There is also the simpler argument that Bitcoin is merely a useful tool and so it has an enabling effect to anyone who uses it, even criminals. Certainly cars, phones, computers, and the Internet are all used by criminals to accomplish illegal activity, but we wouldn't ban those technologies solely to hinder criminal activity.

The Energy Costs of Bitcoin

Another ethically contentious facet of Bitcoin is that miners expend enormous amounts of energy when mining for bitcoins. These energy costs are significant, and some people have argued that this makes Bitcoin wasteful and harmful to the environment.

However, this argument does not take into account the massive costs that are expended by our existing financial system for security. Every armored van, security officer, and bank vault that is used to protect traditional currency uses resources, and if we moved to a currency that leverages modern cryptography for security, many of these traditional security mechanisms that physically deter thieves from accessing this money may in theory no longer be necessary.

Additionally, credit card issuers charge high fees (upward of 2 percent per transaction in the United States), and a large chunk of these fees are used for fraud-prevention purposes. If we widely adopted Bitcoin, that would greatly reduce such fraud, so this 2 percent resource drain on the entire credit card economy would be decreased.

The bottom line is that the energy cost of Bitcoin mining is a necessary component of the Bitcoin currency system, and it serves a real and useful function. Naturally, if a person starts a priori with the assumption that Bitcoin is not useful, no argument will suffice to convince such a person that the energy expended to protect the Bitcoin network is anything but a waste. However, in this book we've described many benefits of Bitcoin that provide some justification for its use of energy.

PROOF-OF-STAKE: A LESS WASTEFUL WAY TO SECURE A CRYPTOCURRENCY?

Bitcoin mining uses a concept called *proof-of-work* to secure the system. In this system, new blocks (and bitcoins) are awarded randomly to miners based proportionally to the number of hashing calculations they perform. However, some developers have attempted to build cryptocurrencies that adopt a different concept called *proof-of-stake*, which awards blocks in a manner proportional to the amount of currency a miner holds (or proportional to a similar metric, such as the number of coins owned multiplied by the days the coins have remained unspent). Two currencies that use this approach are Peercoin* and NXT.**

A proof-of-stake mining reward doesn't require the same considerable energy expenditure required by a proof-of-work currency, like Bitcoin. However, it isn't clear whether proof-of-stake-based currencies are as secure as proof-of-work-based ones. Just as proof-of-work-based systems are "vulnerable" to a 51 percent attack, proof-of-stake-based systems have their own vulnerabilities (51 percent attacks are described in detail in Chapter 8). Although we know that a 51 percent attack in a proof-of-work-based system requires extraordinary resources and is economically irrational for the attacker, attacks on proof-of-stake-based systems may be easier than on proof-of-work-based system. Peercoin mitigates this issue by combining proof-of-stake with some additional proof-of-work to maintain stronger security. NXT addresses this issue by adding nuances to the consensus mechanism to decide which blocks are valid, potentially sacrificing some decentralization in the process.

The bottom line is that no consensus yet exists among cryptocurrency experts as to the practicality of proof-of-stake. Even so, it is an interesting concept with the attractive benefit of dramatically reducing the energy requirements for operating cryptocurrency.

---

* *http://www.peercoin.net/*

** *http://www.nxtcommunity.org/*

Bitcoin and the Dangers of Deflation

Another common criticism that is leveled against Bitcoin is that, since the total number of bitcoins is capped at 21 million, their value will continually increase and nobody will actually want to spend them, making the currency useless (or worse, leading to dangerous deflation).

This argument relates to the economic concept of *Keynesian economics*,[13] which maintains, among other ideas, that frequent injection of new currency into the economy helps promote its growth. Regarding Bitcoin, Keynesians will argue that the inability of governments to print more currency units would seriously damage economic growth.[14] They contend that the scarcity enforced by Bitcoin's cap would drive *nominal deflation*, which is when the price of everyday goods denominated in bitcoins would drop over time, causing the circulation of the currency to freeze up and forcing the economy into a depression. The rationale is that individuals would postpone their purchases in anticipation of lower prices for goods in the future.

Bitcoin supporters counter the Keynesian arguments with ideas based in the philosophy of *Austrian economics*. This economic philosophy argues, among other ideas, that the price of a unit of currency has the ability to adjust appropriately on its own, guaranteeing that purchases and savings in an economy will remain at desirable levels, no matter how many units of currency exist at any point in time in the economy.

Bitcoin and Government Stability

Some contend that a successful Bitcoin system would be harmful because it could destabilize governments. It has been debated that Bitcoin is part of a larger movement, recently termed *radical decentralization*, which maintains that all decentralization (including the functions of the government) is desirable and possible. This idea is a direct extension of the philosophies of Friedrich Hayek, who reasoned that local control is usually preferable to central control, because local people have more knowledge about local conditions and can therefore behave more efficiently in most situations. However, it is true that governments benefit from having control over their currency supply. Governments encounter challenges when they attempt to raise funds via direct taxation, and printing money to fund government projects is known as "taxing by inflation," which is both easier for governments to do and harder for citizens to stop. The loss of this means of raising money for government projects (including military defense) could reduce the financial viability of some governments.

---

13. Named after John Maynard Keynes, the economist who is most strongly identified with this particular approach to monetary policy

14. One well-articulated version of this argument is given by Paul Krugman in the article "Bitcoin Is Evil," *New York Times*, December 28, 2013, *http://krugman.blogs.nytimes.com/2013/12/28/bitcoin-is-evil/*.

However, Bitcoin is not the only recent technology that is decentralized by design: BitTorrent, Gnutella, Tor, and Freenet are similarly immune to central control. Clearly, computers allow us to explore the idea of decentralization, and its merits and potential faults, in ways that were not possible before the Internet revolution. Many of these decentralized systems were thought to pose risks to government stability (especially the Internet in countries with oppressive laws against free speech), but we accepted them anyway due to the enormous benefits they brought to society. The loss of control by governments, in the case of the Internet, was compensated (and then some) by increased economic productivity. Computer engineers are continually pushing the boundaries of what's possible with decentralized networks, trying to drive financial contracts (such as software projects like Ethereum[15]) or communication systems (such as Bitmessage[16]) toward decentralized systems as well. Only time will tell what kind of impact these systems will have on governments, good or ill.

In the next chapter, we'll explore some of the underlying technology in Bitcoin in more detail, starting with Bitcoin cryptography.

---

15. *http://ethereum.org/*

16. *http://bitmessage.org/*

7

THE CRYPTOGRAPHY BEHIND BITCOIN

Bitcoin relies on cryptography to function, which is why it is sometimes called a *cryptocurrency*.[1] But what role does cryptography play in Bitcoin, and why is it needed? We'll begin with a short introduction to some necessary cryptography concepts (if they are familiar to you, you can just skip to "The Reasons Bitcoin Needs Cryptography" on page 137), and then we'll explore the specific cryptographic methods used in Bitcoin.

If you flipped to this chapter only because you wanted to know whether the cryptography used by Bitcoin is safe, you can rest easy knowing that Bitcoin uses only tried-and-tested cryptographic techniques: All of the cryptographic methods used by Bitcoin have been widely used in the past by governments and major corporations to secure financial, medical, and other sensitive information, as well as personal identification data.

1. This term is used in addition to the many others for Bitcoin, such as *digital currency*, *math-based currency*, and among those who don't think bitcoins are real money, *virtual currency*.

In fact, the cryptography in Bitcoin could be described as *boring*, simply because it relies on very conservative cryptographic algorithms. But in some fields of study, such as accounting and dentistry, boring is good; in the case of Bitcoin, conservative and well-established cryptography helps make it more secure. The interesting part is what Bitcoin *does* with cryptography.

Fortunately, as you'll see, although Bitcoin cryptography may be old hat to the experts, it is still immensely fascinating to a novice!

A Brief Cryptography Overview

Historically, cryptography was used to send secret messages when necessary to protect information. Messages were systematically scrambled, or *encrypted*, in a way that hopefully only the recipient of the message knew how to *decrypt*. A well-encrypted message might be intelligible as battle plans to the intended recipient, but to anyone else it would just be a well-tossed word salad with a side order of alphabet soup. Historically, encryption and decryption were laborious tasks and were reserved only for secure clandestine communication (usually of a military or illicit romantic nature). With the advent of computers, which could do in milliseconds what used to take hours manually, cryptography is now used routinely by the masses to encrypt/decrypt very important (e.g., financial) and not-so-important (e.g., pay-per-view TV) communication. Perhaps surprisingly, the convenience and speed of computers has led to the adoption of cryptographic methods for more than just encrypting secret messages. Common examples include logging in to websites with a username and password combination and using a registration key to install software. Both use cryptographic methods, but no message encryption is involved in either case.

In addition to encrypting messages, modern cryptography is used to verify the validity of information (through *cryptographic hash functions*) and to prove one's identity (through *digital signatures*). For example, without modern cryptography, you wouldn't be able to distinguish between two identical websites that both claimed to belong to your bank. One might be phony and run by thieves to steal your money. But only your bank's website can provide the correct digital signature. Before we explain how digital signatures and cryptographic hash functions work, let's explore one-way functions, a feature that both rely on.

One-Way Functions

One-way functions are mathematical functions that make it easy to calculate an output based on the input but difficult to do the reverse. A precise mathematical definition of what is easy or difficult doesn't exist but depends on the complexity of the calculation and the effort required to solve it.

A typical example is called *integer factorization*, which asks you to write an integer[2] as the product of only prime numbers—for example, the factors of 6 are 2 and 3, which are both prime. Given the prime factors as input, it is easy to multiply them to produce an output integer, but the reverse is not true (at least for larger numbers). Given a large integer, finding its prime factors is very difficult. The only known methods involve systematically guessing different combinations of prime factors, but the amount of time required to find the right answer increases exponentially with the number of digits. Imagine trying to multiply $2 \times 7 \times 7$ in your head. It is not that difficult to calculate the answer of 98; however, if you were given the number 98 and were required to find its prime factors, generating 2, 2, and 7 would be more difficult. A typical laptop can factor a 60–80 digit number in less than a second, but the required time grows exponentially: To factor a 300-digit number or greater would take a modern supercomputer decades.

```
Prime factors (2,7,7,13) → 2x7x7x13     → Output integer 1274       (easy)
Output integer 1274      → ???????????  → Prime factors (2,7,7,13)  (hard)
```

Another one-way function, which is a bit more complicated but is commonly used in cryptography, involves the *discrete logarithm*. Consider a set of integers $\{0, 1, 2, 3, \ldots, n-1\}$ where n is a prime number and where we only use modular arithmetic with modulo n:[3]

```
Example: n = 7    3 + 6 (mod 7) = 2         3 x 6 (mod 7) = 4
```

2. An integer is a number that can be written without a fractional or decimal component (e.g., –4, 2, or 17 but not 4.23 or 1.5).

3. In modular arithmetic, whenever a number becomes too large, it "wraps around" like the hour hand on a clock once it moves past 12; instead of pointing to 13, it starts over and points to 1. However, whereas clocks start over at the number one, the common convention among mathematicians is to start over at 0. So $3 + 6 = 9$, but $3 + 6 \pmod 7 = 2$ because after reaching 7, the next three numbers are 0, 1, and 2.

It is easy (as in, you can do it with a pocket calculator) to raise an integer, *a*, to the *k*th power to calculate the integer *b*:

```
Example: a^k (mod n) = b    3^2 (mod 5) = 4
```

However, the discrete logarithm, which is finding *k* given only *a, b,* and *n,* is difficult to calculate. The only known methods to find *k* are variations on trying to guess every value between 0 and *n* that satisfy the preceding equation. The larger the value of *n*, the harder it is (and the more time it will take) to calculate *k*.

```
Example:
a = 4; k = 4781; n = 17627 → 4^(4781) (mod 17627) = 2685 → b = 2685 (easy)
a = 4; b = 2685; n = 17627 → ?????                       → k = 4781 (hard)
```

In the early days of computers, people started applying the asymmetry in these one-way functions to build various classes of cryptographic algorithms, which is what we'll discuss next.

Cryptographic Hash Functions Verify Information

Cryptographic hash functions are one-way functions designed to take arbitrary data as input (e.g., a number, a short message, an image, or the collected works of Shakespeare) and generate fixed-length output (e.g., a 128-bit or 256-bit number). The output is called a *hash* or *hash value.* Hash values can act like a fingerprint—a unique identifier—for files or texts. They're designed in a way that makes it extremely unlikely that any two non-identical inputs would output the same hash value (when this does happen, it is called a *collision*). In particular, even a small change to the input data, such as changing one letter in the entire collected works of Shakespeare, would result in a new hash value that is completely unrelated to the original hash.

A commonly used cryptographic hash function is MD5 (message digest algorithm, iteration five), which takes any data as input and outputs a 128-bit hash value, like this:

```
MD5("hello world")             = 5eb63bbbe01eeed093cb22bb8f5acdc3
```

As you can see, changing just one character in *mysecretpasswordisCATS* results in a completely different hash output:

```
MD5("mysecretpasswordisCATS") = 399257907fd42e2ee3fcb39b04192b04
MD5("mysecretpasswordisBATS") = b12d76c8b8c063616dbf7b8b7349aed0
```

This property enables hash functions to be used to verify that certain information is correct or to match what someone else claims is correct, without needing to scrutinize the actual information. For example, MD5 is used to check whether a downloaded file is safe to use and is free of errors that might have occurred during data transmission. If the MD5 hash value of the downloaded data matches the hash value provided by a reputable source, you can be certain that data does not contain any hidden viruses and was not corrupted during the file transfer. The slightest alteration to the file would cause a noticeable change to the hash output. A hash is like a tamperproof seal: If it's broken, don't buy the product.

Another, more exciting, use of cryptographic hash functions is proving that you know a secret password without giving it away. Imagine you are a spy behind enemy lines. After many days of traveling under the cloak of darkness, you finally reach a guarded warehouse to meet with fellow agents. A guard at the front door asks you for the secret code, but you aren't sure whether the guard is on your side. You need to prove that you know the code without risking the mission by letting your secret code fall into the wrong hands! What do you do? You give him a hash of the secret code. If he knows the code, he can calculate the hash and verify that you also know it. If he doesn't and isn't supposed to know the code, you haven't revealed it.

This dramatic example describes current standard procedure whenever you create a new account with a username and password for a website. The password is never stored on the website's servers; instead, the hash of the password is stored, and the server checks whether the hash of what you typed matches what is on record. As a result, if the server is ever stolen or hacked into, no passwords will be revealed.

Public Key Cryptography

The invention of public key cryptography in the 1970s was a significant breakthrough, allowing for much of the technology we take for granted today. Until then, all methods of encryption required the sender and receiver to know the same secret encryption key to encrypt and decrypt the message (also known as *symmetric key* cryptography). However, this method presented a problem because it assumed that, at some earlier time, the sender and receiver had a safe way of communicating to decide on an encryption key without the fear of anyone eavesdropping.

In public key cryptography (also known as *asymmetric key* cryptography), two different keys are created: a public key that is shared to *encrypt* the message and a private key that is confidential to *decrypt* the message (yes, the same private key that is used to spend bitcoins). With asymmetric key cryptography, communicating securely with anyone using an unsafe channel, like the radio or Internet, is easy: You share your public key with others who want to communicate with you, and then anyone can send you encrypted messages that only you can read using your private key. Because the public key cannot be used to decrypt messages, no danger occurs if it falls into the wrong hands. If others want you to send *them* encrypted messages, they give you *their* public key, and so on.

How does asymmetric key cryptography work? The original method, called *RSA encryption* after its developers—Ron Rivest, Adi Shamir, and Leonard Adleman, is based on integer factorization.[4] Let's imagine that

4. Ron Rivest, Adi Shamir, and Leonard Adleman, "A Method for Obtaining Digital Signatures and Public-Key Cryptosystems," *Communications of the ACM* 21, no. 2 (1978): 120–126.

Crowley wants to communicate with others using the RSA method. Crowley first needs to create a public and a private key (see Table 7-1). He can do this at any time before he starts his communications.

Table 7-1: Sending an Encrypted Message Using the RSA Method

Step	Instruction	Example
1	Crowley chooses two prime numbers, p and q, and multiplies them to get the prime product n. Recall that this is a one-way function; there is no easy way to obtain p and q given only n.	$p = 71$, $q = 149$ $n = 71 \times 149 = 10579$
2	Crowley calculates $t = (p - 1)(q - 1)$.	$t = (71 - 1) \times (149 - 1)$ $= 10360$
3	Crowley chooses an integer e such that e and t do not share a common denominator (other than 1 of course). He has many possible values of e from which to choose. This is Crowley's public key.	Choose $e = 3453$
4	Crowley finds d such that $d \times e \pmod{t} = 1$. This is Crowley's private key.	$d \times 3453 \pmod{10360} = 1$ satisfied when $d = 10357$

Once the public and private keys are generated, Crowley can distribute the public key widely (along with the prime product, n). Then anyone can use this key to encrypt a message meant only for Crowley.

Of course, to encrypt and decrypt messages, you need some way of converting text into a mathematical form, which is called *encoding*. Converting a number back to text is called *decoding*. Encoding and decoding should not be confused with encrypting or decrypting because you are not scrambling the information. Many different encoding schemes exist, and it doesn't matter which one you use, but all parties involved need to use the same one.

Let's assume that the letter *a* becomes a 0, the letter *b* becomes a 1, the letter *c* becomes a 2, and so on through the alphabet. In Table 7-2 we've encoded the message "fade" using this technique.

Table 7-2: Encoding the Word "Fade" Using a Simple Scheme

Letter	Position in alphabet starting with zero
F	5
A	0
D	3
E	4

Now that we have an encoded message we want to send to Crowley, as well as Crowley's public key, we can encrypt his message so that only Crowley can decrypt it, as shown in Table 7-3.

Table 7-3: Encrypting the Word "Fade" Using Crowley's Public Key

Step	Instruction	Example
1	To encrypt a message, use the public key, e, to calculate: $c = m^e \pmod{n}$ c is referred to as the ciphertext	c = 5034^3453 (mod 10579) = 5272 decoded as *fchc*
2	To decrypt a message, use the private key, d, to calculate $m = c^d \pmod{n}$ m is the original message	m = 5272^10357 (mod 10579) = 5034 decoded as *fade*

Almost an identical scheme can be used to prove one's identity, using what is referred to as a *digital signature.*

Digital Signatures

In the public key encryption scheme described earlier, anyone can send you encrypted messages without you knowing who they are. Consider Crowley on his island trying to arrange a transfer of pineapples with Satoshi on another island. If Crowley receives two messages with contradictory information both claiming to come from Satoshi (for example, "Send pineapples to the north island. —Your friend, Satoshi" and "Send pineapples to the south island. —Your friend, Satoshi"), how does Crowley know which message really came from Satoshi?

Fortunately, Satoshi can use a trick to prove his identity *and* the authenticity of his messages: He can encrypt messages not only with his public key but also with his private key. This backward encryption method reverses the mathematics of encryption, just as you'd expect: Although it's very difficult to encrypt a message (only the person with access to the private key can accomplish this), it's very easy to decrypt a message (anyone with the public key can do so).

Therefore, if Satoshi uses this backward method to encrypt the message: "My name is Satoshi, I live on the south island, and I double-pinky-swear to pay you for some pineapples," anyone, including Crowley, can decrypt this message using Satoshi's public key (which, let's assume, was previously established to be 100 percent authentic). Crowley can then say, "I know Satoshi is the only person on Earth who has access to his private key, and this message was written by someone who must have access to this private key; therefore, these words are Satoshi's words."

When you use this method to prove your identity, the functions of the public and private key are reversed. Satoshi can use his private key to encrypt a message, and everyone else can decrypt it using his public key. Because others have Satoshi's public key, the contents of the message wouldn't be secret, but the fact that it was encrypted using Satoshi's private key proves that it could not have been sent by anyone else.

Whis Is It Called a Digital Signature?

The term *digital signature* is used because the most convenient way to send a reverse encryption is to send two separate bits of information: a *message* and a *message signature.*

Think about it: Satoshi has nothing to hide in the message he is sending (in fact, he explicitly wants everyone to be able to read his message); therefore, it is arguably more convenient for Satoshi to send the message in an unencrypted form and then a duplicate it in encrypted form. Crowley can easily read the message and only bother using Satoshi's public key to decrypt the duplicate if he is suspicious of whether Satoshi actually wrote it.

However, it seems inefficient to send a message twice. Clearly, Satoshi must send the entire *unencrypted* message to get the message out to the world. But could the *encrypted* message be shortened? In fact it can, by using cryptographic hash functions. Remember that if anyone tries to tamper with a message, the hash of that message will be different as a result. Satoshi can therefore simply calculate the hash output of his message and then encrypt *only that hash* using his private key. Then anyone who reads the message can decrypt Satoshi's hash output (using his public key) and also calculate the hash of the unencrypted message, checking whether the two agree.

Keep in mind that a hash of a message, no matter how long the original message, is a short piece of data. Therefore, by only encrypting the hash of the original message, you can create a short digital signature of a much longer message. More important, even the slightest alteration to the unencrypted message would cause the cryptographic hash to be completely different, thus preventing any interceptor from modifying the signed message. As a result, not only does a digital signature prove that the real Satoshi signed the message, but it also proves that he signed a very specific message. In this regard, digital signatures are even better than analog handwritten signatures.

Using Digital Signatures

Using the RSA encryption scheme, implementing digital signatures is straightforward. Let's assume that we are using the same encoding scheme as in Table 7-2 and we want to send the message "fade" unencrypted but signed. Table 7-4 shows how to use a digital signature to prove authorship of the message.

Now we can send the message "fade" and sign it with *ifda*. The recipient doesn't need any additional information to read the message, because it can be read plainly. But to verify the identity of the sender, the recipient needs to know the hash function used (in this case MD5), the prime product n, and the public key of the sender, e. The recipient then decrypts the signature with the public key to obtain the hash value, in this case 8808, and checks to see whether it matches the MD5 hash of the message "fade." If a match is made, the recipient knows who the message came from and that the message was not altered in transit.

Table 7-4: Signing the Message "Fade" Using RSA Encryption

Step	Instruction	Example
1	Calculate the hash of the message using a suitable cryptographic hash function (e.g., MD5). The hash output must be less than the prime product *n*, which can be accomplished by calculating the modulus of the output.* h = MD5(*message*) (mod n)	*fade* encoded as 5034 h = MD5(5034) (mod 10579) = 8808
2	Encrypt the hash, h, using the RSA encryption method, namely calculate: $s = h^d \pmod{n}$, where s is the signature (it is a ciphertext)	s = 8808^10357 (mod 10579) = 8530 decoded as *ifda*

* If you are following along, keep in mind that the input format for a hash function is important. The MD5 hash of the integer 5034 is not the same as the MD5 hash of the word *5034*, which is in text format. For numbers, the base of the number needs to be specified as well.

This is how digital signatures work. Of course, in this example, the prime product chosen was a low number so the examples were easy to follow. In practice, RSA cryptography uses 512-bit or 1024-bit prime products (or even higher for military communications), which looks something like this:

```
Example RSA-1024 key:
5708540643351253003745803928442300669566321160974683770675705367947951077337302
555449467671585284876326135547312465091842513308062672649065703073156201588336
794409395089283404219568759916726604265635656153071866002944861048200509043191
065262154874848937338866257399506142323572694928592907380693479819082939185
```

Other small details differ in practice to further increase the security of the procedure.

Why Bitcoin Needs Cryptography

So why is cryptography necessary to make Bitcoin work, even though Bitcoin does not involve sending secret messages? In Bitcoin, hash functions and digital signatures are used for the following important purposes:

- Authorizing transactions with digital signatures
- Verifying the validity of the transaction history
- Proof-of-work in Bitcoin mining
- Extra protection for Bitcoin private keys

Let's explore the functions of Bitcoin that require cryptography and then delve into the specific methods that Bitcoin uses.

Authorizing Transactions with Digital Signatures

Bitcoin uses digital signatures to authorize transactions so that you, and *only* you, can spend the bitcoins you own. With credit card payments and bank transfers, you authorize a transaction by providing proof of your personal identity (and these days, the amount of proof you have to show is getting quite burdensome). With Bitcoin, no personal information is tied to any Bitcoin address; instead, you must prove that you own the private key. Showing people your private key would certainly be valid as proof, but by knowing the private key, the people you've shown could then claim *they owned* the bitcoins at that address. Therefore, you need to prove that you have the private key without actually sharing it. But there's more to it than that.

A Bitcoin transaction contains a fair amount of information: the number of bitcoins transferred, the address they are being transferred to, the transaction fee, and so on. You don't want any of that information to be altered without your permission, so in addition to proving you own the bitcoins you are sending, you also need to ensure that the transaction details are followed exactly a you wrote them. A Bitcoin transaction is a message with instructions, and by signing it with a digital signature, you simultaneously prove tat you have the private key and ensure that the transaction details are what you intended. If the signature is missing or doesn't match the public key, nodes on the Bitcoin network will consider the transaction invalid and will not ad it to the blockchain.

Verifying the Validity of the Transaction History

Bitcoin depends on the blockchain being widely distributed among the nodes in the network. But how can you be sure that any individual node in the network with a copy of the blockchain has not been surreptitiously altered? A malicious attacker cold try to distribute a fraudulent blockchain where just a single transaction has been modified in the attacker's favor. However, such an attack could never work for several reasons. One reason is that the slightest change in the transaction history would completely change the *block hash* of all the blocks after it in the chain.

Each block in the blockchain contains a list of transactions and a hash of the transactions in the previous block in the chain. Hence, it's impossible to alter just one transaction in a block in the middle without causing a mismatch between the expected block hash and the hash recorded in the next block.

This verification provides an efficient way for a single node to check whether transactions in its copy of the blockchain have been tampered with. Rather than checking every transaction in the entire transaction history, a node can simply check whether the hash of each block matches the recorded hash of subsequent blocks.

Proof-of-Work in Bitcoin Mining

Bitcoin mining is based on a lottery system that you can win only by guessing numbers repeatedly, but that makes it is easy for others to check when you're right. If this sounds similar to a one-way function, that's because it is. The one-way function used in Bitcoin mining is a cryptographic hash function. Miners are given the output criteria (the output can be any number less than some threshold), but by design, cryptographic hash functions make it difficult to reverse calculate what the corresponding input needs to be. Therefore, Bitcoin miners can only randomly choose different inputs, hoping that the output will be a number below the threshold. Once a miner determines the correct input value, it is easy to prove his or her work to others by sharing that value with others who can easily recalculate the hash.

Extra Protection for Bitcoin Private Keys

Authorizing transactions with digital signatures requires sharing your public key with others. Although it is thought to be computationally infeasible to calculate a private key from a public key, it is similarly difficult to calculate the input of a hash function given just the output, and it is doubly difficult to do both. Instead of sharing a public key, users share a *Bitcoin address*, which is a cryptographic hash of a public key. In fact, the public key is hashed twice using two different cryptographic hash functions to create a Bitcoin address. This extra protection ensures that no amount of analysis of a Bitcoin address can reveal the underlying private key.

Bitcoin uses cryptographic hash functions to accomplish a variety of other important tasks as well. Next, you'll explore the specific cryptographic methods Bitcoin uses.

Cryptographic Methods Used in Bitcoin

Public key cryptography is a high-level framework that can be implemented many different ways. You learned how the RSA method, using integers factored into large prime numbers, could be used to implement digital signatures. But how are digital signatures implemented in Bitcoin? Many different cryptographic hash functions exist, and although the MD5 method mentioned earlier is widely used, it is not sufficiently secure for a cryptocurrency (collisions have been detected in MD5, resulting in two different inputs leading to the same output).

SHA256 and RIPEMD160 are the two cryptographic hash functions used in the Bitcoin protocol.

Cryptographic Hash Functions: SHA256 and RIPEMD160

Secure Hash Algorithm (SHA) was developed by the US National Security Agency (NSA). Race Integrity Primitives Evaluation Message Digest (RIPEMD) was designed in the academic community by Hans Dobbertin, Antoon Bosselaers, and Bart Preneel at the Katholieke Universiteit Leuven.[5]

The prefixes *SHA* and *RIPEMD* refer to the underlying algorithms, and the numerical suffixes 256 and 160 refer to the bit-length of the output. A spectrum of other SHA functions, like SHA224 and SHA512 output other bit-length hashes as well.

Both SHA256 and RIPEMD160 are widely used, but the SHA methods are more popular and have undergone a higher degree of scrutiny from cryptographers. At the time of this writing, nobody has detected a collision in either SHA256 or RIPEMD160, which is an important measure of the security of a cryptographic hash function.

In the Bitcoin protocol, SHA256 and RIPEMD160 are used together to protect the public key used in digital signatures. The SHA256 method is also used for the proof-of-work function in Bitcoin mining and as part of the digital signature algorithm. Here are some examples of encrypting a sentence with a slight variation in both SHA256 and RIPEMD160 (all of the following outputs are in base 16 format):

```
SHA256("Crowley is trapped on an island")
= 1e8f7e62b42f07766c3c4367e670a328d73b7eb596602198f126324f013f30a5
```

A completely different result is produced with a single character change:

```
SHA256("Crowley is trapped on an Island")
= 91a382b6584261e0e7690da2c43cec9f7ce251b47396b543bddb3ed6ada8c9cc
```

The same happens using RIPEMD160:

```
RIPEMD160("Crowley is trapped on an island")
= 64d50d0853d09d97c4567117a616954ca648e46c
```

This hash is completely different:

```
RIPEMD160("Crowley is trapped on an Island")
= b84aec162a0aa5786541b5e4f3286f8734e3bc3c
```

As you'd expect and appreciate in an effective hash function, a minor change to the text (capitalizing the word *Island*) completely changes the resulting hash value in both methods.

5. Hans Dobbertin, Antoon Bosselaers, and Bart Preneel, "RIPEMD-160, a strengthened version of RIPEMD," in *Fast Software Encryption*, ed. Dieter Gollmann (Berlin: Springer-Verlag, 1996), 71–82.

Now that you understand the hash functions Bitcoin uses, let's discuss the algorithm Bitcoin digital signatures use.

Crowley and the Unfortunate Jelly-Filled Donut Incident

For the remainder of this chapter, we'll discuss the details of elliptical curve cryptography (ECC). But before we delve into the details of this algorithm, and to help you understand the basic concept behind it, let us tell you a story.

One day Crowley was driving through Cryptoville in his car, minding his own business, when suddenly, BAM! His car was thrown into the air!

He had been driving by a donut shop that was trying to beat the world record for the largest jelly-filled donut. Unfortunately, the bakers miscalculated the correct pressure of jelly to inject into the donut, causing the explosion.

After tumbling through the air, Crowley landed safely and was relieved to realize he wasn't hurt. However, he was a bit shaken from this frightful incident, and his car was covered in jelly. Because he had tumbled through the air, he was lost and no longer knew where he was in Cryptoville. What was he going to do now?

Suddenly, Satoshi stepped out of a nearby house. Quite by accident, Crowley had found out where the secretive Satoshi lived!

Crowley proceeded to explain to Satoshi what had happened to him and his car. Satoshi was concerned to hear that Crowley was lost but also a bit relieved because it meant that his home address was still a secret.

Crowley asked Satoshi to give him a ride home or call a tow truck. But Satoshi refused, saying, "If I do either of those things, you'll be able to figure out where you are in Cryptoville, and then you'll be able to figure out my secret home address. Luckily I have another idea: Why don't you come into my home as a guest and enjoy a cup of coffee as you regain your wits from your harrowing experience today. I'll be back in a couple of hours and will then share my plan to get you and your car home again."

Sure enough, Satoshi returned to the house after a while carrying an iPod, of all things. "OK, Crowley, here's what I did. I just drove to your house with my own car. While doing so, I recorded my drive on this iPod and recorded every action as I drove along. When I turned the steering wheel 10 degrees to the left, I said this on the recording. If I accelerated from 20 mph to 40 mph, I recorded this as well. Everything I did I recorded at the exact time I did it."

Crowley then understood the plan: Even though his car was covered in jelly and it was impossible for him to see through the windows, he could still follow the simple instructions on the tape. After all, his car motor still ran fine, and he could see the speedometer on his car's dashboard. Satoshi added, "It'll be very hard for you to reverse engineer the exact physics of how the car was driving based solely on the instructions I recorded on the iPod. Therefore, the location of my home will remain unknown to you. However, to make it extra hard, I also took a very circuitous route, driving through almost all of Cryptoville along the way to your house!"

But sure enough, using Satoshi's iPod, Crowley was able to drive his car back home without being able to see a thing through his car windows. He simply followed the instructions, and when the recording finished, he was back home. He still didn't have the slightest clue where Satoshi lived, and he miraculously avoided hitting any pedestrians or other cars in the process!

To thank Satoshi for helping him, Crowley sent Satoshi an email inviting him to lasagna at Crowley's house on Saturday night and asking him to suggest a time for dinner. Here is the email Satoshi wrote back:

> Thanks Crowley—Dinner sounds great, and I love lasagna! Let's meet at 9:25 P.M.
>
> Oh, and to prove that this email is legit, I can tell you that I was on the 300 block of Main Street driving north at exactly 38.7 mph when the iPod displayed 9 minutes and 25 seconds.

Being a stickler for verifying identities, Crowley tested this fact: He first had his car (still covered in jelly) towed to the location mentioned in the email and then started the iPod at the 9 minute and 25 second mark. Following the instructions on the iPod explicitly until they completed, he once again stepped out of the car and found he was back at home!

This silly parable is meant to give you a rough outline of one way you could create a digital signature: Imagine that Satoshi's home address is Satoshi's private key, and Crowley's home address is the public key. The instructions on an iPod are a one-way function that's difficult to reverse. Using this information, you could *sign* an arbitrary message (in this case the number *925*, which corresponds to the meeting time). Only the person who knows the private key (Satoshi's home address) could generate this signature.

As you'll see, with ECC, we'll instead "drive around town" by jumping between points on a special two-dimensional curve, which makes it even harder to reverse engineer the directions. However, the overall process will remain roughly analogous to that in the story.

Moving Around on a Line

Before we start thinking about what's involved in driving around on a curve, let's use an easier scenario and imagine driving around on a line (see Figure 7-1).

If we have a straight line that passes through the origin (i.e., the point at $x = 0$, $y = 0$), we can create a new point on the line by using two points A and B to create a point C by simply adding A and B. Here is the obvious formula for adding two points:

$$A(x_1, y_1) + B(x_2, y_2) = C(x_3, y_3) \qquad x_3 = x_1 + x_2 \qquad y_3 = y_1 + y_2$$

We need to add the two x-coordinates to get a new x (simply $1 + 3 = 4$) and add the two y-coordinates (also $1 + 3 = 4$). Note that we can also use a simple geometric trick to generate point C without using arithmetic: Simply start at point B and then move at the same angle and amount as point A is from the origin.

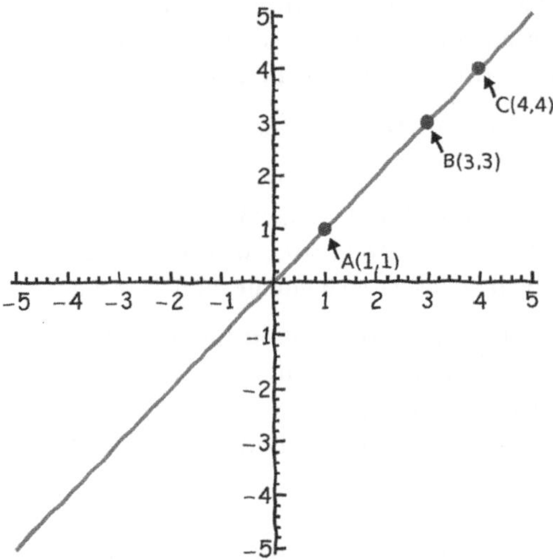

Figure 7-1: Adding two points (A and B) on a line to get point C

For a line, this addition process is very simple but is not useful for cryptography (and equally not useful for creating driving instructions for our "car" that are hard to reverse engineer). But as you'll see, the process for adding points is very different with elliptical curves.

Elliptic Curve Digital Signature Algorithm (ECDSA)

Instead of integer factorization-based schemes, digital signatures in Bitcoin are based on ECC. Although integer factorization works well in principle, faster computers and better algorithms to factor integers have over time increasingly required the use of ever larger prime factors to ensure reasonable security. The recommended size of encryption keys used for RSA encryption is between 1024 and 4096 bits. In contrast, elliptic curves offer the same functionality but are not affected by advances in factoring integers; therefore, shorter keys can be used (a 256-bit key in ECC is believed to offer comparable security to a 1024-bit key in an RSA-type scheme). In short, ECC is thought to be stronger than methods based on factoring integers for the same key length.

Bitcoin uses elliptic curves to create digital signatures, specifically by using a protocol called the Elliptic Curve Digital Signature Algorithm (ECDSA). An elliptic curve is any two-dimensional curve that satisfies the equation:

$$y^2 = x^3 + ax + b$$

A few sample curves that satisfy this equation are shown in Figure 7-2. Public/private key pairs are generated by choosing points on these elliptic curves that are mathematically related to each other.

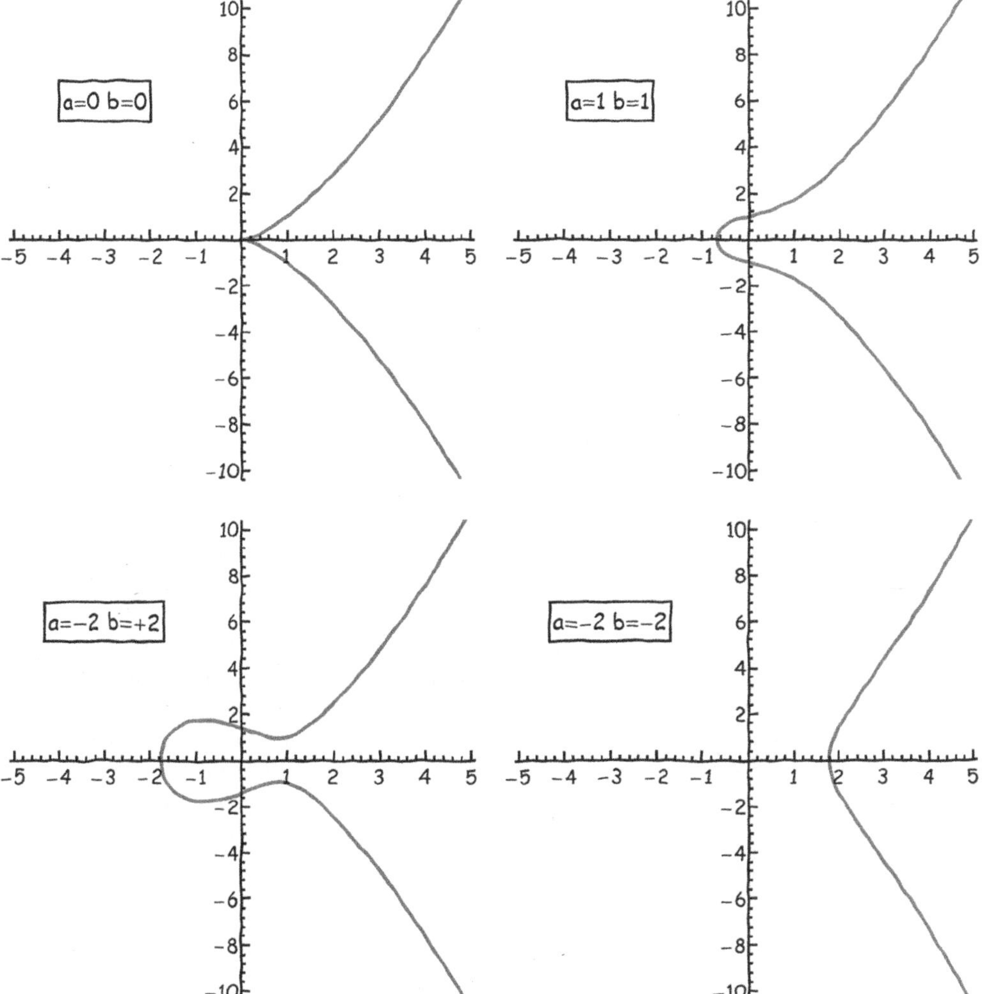

Figure 7-2: Different elliptic curves can be generated using different parameters in our starting equation.

As with the property of a straight line, when you add the coordinates of any two points on the curve, the result is another point on the curve.

However, with elliptic curves *addition* has a special meaning and is defined as follows:

$$A(x_1, y_1) + B(x_2, y_2) = C(x_3, y_3) \qquad x_3 = \left(\frac{y_2 - y_1}{x_2 - x_1}\right)^2 - x_1 - x_2 \qquad y_3 = -y_1 + \left(\frac{y_2 - y_1}{x_2 - x_1}\right)(x_1 - x_3)$$

Clearly, this formula for adding two points is much more complex than the addition formula we used for straight lines. Figure 7-3 shows an example elliptic curve with two points A and B and the resulting point C created by following these addition rules.

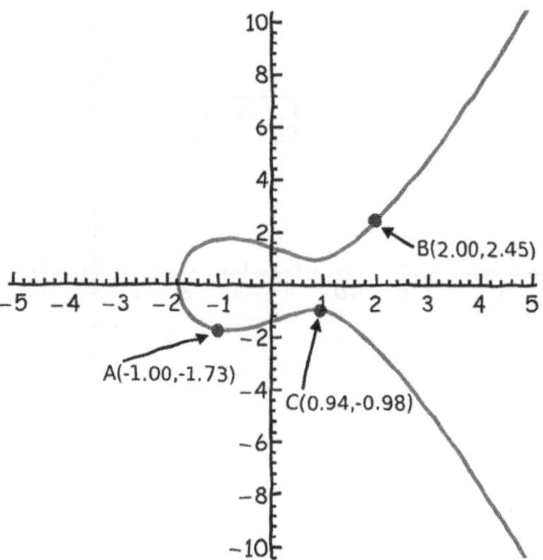

Figure 7-3: Two points (A and B) on an elliptic curve are added to create point C, using our special method of addition.

In the example in Figure 7-3, points A and B are not special in any way. Choosing different A and B points would lead to a different point C (Figure 7-4), which is the whole point of using this type of addition for cryptography: In the earlier jelly donut incident, Crowley had to drive a long, circuitous route back to his house so Satoshi's home address would remain obscured. Repeatedly jumping between points on the elliptic curve using this method of addition can help you obscure your private key in a digital signature system in the same way, as you'll soon see.

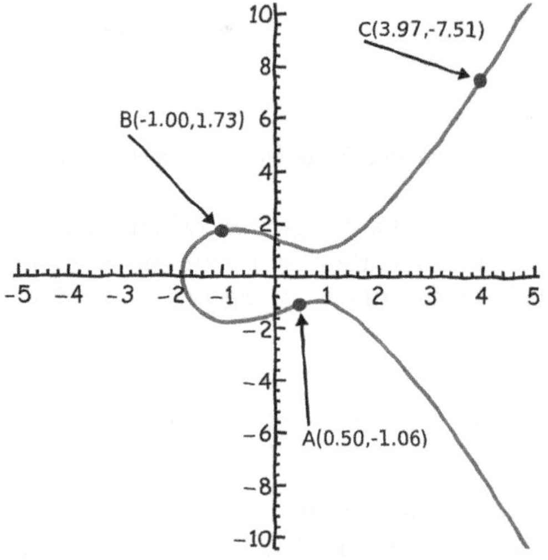

Figure 7-4: When different points A and B are chosen, a different point C is created.

Similar to lines, you can use a geometric trick to calculate the sum of adding two points on elliptic curves (i.e., without needing to do the tedious arithmetic). Simply draw a line through points A and B, and find another location where the line intersects the curve. Then draw a vertical line starting at this point of intersection and see where else it crosses the elliptic curve. This second crossing is point C (Figure 7-5).

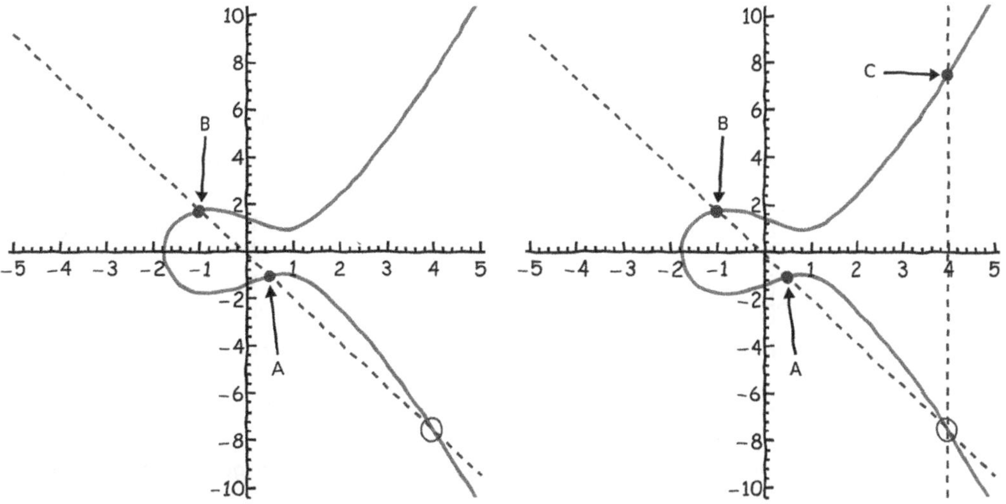

Figure 7-5: Using simple geometry, you can find point C by just drawing a line through points A and B and then moving vertically to find point C.

A fundamental property of elliptic curves is that any line that intersects at least two points must also intersect a third (except for vertical lines and lines that are tangent to a point on the curve[6]).

Of course, if we want to "drive around" our elliptic curve, as in our conceptual example involving a car, it's somewhat awkward that we need two points to generate every new point: As with a car, it would be ideal to go from a single point to another single point so our "car" only has to be in one place at a time. Fortunately, this is possible with elliptic curves as well by using a form of multiplication to multiply a point on the curve by an integer, which is the same as adding a point to itself multiple times. It might seem like the geometric trick does not work in this case. How do you draw a straight line through two points if they are in the same place? You can probably guess by imagining what happens when you consider adding two points, A and B, that are very close together: The line that passes through A and B will resemble the tangent to the curve near those points. So when

6. Exact vertical lines are considered to hit a third point at y = infinity. Points where the line is tangent to the curve count as two intersection points (even though it looks like only one in Figure 7-6), so if a tangent line touches the curve only one more time it is still counted as "intersecting three times."

we add A + A (or equivalently, multiply A by 2), we draw a tangent to the curve at point A and find where else it intersects. Then we draw a vertical line, as before, to find the resulting point, 2A (Figure 7-6).

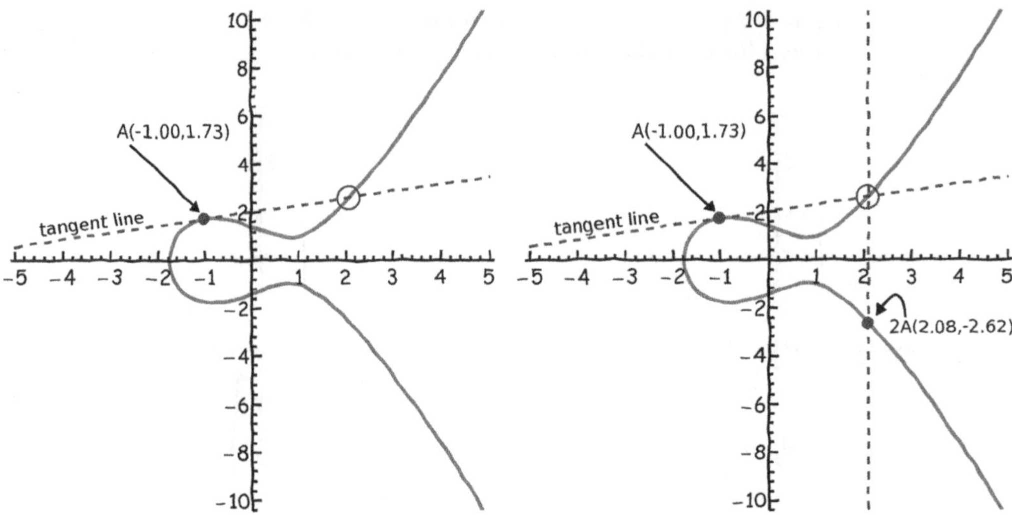

Figure 7-6: With only one starting point, we can point multiply by 2 by using the tangent line through point A.

To calculate 3A, you first calculate 2A, as we just did, and then adding an additional A is just like adding any two nonoverlapping points. In elliptic curve terminology, calculating *k*A, where *k* is an arbitrary integer, is called point multiplication. Calculating *k*A for large values of *k* is computationally expensive without efficient implementations.

So as with our conceptual example, we'll now use point multiplication to "drive" from one point on the curve to another. In ECC, point multiplication is used to generate the public key from the private key. However, there will be one important difference between our jelly-filled donut story and how ECC really works. In our story, Satoshi's house represented a private key and Crowley's house a public key, but in ECC the starting point and destination point are *both* publicly known—it is only the path between them that is secret. So it is in fact the *path* that is the private key; the destination point is the public key (as it was before), and the starting point is simply a standard location that everyone agrees to use. In ECC it's as if Satoshi's home address were widely known to be in the center of a very complex labyrinth—everyone knows where he lives, but no one knows how to get there. Given a previously agreed-upon point on the curve, G, and a private key, *d*, the public key, Q, is calculated by point multiplication such that Q = *d*G. Note that the public key is a point on the curve but the private key is just an integer.

So far we've been depicting elliptic curves as smooth, continuous functions that extend into infinity. However, computers have limited memory, and it isn't possible to use real-valued numbers as coordinates for points on the curve without introducing rounding errors (which are unacceptable in cryptography). For practical implementations, only integer-valued points on elliptic curves are allowed, and modular arithmetic is used to keep all of the points within certain bounds (from 0 to 512, for example). This technique of using only integer-valued points is best illustrated with an example. Let's first choose the same elliptic curve that Bitcoin uses, which is called a *Koblitz curve* (Figure 7-7), using the parameters $a = 0$ and $b = 7$.

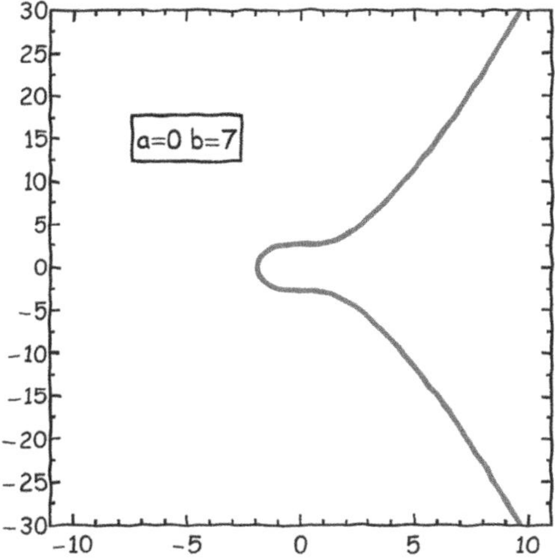

Figure 7-7: A Koblitz curve

We then choose a prime modulo p so that the elliptic curve satisfies this equation:

$$y^2 = x^2 + ax + b(\text{mod}p)$$

NOTE *In this type of math notation, the modulo operation is performed after the additions so first you calculate* $x^2 + ax + b$ *and then you perform mod* p *on the result.*

Bitcoin uses a very large p value (specifically $p = 2^{256} - 2^{32} - 2^9 - 2^8 - 2^7 - 2^6 - 2^4 - 1$), which is important for cryptographic strength, but we can use a smaller number to illustrate how "driving around on integer-valued points on a Koblitz curve" works. Let's choose $p = 67$. In fact, many curves satisfy the modular equation (namely, every curve where p is added to or subtracted from the b parameter any number of times; see the left-hand chart in Figure 7-8), and from those curves we can use all of the points that have integer-valued coordinates (shown in Figure 7-8 as dots).

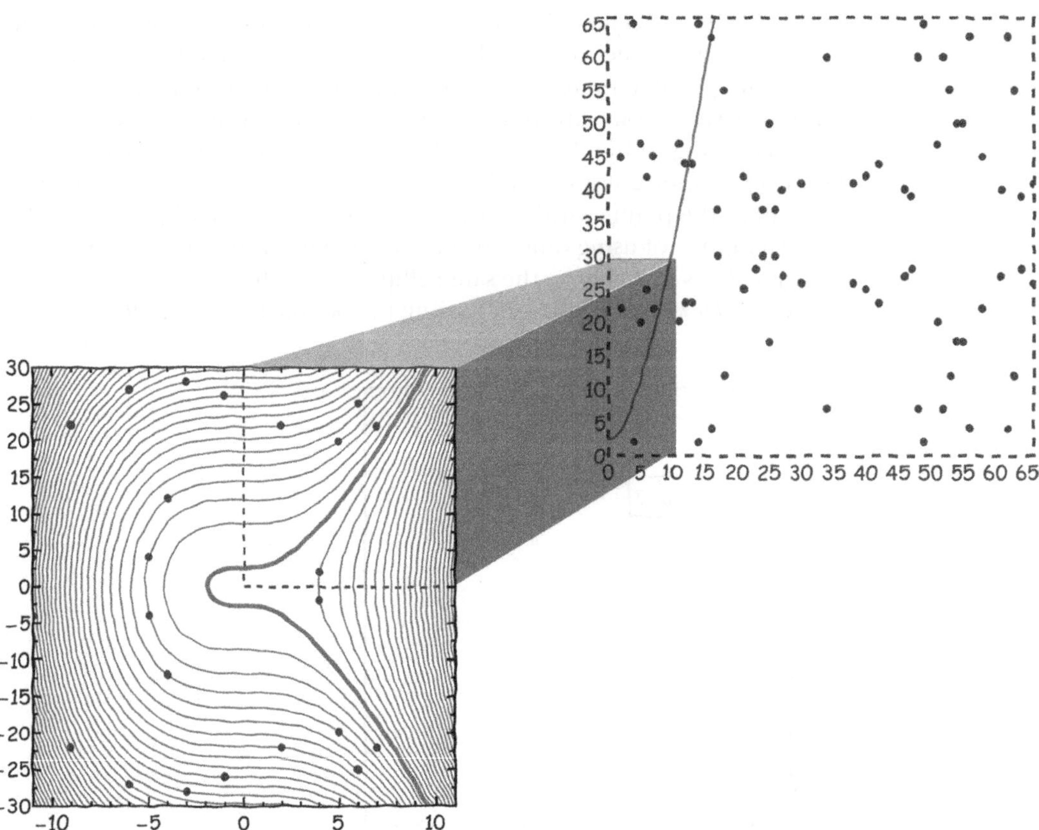

Figure 7-8: On the left is a standard picture of the elliptic curve in the form we're familiar with (the bold curve) with additional curves that are drawn by using other multiples of p (the thin curves.) On the right, we've taken a larger section of the coordinate plane that is an expansion of the upper-right quadrant. This is the section of the curve that is most convenient when using the integer-based variant of ECC.

Given the choice of $p = 67$, only 79 unique points with integer-valued coordinates exist, and 78 of them can be found in the upper-right quadrant from $0 < x < 66$ and $0 < y < 66$ (shown in the chart on the right in Figure 7-8; note that the left chart shows the entire range). The number of unique points, n, is called the *order* of the curve. The 79th point is the *zero* point, which is not at (0,0) as you might expect but rather is the point at y = infinity. The zero point is important because it is valid output from an addition or point multiplication operation and therefore needs to be carefully accounted for (see the sample code in "Pseudocode for Elliptic Point Summation and Point Multiplication" on page 158).

As a last step before we can generate public/private key pairs, we need to choose one of the 79 points to be a *generator* point, G. The generator needs to have the property that one can calculate every one of the other 78 points by multiplying G by some integer, k (i.e., so you can *generate* every point by calculating G, 2G, 3G, ..., 79G). If we choose the point (5,47) as our generator point, we can check whether by successively incrementing k we can travel to every point in the set (see Figure 7-9).

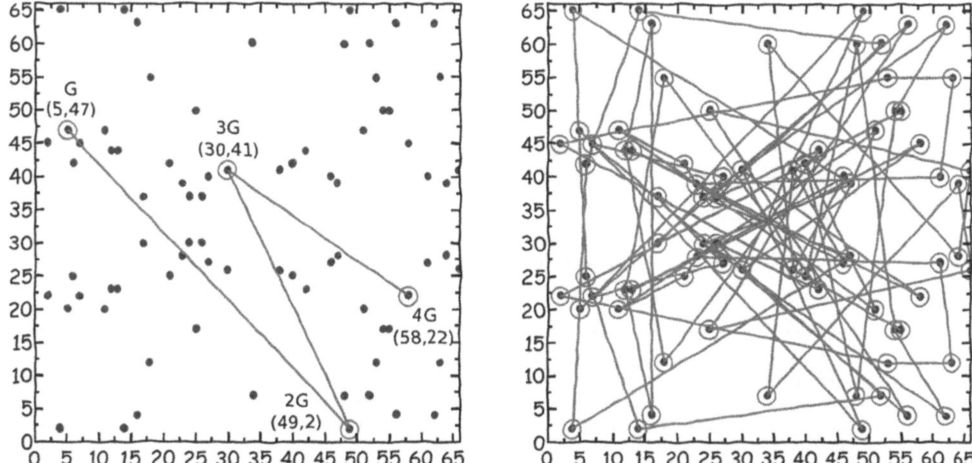

Figure 7-9: On the left, starting with point G, we multiply G successively to create new points at 2G, 3G, and 4G. On the right, you see what happens when this multiplication is repeated even further.

If the order of the curve is prime (i.e., there is a prime number of points), any point except the zero point works equally well as a generator. If the order is not prime, regardless of the *k* value, some points will travel only to a subset of points (which can lead to a reduction in cryptographic strength). In our case, we can safely use the point (5,47) because it generates all the other 78 points (as depicted in the chart in Figure 7-9).

To return to our conceptual car example, point G in this figure could be Satoshi's house and point 4G, for example, could be Crowley's house. The points between represent the complicated drive through Cryptoville. Until you carry out the point multiplication operation, it certainly isn't obvious what the path from G to 4G is. The 4 in 4G gives away the answer, namely that the path connecting those points can be found by taking three steps from G. However, if G and 4G were instead labeled A and B, it would take a long time to guess how to get from one to the other. In other words, if you know only the start and end points (i.e., the public key), it would take a long time to guess the path (i.e., the private key). But if you know the starting point and the path, then calculating the end point is easy. In terms of Bitcoin, it means that if someone knows the Bitcoin address that contains your money (which is based on the public key), it is still impossible for that person to figure out your private key to spend the bitcoins at that address.

Signing a Bitcoin Transaction Using ECDSA

Now that we've chosen *p*, *a*, *b*, and G and determined the order, *n*, we have all the information we need to create a public/private key pair following the steps in Table 7-5.[7]

7. If are you trying to follow along but don't know how to perform a point multiplication calculation, see the pseudocode at the end of this chapter.

Table 7-5: Creating a Public/Private Key Pair with ECDSA, Assuming p = 67, a = 0, b = 7, G = (5,47), n = 79

Step	Instruction	Example
1	Generate a private key, d, which can be any integer from 1 to (n − 1). It should be hard to guess. This can be done using a random number generator or other clever means.*	d = Random # from 1 to 78 Choose d = 13.
2	Generate a public key, Q, by point multiplication of the private key, d, and the generator point, G. Note that this is a one-way calculation. It is very hard to determine d given G and Q.	Q = d × G = 13 × (5,47) = (7,22) (see Figure 7-10)

* A clever way to generate a seemingly random but memorable private key is by coming up with a passphrase (i.e., *Crowley and Satoshi sitting in a tree*) and feeding it into a cryptographic hash function, which outputs an integer. This is called using a brainwallet. Because there are just slightly fewer than 2^{256} points on the curve Bitcoin uses (because the p value is much higher than the one we are using), brainwallets can use the SHA256 hash function (due to its 256-bit output).

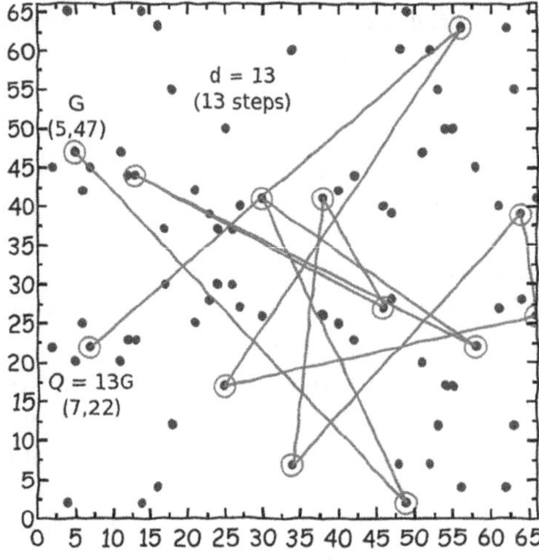

Figure 7-10: Here are the 13 points we "drive through" as we point multiply to create a digital signature.

Now let's look at how we sign messages with our private and public keys (or Bitcoin transactions): The receiver of our message will need all the values we have calculated so far except the private key, namely p, a, b, G, n and Q, in order to verify that the signature is valid. Let's assume that our message is this: *Please update the blockchain so that 5 bitcoins from Crowley are given to Satoshi.* The steps to sign the message are listed in Table 7-6.

Table 7-6: Signing a Message with ECDSA, Assuming $p = 67$, $a = 0$, $b = 7$, $G = (5,47)$, $n = 79$, $d = 13$

Step	Instruction	Example
1	Calculate the hash of the message, h. The Bitcoin protocol uses the SHA256 function for this purpose. The output of the hash needs to be less than n, so we need to calculate h = SHA256(*message*) (mod n).	h = SHA256("Please update the blockchain so that 5 bitcoins from Crowley are given to Satoshi")(mod 79) = 46
2	Choose a random integer, k, between 1 and $(n - 1)$.	k = Random integer from 1 to 78 Choose $k = 6$.
3	Calculate the point $(r,s^*) = kG$.	$(r,s^*) = k \times G = 6 \times (5,47)$ $= (46,27)$
4	Find s such that $s \times k \pmod{n} = (h + (r \times d)) \pmod{n}$. The signature is the pair of numbers (r,s) (not a point on the elliptic curve unless by coincidence).	Left side: $s \times k \pmod{n}$ $= s \times 6 \pmod{79}$ Right side: $(h + (r \times d)) \pmod{n}$ $= (46 + (46 \times 13)) \pmod{79}$ $= 12$ Left = Right when $s = 2$

When the message is signed, the receiver will need p, a, b, n, G, Q, and the signature pair (r,s) (and the message, of course). However, the parameters p, a, b, n, and G are standard to the Bitcoin protocol and therefore don't need to be shared with every transaction. The only information specific to your message that needs to be shared is Q, (r,s), and the message. The message recipient can verify that you signed the message with your private key by using the steps in Table 7-7.

Table 7-7: Verifying a Signature with ECDSA, Assuming the Receiver Gets $Q = (7,22)$, $(r = 46, s = 2)$, and the message

Step	Instruction	Example
1	Repeat the hash calculation of the message to get the hash: h = SHA256(*message*) (mod n)	h = SHA256("Please update the blockchain so that 5 bitcoins from Crowley are given to Satoshi") (mod 79) = 46
2	Find w such that $w \times s \pmod{n} = 1$ (w is called the *modular inverse* of s).	$w \times s \pmod{n} = 1$ $w \times 2 \pmod{79} = 1$, $w \rightarrow 40$
3	Calculate $u = h \times w \pmod{n}$.	$u = h \times w \pmod{n}$ $= 46 \times 40 \pmod{79}$ $= 23$
4	Calculate $v = r \times w \pmod{n}$ (if u and v are the same, it is just a coincidence).	$v = r \times w \pmod{n}$ $= 46 \times 40 \pmod{79}$ $= 23$
5	Calculate $(tx,ty) = uG + vQ$.	$(tx,ty) = u \times G + v \times Q$ $= 23 \times (5,47) + 23 \times (7,22)$ $= (11,47) + (2,22) = (46,27)$
6	If $tx = r$, the signature is valid.	$tx = 46$, $r = 46$, signature is valid

In our car example, we were able to *sign messages* in a similar way by relating a message to a point that the car passed as it traveled toward its destination. However, this is where this analogy reaches its limits: In the car example, providing information about where the car traveled conveys some clues as to the path the car took, compromising the secret of Satoshi's address a bit. Using the math in Table 7-7 shows that signing a document does not provide any useful information that compromises the private key. We can sign as many documents as we want, and the private key will continue to remain fully obscured.

So this is how bitcoins are spent. When you sign a Bitcoin transaction with your private key, other nodes in the Bitcoin network can check that your signature is valid (by matching your public key and the contents of the transaction) and safely know you authorized it. Of course, if your private key falls into the wrong hands, someone else can sign transactions and steal your bitcoins.

Note that until you actually need to spend bitcoins, there is no need to share the public key. Although in principle sharing your public key far in advance of signing a transaction should be no problem, it's possible that a weakness in ECC will be discovered that could allow an attacker with enough time and computing power to figure out your private key from your public key (i.e., figure out d, given G and Q in the equation $Q = dG$). So why give an attacker the extra time if it isn't necessary? If an attacker doesn't know your public key, the ability to determine your private key is drastically reduced. For this reason, Bitcoin users share *addresses* instead of public keys.

The Bitcoin address described at length earlier in this book is actually a hash of the public key, using the SHA256 and RIPEMD160 hash functions. The public key is first input into the SHA256 hash function, and then the output is fed as input into the RIPEMD160 hash function. The resulting double hash is used to generate the Bitcoin address in a standard way.[8] When you spend bitcoins from a Bitcoin address, you must provide your public key, and others can check that the public key corresponds to the Bitcoin address by repeating the same double hash calculation (and of course, the signature proves that you have the private key).

In cryptography, the double hash scheme results in extremely strong security. Given only a Bitcoin address, it would require a simultaneously discovered weakness in three different cryptographic methods—SHA256, RIPEMD160, and ECDSA—for an attacker to guess a private key. If a weakness was discovered in one method but not the others, there would be time to update the cryptographic methods used in Bitcoin before anyone's bitcoins were at risk.

---

8. In addition to hashing the public key with SHA256 and RIPEMD160, some additional steps are involved (like appending the Bitcoin *version number*) to the hash to generate the actual Bitcoin address. However, the cryptographically significant step is the SHA256/RIPEMD160 double hash.

The Security of Bitcoin's Cryptography

A common anxiety among those new to Bitcoin is to wonder whether the cryptography used in Bitcoin is secure enough to protect against threats. Could a big, powerful government with huge computing resources break Bitcoin's cryptography? What about a very clever hacker who might bring down the entire system? What about super powerful computers of the future, like quantum computers?

These are healthy concerns to have when a person is deciding whether Bitcoin is a sound protocol and worth investing in. Every Bitcoin private key is some number between 1 and 2^{256}, and *in principle* a computer could continue generating numbers billions or trillions of times per second until it found one that could access your bitcoins. However, 2^{256} is a *very* big number; in fact, it's approximately 10^{77} or a 1 with 77 zeroes behind it. Putting that in perspective, approximately 10^{50} atoms make up the earth. If you chose a single atom in the earth at random, and then chose a second atom, also at random, the odds that you picked the same atom twice would be *significantly* greater than randomly guessing someone's private key.

Could an extremely powerful computer, based on futuristic technology that is yet to be invented, guess a private key? Theoretical physicists have estimated that the smallest amount of energy to perform the simplest computation (changing a 0 to a 1 or vice versa) requires at least 3×10^{-21} joules (this is known as the Landauer limit[9]). A computer that used this amount of energy per computation would theoretically be the most efficient computer allowed by the laws of thermodynamics. If you then could harness 100 percent of the energy of the sun (not just the tiny fraction that falls on the earth, but the entire amount, by building a sphere of perfect solar panels surrounding the entire star), with no losses, you could theoretically capture 10^{34} joules per year. If you harvested that energy for 100 years and fed all of it into your maximally efficient computer designed for the single purpose of guessing someone's Bitcoin private key, it would be able to perform only 10^{55} computations. Of course, calculating a private key is more complicated than flipping a 0 into a 1, but even if we assume that this computer could calculate 10^{55} private keys, it would run out of energy before it would even have one-trillionth of a chance of correctly guessing yours.

In summary, it is physically impossible, independent of future technological developments, to create a computer that could steal bitcoins by randomly guessing private keys. However, that does not eliminate the concern that a weakness exists in the cryptographic methods that Bitcoin uses. Perhaps it is easier than we think to work backward from a Bitcoin address to calculate the underlying private key. Here, it is important to note that the cryptographic methods used by Bitcoin are standard methods used by governments and major corporations to ensure security in

9. Rolf Landauer, "Irreversibility and heat generation in the computing process," *IBM Journal of Research and Development* 5 (1961): 183–191.

communications, financial transactions, and network security. If a weakness exists in the methods that Bitcoin uses, a weakness exists in the methods the entire world uses.

Also, if weaknesses *are* discovered in the cryptographic standards, such that new methods need to be used, it is possible to update the methods that Bitcoin uses without affecting how Bitcoin functions. A new version of the SHA256 algorithm may be used in the future, or ECDSA might be replaced with a different digital signature algorithm. However, Bitcoin's reliance on cryptography in general will not change.

The bottom line is that Bitcoin's cryptography has a solid technical foundation. If a hacker ever does steal your bitcoins, it is far more likely the hacker would do so by finding a bug in a *specific implementation* of this cryptography that is flawed or by using the many other ways we've discussed, such as simply stealing your private key through a computer virus. It is far less likely that a hacker would be able to steal your money by finding a flaw in the mathematics of the cryptography.

Pseudocode for Elliptic Point Summation and Point Multiplication

To follow along with the elliptic curve digital signature examples earlier in the chapter, you'll need to be able to correctly calculate elliptic point summations and point multiplication operations using modular arithmetic. Pseudocode for the implementation of these operations follows:

```
Assumptions: p, a, b, G, and n are defined elsewhere
Elliptic curve point summation (ECPS): A + B = C
ECPS(A,B) returns a point on the elliptic curve, C
Begin
    If A is the zero point then return C = B❶
    If B is the zero point then return C = A
    If Ax != Bx then❷
        find inv such that inv*(Bx - Ax) (mod p) == 1
        lambda = (By - Ay)*inv (mod p)
        Cx = lambda^2 - Ax - Bx
        Cy = -Ay + lambda*(Ax - Cx)
        return C = (Cx (mod p), Cy (mod p))
    If Ax == Bx and Ay != By then return C = the zero point❸
    If Ax == Bx and Ay == By then❹
        find inv such that inv*2Ay (mod p) == 1
        lambda = (3*Ax^2 + a)*inv (mod p)
        Cx = lambda^2 - 2Ax
        Cy = -Ay + lambda*(Ax - Cx)
        return C = (Cx (mod p), Cy (mod p))
End
```

In this elliptic curve point summation (ECPS) pseudocode, which allows you to add two points on the elliptic curve to generate a third point, we first check whether A or B is the zero point ❶ (recall that this is the single weird point that's part of an elliptic curve that is essentially at infinity). Next, we handle the typical case where two points have different *x* locations, and we don't need to worry about the slope between the points being divided by zero ❷. Then, we handle the case where the slope is indeed zero, which forces C to be at the zero point ❸. Finally, we handle the case where A and B are the same, in which case we need to calculate the answer differently using a mathematical derivative to calculate C using the point's tangent line ❹.

```
Elliptic curve point multiplication (ECPM): kA = C
ECPM(k,A) returns a point on the elliptic curve, C
Begin
    C = A
    Do the following k times:
        C = ECPS(C,A)❶
    return C
End
```

For elliptic curve multiplication, we simply run the ECPS function repeatedly ❶. This is really inefficient! In fact, this method of point multiplication is so inefficient that it ceases to be a "one-way" function. It is just as computationally difficult to calculate the public key (knowing the private key) as it is to guess the private key (knowing the public key). For the small number of points we were using in this chapter, it's fine to use our brute-force approach, but for practical applications, more efficient schemes for point multiplication need to be used. We leave this as an exercise for the reader.

8

BITCOIN MINING

New bitcoins are created through Bitcoin mining. In some sense, Bitcoin mining is similar to digging for gold: It takes time and effort—hence the term *mining*. The difference between mining gold and mining bitcoins is that a Bitcoin miner uses electricity and computational labor rather than physical labor. Mining is also the process by which new Bitcoin transactions are added to the blockchain, or the public ledger. By adding a new block of transactions to the blockchain, the miner who added the block is rewarded with newly minted bitcoins (as well as old bitcoins in the form of transaction fees).

The number of new bitcoins being mined from each block is diminishing slowly over time and will continue to do so until all 21 million bitcoins have been excavated. But unlike mining for gold, Bitcoin miners know exactly how many bitcoins are left to be mined. By 2140, every bitcoin will have been extracted and will be in circulation.

Although it is *potentially* lucrative to mine bitcoins, it is not for everyone. As with gold, most people, regardless of how much they want gold, would not mine it themselves. Similarly, earning a profit mining bitcoins is challenging and risky. Should you mine bitcoins? Probably not. In this chapter we'll explore the difficulties and hazards, but the short answer is that deciding whether to mine bitcoins is like deciding whether or not to mine gold. Mining gold in financially meaningful quantities requires a high degree of expertise, access to cheap labor and electricity, raising (and risking!) significant capital, and waiting years for a return on investment. If you are reading this book, it's best for you to leave Bitcoin mining to the professionals. *However,* if you are not motivated by profit and just want to mine (a trivial amount of) bitcoins for fun, you can certainly do that!

Why Is Bitcoin Mining Needed?

Whenever someone creates a new currency, one awkward problem usually surfaces at the outset: They need to figure out how to distribute newly minted money. If a government creates the money, this problem is easily resolved because the government can simply compensate itself and use the money to pay for government services. (Or, as in the United States, a government can use a complex scheme involving a Federal Reserve and treasury bond underwriting to lead to the same end result, giving the federal government capital it can spend that originated through the minting process.) However, if you're creating a distributed currency like Bitcoin, without a central party, dispersing newly minted money is surprisingly difficult. Part of the genius of Bitcoin's design was that Satoshi found a sensible way to distribute bitcoins. The currency would be given to those people willing to do computational work to protect the network, aka *the miners.*

Because protecting the Bitcoin network requires effort, time, and money, anyone willing to do this work would merit a monetary incentive. Therefore, Satoshi's strategy of using bitcoins as an incentive for miners acted as a decentralized mechanism for *giving away* new coins and created a community dedicated to protecting the network through the mining process. Let me tell you a little story to help you understand how mining protects the Bitcoin network.

A Parable of Two Generals

"The fat king is dead!" they yelled through the streets of the Principality of Cryptoville the day the king died. King Karl was not popular among the common folk for his cruelty to the peasants of his kingdom was exceeded only by his girth. Unfortunately, his son Crowley was crowned that same day, and he was believed to be very much his father's son.

For this reason and more, two generals, the General of the North and the General of the South, banded together in a plan to overthrow the monarchy. Quickly, they were able to conquer most of the lands outside the castle walls. All that remained to free the land from tyranny was to storm Castle Cryptoville!

The two generals' armies gathered at the north and south sides of the castle. On the east and west sides of the castle were the Kraggly Mountains, a treacherous mountain range with steep cliffs that had taken the lives of many Cryptovillians through the ages.

On the south side of the castle, the General of the South exclaimed, "Yes! This is the time to strike! I shall send a message to the north to begin the attack!" However, it then occurred to the general that his messenger would have to cross the Kraggly Mountains. What if a mishap prevented the message from getting through? If this happened, he, the General of the South, would attack the castle on his own and might be defeated by the foe. So the General of the South revised his plan: "I will send a message to the north to attack and will ask the General of the North to send a confirmatory reply indicating that he received my message!"

When the General of the North received the message, he declared, "Splendid! Surely we will be victorious! I shall send the confirmation to the south. Oh, but just to be sure, I'll ask the General of the South to return a message so I know he received my confirmation. I definitely wouldn't want to attack the castle on my own."

After receiving the confirmation, the General of the South asserted, "Great, we're almost ready. Now all I need to do is wait for the north to send a confirmation that the general received the confirmation of my confirmation. Victory shall be ours after I get my answer—maybe sometime tomorrow!"

That night, King Crowley's henchmen snuck into the north and south camps and assassinated both generals as they slept.

Applying the Parable to Bitcoin

In the story of the two generals, two parties needed to achieve a consensus on a plan. However, their mode of communication was based on unreliable mediums—the messengers who had to cross the perilous mountains. As a result, their naïve attempt to attain this consensus created an infinite loop of confirmations for confirmations that led to their doom. Could the generals have used another strategy to coordinate their attack?

The parable is based on an old math puzzle that was studied long before the existence of Bitcoin. The short answer to the question is that the generals would never be 100 percent certain that the other general had agreed to participate in an attack, and this can be proven mathematically.[1]

A more generalized version of this puzzle, called the *Byzantine Generals Problem*, is the same as the preceding parable except more is at play than just two generals. With this generalized version of the puzzle, with more than two armies, we can posit not only that the messages are unreliable but also that one or both of the generals may be in cahoots with King Crowley, sending misleading messages to the other generals.

This is precisely the problem a decentralized cryptocurrency needs to solve to determine which Bitcoin transactions sent across the network are valid: That is, if two conflicting transactions are sent via the network and involve the same coins, which of those transactions should take precedence? In fact, Bitcoin offers a probabilistic solution to the Byzantine Generals Problem.

1. For an early formulation of such a proof, see Jim Gray's, "Notes on Data Base Operating Systems," lecture notes in *Operating Systems, An Advanced Course* (London: Springer-Verlag, 1978).

In essence, the generals need to mine *blocks* that require significant computational resources to solve. In those blocks, they state the exact time the attack should occur. Also, as soon as a general finds out that another block has been completed, that general should cease his effort to create a new stand-alone block. Instead, each general should simply create a block containing the message "I confirm that I agree with the time in the block by general ABC." Then other generals should create their block to link to this new block and include the message, "I confirm with the confirmation by general XYZ of the time by general ABC." By continuing this process indefinitely, these blocks will form a *blockchain*, adding weight to the time suggested in the initial block (a *genesis block*). This exact blockchain strategy was described by Satoshi soon after he created Bitcoin.[2]

However, a couple of open questions remain about this algorithm's description: Aren't we back to square one, piling confirmations on top of confirmations ad infinitum? Surprisingly, the answer is *no*. Because of the computational effort involved in creating blocks, every new block generated as a confirmation of a previous block provides statistical information about the total computational power possessed by the entire population of generals. Consequently, when a given genesis block has approximately six more confirmations amassed on top of it than any other genesis block, the result is almost (but not quite) absolute certainty that the majority of generals are in agreement with the suggested attack time. (However, because this is a probabilistic solution, certainty will always be a bit less than 100 percent, which is why the original Two Generals Problem is still considered unsolved in a purely theoretical sense. But with Satoshi's approach, certainty can be arbitrarily close to 100 percent.)

However, this approach of using proof-of-work and a blockchain to coordinate the attacks of the generals still has a subtle flaw: A general who is lazy could cheat the network by never using her computer to mine blocks. Because blocks are awarded randomly by solving the mining puzzle, any one general could just leave her computer turned off during the entire process—saving electricity—but still benefit from the consensus. No one would discover that she shirked her duty, because not every participant will successfully mine blocks in either case. But in the case of Bitcoin, Satoshi had the genius to add an extra detail that solves this freeloader problem: The system pays miners with bitcoins as a reward! By paying a handsome reward, the Bitcoin network maintains an adequate number of miners at all times, a reward that is not possible in the simpler solution to the Byzantine Generals Problem without a currency built into the network.

Now that you have a good conceptual understanding of Bitcoin mining and why it's important, let's dive into the details of how Bitcoin mining helps prevent attacks against the network and how it enables the distribution of new currency.

---

2. A formulation of this puzzle by Satoshi is available at *https://bitcointalk.org/oldSiteFiles/byzantine.html*.

Preventing Attacks with Mining

How does mining prevent attacks? When designing a peer-to-peer payment network, the creator must assume that some peers on the network will try to deceive other, and that all peers in the network will act in their own self-interest. So what might go wrong with the Bitcoin network? One obvious problem is that someone might create a transaction assigning himself a million bitcoins. However, because a public record of all Bitcoin accounts exists in the blockchain, everyone can easily identify when someone is trying to give himself money that he doesn't own; unless a person can provide a valid signature for the transaction using a Bitcoin address that contains a million coins, no other node on the Bitcoin network will accept this transaction.

However, a more difficult problem to pinpoint is when a peer creates one ledger that includes a transaction spending her own bitcoins (for which she can create a digital signature) and then produces a second ledger in which those bitcoins were never spent (or sent to a different person). An abusive peer could first add a transaction to the blockchain to send bitcoins to you, and then after you gave her something of value (e.g., a cake), she could produce a new ledger in which that transaction never happened. The second ledger would conflict with the first ledger, so this abuse would certainly not go unnoticed, but it wouldn't be clear which ledger was correct. Presumably, the first ledger would be correct and any subsequently created ledger that conflicts would be invalid (after all, you already gave away your cake). But peers on the network may disagree as to which ledger came first (especially those with malicious intent), and without a central authority, who is to say which peers are correct? Bitcoin mining solves the problem of ordering transactions so everyone can agree which ones came first.

Every Bitcoin user constantly receives blocks from other users on the network. These blocks may be part of different, competing branches in the main Bitcoin blockchain and therefore represent conflicting versions of the *true ledger*. Hence, the software running on every user's computer constantly evaluates blocks as they appear on the network and decides which one is the most trustworthy and likely to be part of the accepted blockchain in the future. How does it decide?

It simply picks the one that has the most blocks (i.e., has the longest blockchain). This is considered the oldest and so came first. A blockchain with 12 blocks has existed for longer than one with 7 blocks. However, this method of deciding which chain to trust works only if a malicious peer cannot create a second ledger, immediately add 10 (or more) blocks to it, and make it seem as though the second ledger predated the first.

For this reason, the Bitcoin software checks how much computational work was required to add each block in competing branches. The amount of work used to add a block is easy to verify (they call it a proof-of-work algorithm because you can prove that you did the work). The branch with the "most work" is usually the longest one (i.e., the one with the most blocks), but if someone cheated by making a long branch with lots of "easy" blocks, it wouldn't count. For a malicious peer to create a second ledger, erase his old transactions, and convince everyone his ledger was first, he would have to add blocks to it *more quickly than the rest of the network*. The only way to accomplish such fraud would be to privately control more computational power than the entire Bitcoin network. This type of abuse is called the *51 percent attack*, and there is a good reason why it has never happened.

The only way to carry out a 51 percent attack is to invest more heavily in Bitcoin mining than everyone else on the network combined, and the only advantage gained is being able to *double-spend* your own bitcoins. But the rewards of doing so are limited: Such an attack would undermine people's confidence in the Bitcoin system, and the attacker's bitcoins would become devalued.

Let's suppose that a malicious attacker decided to make such an investment. What would be more lucrative: to abuse the ledger or to collect mining rewards? The economic incentives of Bitcoin mining strongly favor the latter. So if someone did amass the power to abuse the system, the only economic advantage would be to use that power honestly and simply mine Bitcoins better than everyone else.

Distributing New Currency with Mining

As mentioned in the beginning of the chapter, besides ordering transactions correctly, Bitcoin mining also serves as a mechanism to distribute a new digital currency. It is not an easy task to create a new currency and distribute it widely. Satoshi could have initially given himself 21 million bitcoins and then arbitrarily handed them out. But that would have been a bit random and most likely wouldn't have created a meaningful, valued currency.

Because Bitcoin was intended to be a currency with a finite supply, miners can't generate new bitcoins forever. This means that Satoshi needed to somehow choose a point in time by which all the bitcoins would be generated. If all bitcoins were generated in the first year of Bitcoin's existence, the currency would have favored early adopters too much. Conversely, if bitcoins were generated too slowly, newcomers might not have had enough incentive to take a chance and devote their computing power to this strange, new project called Bitcoin. Also, if bitcoins were generated so slowly that it would take thousands of years before they were all mined, bitcoins might not have been perceived as a finite commodity but rather one whose supply was constantly being inflated. For better or worse, Satoshi chose a scheme in which bitcoins would be distributed over a century at a rate that is reduced by half approximately every four years[3] until the total number eventually reaches 21 million (see Figure 8-1).

3. The number of bitcoins mined in each block is cut in half exactly when the blockchain grows by 210,000 blocks, which takes approximately four years.

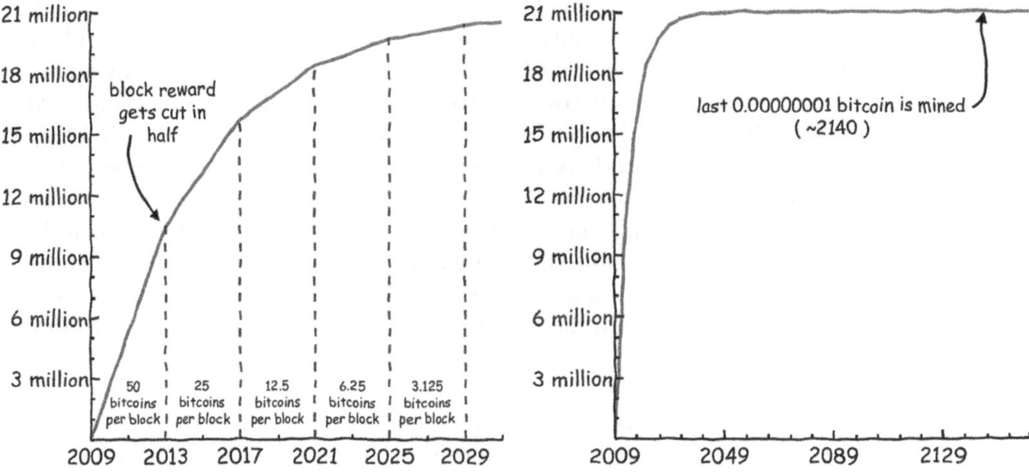

Figure 8-1: Bitcoin awarded over time: The left graph shows the reward schedule for bitcoins until the year 2031. The right graph extends the time range until the year 2169.

The graph on the left shows the total number of bitcoins in circulation until the year 2031. As you can see, the amount in circulation continues to increase, but the pace slows over time because the block reward is cut in half at regular intervals. Consequently, the bitcoins a miner receives every few minutes, as she wins the mining race, will be much less in future years.

Nearly all of the approximately 21 million bitcoins will be distributed by 2031. However, small amounts of the currency will continue to be distributed long past that date. The graph on the right shows the distribution schedule to the year 2169. Bitcoin's success in its first five years suggests that Satoshi was at least in the right ballpark when he estimated how rapidly bitcoins should be distributed.

When all the bitcoins have been mined, Bitcoin mining will no longer serve its distribution purpose; rather, it will just be a mechanism for securely processing transactions.

Will people still mine bitcoins then? What happens to the public ledger? Instead of new bitcoins, the reward for being a Bitcoin miner will only be the transaction fees paid by the users (which may be substantial in years to come).

How Does Bitcoin Mining Work?

Bitcoin involves a network of computers around the world that constantly broadcast and relay new transactions to each other. Each computer on this network is a *node*. Because of Bitcoin's decentralized nature, some nodes can appear or disappear at random times without impacting the network as a whole. No special central nodes exist.

Nodes can be grouped into three categories: those that only broadcast transactions; those that broadcast and relay transactions; and those that broadcast, relay, and create new blocks with transactions. Each type of node requires substantially more computational resources than the previous type. The last of the three includes Bitcoin-mining nodes and requires the heftiest computers.

When a Bitcoin node is launched (i.e., when you launch Bitcoin software on your computer), it connects to other nodes through the Internet to form a somewhat haphazard (but also robust) *mesh network*. A mesh network has no central nodes that manage traffic. Instead, all nodes equally share the responsibility of propagating information across the network.

Figure 8-2 shows what a small piece of the Bitcoin mesh network might look like.

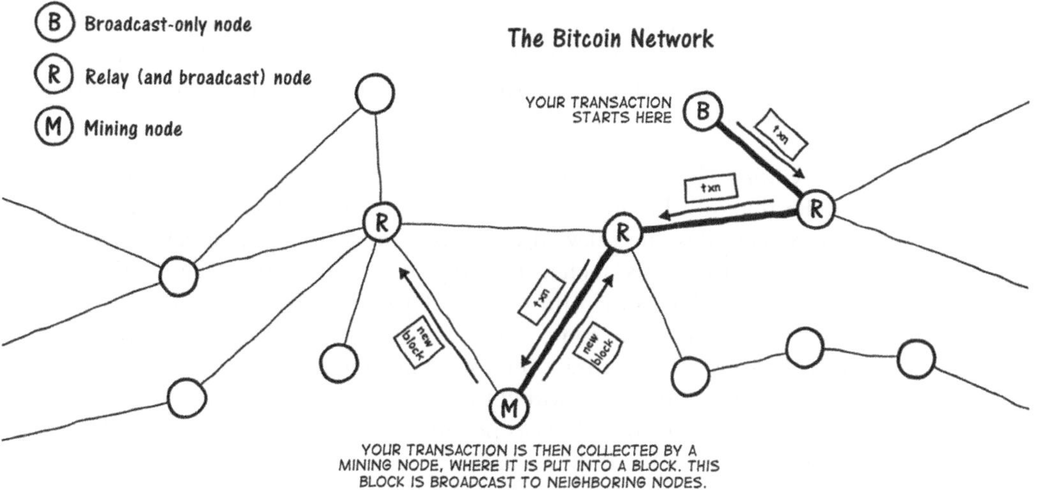

Figure 8-2: A conceptual drawing of the Bitcoin network. The circles represent nodes, all of which are arbitrarily connected to other nodes via network connections, shown as lines. Transactions and newly mined blocks are continuously broadcast over this network.

In this figure, you can see what happens when, for instance, you buy a cup of coffee using bitcoins. Most likely, you would do this from a mobile phone and would be running the most basic type of node, the *broadcast-only node* (shown as the circle labeled *B* at the top of the figure). The transaction steps are as follows:

1. The starting node (your phone) creates a transaction that transfers your coins to the Bitcoin address owned by the coffee shop. This node then immediately sends this transaction to its peers on the mesh network, which are most likely relay nodes.

2. The *relay node* simply propagates this transaction to other relay nodes, allowing the transaction to quickly propagate everywhere and to everyone. Actually, it is not quite that simple, since the relay nodes need to be wary of malicious or spammy transactions: If a relay node just forwarded any message, the Bitcoin network would quickly collapse in a flood of junk transactions. Therefore, all the relay nodes check that the transaction is correctly formatted, make sure it has valid signatures, and look through the most current version of the blockchain to ensure the money being spent is verifiably present in the source account of the transaction.
3. If the transaction passes muster, it arrives within seconds at all the *mining nodes* on the network. These mining nodes add this transaction to a preliminary block, which they will attempt to mine (a process we'll describe in more detail shortly).
4. If the mining is successful, the newly mined block is then broadcast across the network, confirming the block's transactions and giving the miner a mining reward. Although it typically takes a few minutes for a block to be mined, once the block has been found, it will again traverse the entire network within seconds.

Ultimately, every transaction must be recorded on the blockchain. So nodes that only broadcast must link up directly with nodes that mine or indirectly via nodes that relay. Mining nodes may also apply specific arbitrary criteria to transactions, such as favoring those with a larger transaction fee. If the fee is too low, some mining (or relay nodes) may ignore the transaction. However, just because some nodes ignore a transaction doesn't mean others will: As long as the transaction finds a mining node that accepts it, the transaction will eventually be added to the blockchain. Usually, mining nodes collect as many transactions as possible (to collect the most fees). Although each transaction has only a small fee attached to it, many thousands of transactions can be included in a block, and the sum of these fees, which are paid to the miner, can be substantial. But due to memory constraints,[4] the number of transactions that can be included in a block has a maximum limit. For this reason, some miners exclude transactions whose fees are too low (or zero).

Although all mining nodes collect transactions and organize them into blocks, only one of the nodes (the lucky one) adds its block to the blockchain.[5] The fortunate miner then collects the mining reward, which is the sum of the block reward (the newly minted bitcoins in each block) and all the transaction fees for the added block. Nodes that relay transactions and those miners who didn't add a block do not receive any bitcoins from transaction fees or otherwise.

Once the lucky miner is selected, the new block is broadcast to the rest of the network, and all of the other mining nodes stop working on their old

4. The maximum limit has generally been increased over time as concerns about memory constraints have lessened. But there will always be a maximum limit.

5. As mentioned before, two or more miners could possibly add a new block at the same time. This causes a split in the blockchain but is resolved by waiting to see which branch grows by yet another block first.

block and start working on a new one. So how is the lucky node decided on? It is the node that *solves the block* by finding a special input to the SHA256 hash function.

How Miners Solve a Block

Bitcoin mining requires a great deal of computational power, but what do miners calculate? They repeatedly calculate the double SHA256 hash[6] of slight variations of certain information, called the *block header*, in their new block. When a block of transactions is created, the block header contains a summary of information about the block, including the time it was created, a hash of the transactions within the block, and other data, which we'll delve into shortly. Importantly, in the block header is a field for an arbitrary number called a *nonce*,[7] which the miner chooses. In fact, it is *the only part of the block* that is under the full control of the miner. So how does a miner choose a value for this nonce?

A solved block (i.e., a block that will be accepted by others as part of the blockchain and the one the miner is paid for) occurs when the double SHA256 hash of the block header results in a number that is less than some predetermined threshold, known as the *difficulty target*. If the result is greater than the target, the block remains unsolved. When this happens, the miner must try a different nonce, which is contained in the header and hence affects the hash. Because cryptographic hash functions produce completely new outputs when the input is changed by even the tiniest amount, changing the nonce value results in a totally new hash for the entire block header. By repeatedly changing the nonce value, eventually a hash output will be found that is less than the target. Typically, a miner simply increments the nonce by 1 in this search until a successful nonce value is found. When a working nonce is found, the block is solved.[8]

Anatomy of a Block

Let's take a closer look at a block's structure so you can see how the miners' actions fit into the big picture. At the top level, a Bitcoin block essentially has four parts:

```
Anatomy of a Block
❶ blocksize (e.g., 868 KB)
❷ block header (see below)
❸ transaction count (e.g., 1,278)
❹ list of transactions
```

6. A double SHA256 hash is the SHA256 hash of a SHA256 hash. If y = SHA256(x), then SHA256(y) is the double hash. The use of double SHA256 hashes was proposed by Ferguson and Schneier in their book *Practical Cryptography* as a way of preventing a certain kind of cryptographic attack called *length-extension*.

7. Nonce is short for "a number used once."

8. Because a nonce is only a 32-bit number, it is actually possible to exhaust every value without a solution. If every nonce is tried and the block is still not solved, an *extraNonce* field, hidden in the list of transactions, is incremented.

Blocksize is a number at the top of the block that indicates the size of the entire block ❶. This is followed by the block header ❷, which we'll discuss in detail shortly. The rest of a block stores a count of the number of transactions ❸ followed by a list of all the transactions ❹. One of these transactions is the block reward, which the miner adds to assign himself some new bitcoins. These bitcoins are created from nothing. All bitcoins in existence at one point originated as such a block reward.

Including the nonce ❻, the block header consists of six pieces of data:

```
Block header structure
❶ bitcoin version number
❷ double SHA256 hash of the previous block header
❸ double SHA256 hash of all of the transactions in the block
❹ current timestamp
❺ the difficulty target
❻ the nonce
```

At the top is a version number ❶. It exists to facilitate the ability to distinguish blocks in the old and new format if ever a major change in the blockchain structure occurs in the future, as Bitcoin is refined. Next, the block header holds a hash of the previous block's header ❷. It is a very important field because this value links blocks together in a chain: When miners mine a block, not only are they securing the transactions in their own block, but they are also securing the transactions in all previous blocks that make up this version of the chain. By creating this block, a miner is essentially casting a vote stating, "I believe this is the true history of all Bitcoin transactions, and my block builds upon the work of other miners, as indicated by this hash of the previous miner's block."

Next, the header contains a hash of all transactions in the current block ❸. When a node on the Bitcoin network receives a block from other nodes on the network, this hash allows them to verify that the transactions in the block haven't been tampered with; the hash of the transactions must exactly match the value in this field.

Subsequently, a timestamp ❹ indicates when the block was created. For the most part, Bitcoin disregards real-world time. In fact, mining blocks in the blockchain can be thought of as a primitive sequential clock, and the *ticking* of this clock in the form of newly mined blocks is the only concept of time Bitcoin takes into account.

However, setting the block difficulty is one specific instance in which Bitcoin needs to recognize real-world time. Block difficulty ❺ is periodically calculated using the timestamp of previous blocks and is also a field in the block header. Because Bitcoin is designed to solve new blocks roughly every 10 minutes, it needs a way to measure how far apart blocks have been spaced in the recent past, which is the reason the timestamp field exists. If Bitcoin difficulty wasn't periodically adjusted based on real-world time, its block rate would be determined by the currency's popularity. As a result, the Bitcoin network could become unstable if it became too popular or not popular enough. In both of those instances, the block rate would become unreasonable, and the Bitcoin network would no longer function.

So how is the difficulty target value decided? When Bitcoin was created, the target was set to this certain *easy* number:

$$26959535291011309493156476344723991336010898738574164086137773096960 \approx 2.7 \times 10^{67} \text{ or } 2^{224}$$

To put this value in perspective, the SHA256 hash function outputs values between 0 and 2^{256} (~1.16×10^{77}), and this target requires the output to be less than 2^{224} (about one-billionth of the maximum output). This is similar to requiring that a random number generator that generates values between 0 and 1 must output a number less than 0.000000001 to solve a block. This target value is the *easiest* Bitcoin has ever used. Most ordinary personal computers (in 2009) could calculate new hashes at a rate of about 1 million hashes per second, or 1 megahash/s (MH/s). Because the odds of a hash being less than this target value are 1 in a billion, a computer hashing at 1 MH/s would need about 1,000 seconds (~17 minutes) to have a good chance[9] at solving a block.

If a faster computer were to start mining at 2 MH/s, the target would automatically decrease to reduce the odds of finding a block (thereby taking longer). The difficulty stored in the blockchain header is expressed as a ratio between the initial target used by Bitcoin (when it started) and the current target. Initially, the difficulty was equal to 1 (because the initial target *was* the current target), and it has been mostly increasing ever since. If the hash rate decreases (e.g., due to computers withdrawing from the network) so that blocks are found more slowly than ten minutes on average, the difficulty will decrease (which in Bitcoin's first five years has happened very rarely).

As you can see, target numbers are large and unwieldy. Therefore, it is more convenient, when discussing bitcoin mining, to calculate a *difficulty*, which is simply the ratio of the current target number to the target number on Satoshi's very first block, the genesis block:

$$\text{difficulty} = \frac{\text{initial target}}{\text{current target}}$$

The difficulty is not adjusted immediately in response to increases or decreases in the hash rate. Instead, the difficulty is adjusted every time the blockchain grows by 2,016 blocks, which happens approximately every two weeks (2,016 × 10 minutes = 14 days). If it takes less than two weeks to mine 2,016 blocks, the difficulty is increased, but if it takes longer than two weeks, the difficulty is decreased.

During the first five years, the mining difficulty in Bitcoin increased from 1 to over 50 billion. At this difficulty, an ordinary personal computer (tablet, laptop, etc.) would be lucky to solve one block every

9. The odds of finding a one-in-a-billion hash after trying 1 billion times is ~63.2 percent. In precise mathematical terms, the probability is $1 - 1/e$, where e is the irrational mathematical constant, approximately equal to 2.718.

3.5 million years! This difficulty corresponds to a network hash rate that is ~360,000,000,000 MH/s, or 360 petahash/s (PH/s). All of the world's conventional supercomputers combined would hash at a rate less than 1 PH/s.

The incredible rise in computational power used for Bitcoin mining derives from a combination of wider adoption and the use of increasingly specialized hardware. In the first year, most miners used the CPUs on their laptops to mine bitcoins. Then people realized they could repurpose graphics cards designed originally for demanding computer games to mine bitcoins. The graphics cards, specifically the graphics-processing units (GPUs) on them, were thousands of times faster and more energy efficient than CPUs. Not long thereafter, hardware developers discovered they could use field programmable gate arrays (FPGAs), which are specialized devices used for computer chip prototype development, to mine bitcoins even faster than GPUs. Until this point, nobody had manufactured hardware specifically to mine bitcoins. GPUs and FPGAs were off-the-shelf hardware that was just repurposed for Bitcoin mining. However, when the Bitcoin economy became extensive, it became worthwhile for computer chip developers to create *application specific integrated circuits (ASICs)*, like the one in Figure 8-3.

Figure 8-3: An early ASIC Bitcoin-mining machine from the Avalon Corporation. The small chips arranged in a grid are each custom ASIC chips designed to perform Bitcoin hash operations.

These single-purpose computer chips were manufactured specifically to mine bitcoins in the fastest, most energy-efficient way possible. Bitcoin ASICs are optimized to calculate SHA256 hashes. Today, practically all Bitcoin mining is done with ASIC-based hardware. Further increases in speed and efficiency are being achieved continually by designing the chips with smaller and smaller features (from 130 nm to 65 nm to 28 nm features, and so on). Consequently, more calculations can be made per unit of area. Each new breakthrough in hardware performance leads to a network hash rate that increases by many orders of magnitude (see Figure 8-4), especially if the price of bitcoins rises at the same time (further justifying capital investment in mining hardware).

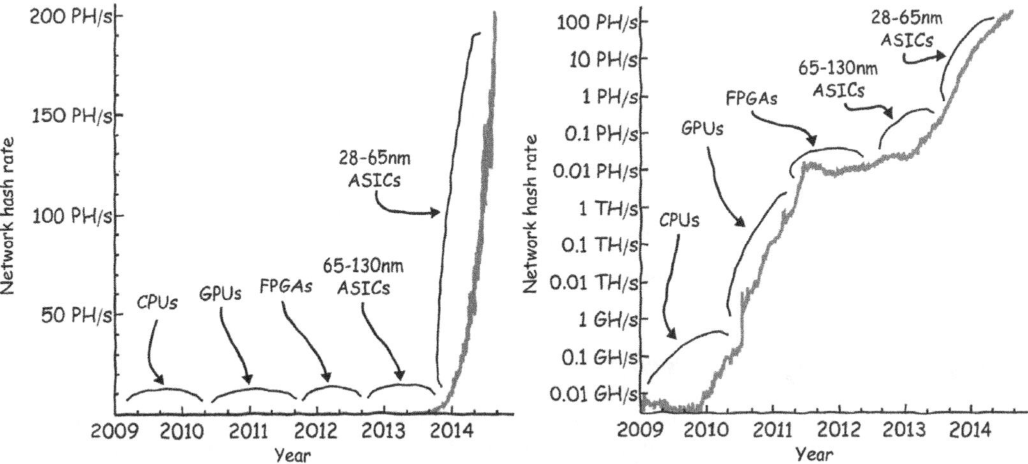

Figure 8-4: The amount of computation performed over time on the Bitcoin network (in terrahashes, or trillions of hashes per second). The left graph uses a traditional linear scale for the y-axis, in which the enormous computing power of ASIC miners in 2013 dwarfs all previous methods of mining. In the right graph, we use a logarithmic scale for showing the hash rate of the network, making it possible to see the progress in computing power on the network more clearly, progressing from CPU, to GPU, to FPGA, and finally ASIC mining.

At a difficulty of 50 billion, a Bitcoin-mining device capable of 10 TH/s could find a block about once every 8 months, which is an average time, and the variance can be significant. For Bitcoin miners who want to receive a more steady income, it is best to join forces with other miners in what is known as pooled mining.

Pooled Mining

Although the network solves blocks about every 10 minutes, individual miners might only solve a block once every few months. With such an unpredictable revenue stream, it can be difficult to plan and operate a Bitcoin-mining operation. To help make the reward more regular and predictable, most miners who don't control enormous computational power (i.e., greater than 1 percent of the network hash rate) join a mining pool.

A *mining pool* is a collection of miners who combine computational resources and then split the block reward. From the network's perspective, a mining pool is a single mining node, but hundreds or perhaps thousands of individual miners are calculating hashes within that node. A mining pool solves blocks more often than an individual miner; therefore, the miners' income is more frequent. When the block reward is divided among the miners, it is usually allocated proportionally based on the number of hashes a miner contributed. Because it is difficult to know exactly how many hashes an individual contributed, the typical measurement of contribution is in the form of calculated *shares*. Although the exact details vary between mining pools, a miner earns a share when she calculates a hash output that is less than a much easier-to-reach target than the real target. As a result, it might take an individual miner years before he would find a hash less than the real target but only a few minutes to find a hash less than the pool's share target. The number of shares accumulated by a miner represents how much of the pool's hashing power that miner contributed.

Using a pool, a casual Bitcoin user can try her hand at mining and collect tiny fractions of bitcoins using a moderately powerful computing device (e.g., a cheap Bitcoin-mining ASIC that can be plugged into a USB slot). Although it may not be profitable, considering the costs of electricity, it can be fun to accumulate a few microbitcoins by contributing computational power to the network.

Bitcoin Mining for Profit

Should you mine bitcoins? In short, probably not. Bitcoin mining requires significant computational power, which requires electricity, expensive hardware, and space. Your return on investment will depend heavily on the number of other miners there are and how much computational power they're providing. Because the number of bitcoins distributed to the network is not affected by the number of miners, the more miners, the more diluted the reward will be.[10] Bitcoin mining can only be profitable for those with the most efficient hardware, in terms of energy and capital efficiency, and cheapest electrical power. Because hardware manufacturers have the lowest capital costs per mining device, many profitable Bitcoin-mining companies manufacture their own hardware. These manufacturers may also hire their own research and development engineers to design newer and more efficient computer chips (i.e., ASICs) for Bitcoin mining. In summary, Bitcoin mining is an extremely competitive business and will likely become more so as Bitcoin adoption increases.

Perhaps if you have your own wind farm or solar panel array and have more electricity than you know what to do with, you *might* be able to mine bitcoins profitably. But it still requires careful consideration of the capital costs and the opportunity cost compared to just buying bitcoins directly. A common mistake in estimating the viability of a Bitcoin-mining venture is to put too much weight on the exchange rate (in whichever other currency you're using). You should always compare the return from Bitcoin mining against the number of bitcoins you could have purchased for the same initial investment. The future exchange rate should make little difference in

10. Strictly speaking, the number of individuals involved in mining is irrelevant, of course; only the amount of computational power applied to mining matters.

your investment decision. If it is not profitable to mine bitcoins today when the rate is $200 per bitcoin, it makes no difference if they will be $1,000 per bitcoin tomorrow; you should just buy bitcoins instead of mining them.

It is also important to reasonably project the future hash rate. Although it is impossible to predict the future, more than likely the network hash rate will continue increasing very quickly during Bitcoin's first 10 years.[11] See the following example calculation, keeping in mind that even if mining is more profitable than buying bitcoins directly, it's still a lot more work!

```
Example calculation: To mine or to buy?
Equipment: One super-duper-hashing-miner made by Miners-R-Us
      Hash rate: 1 TH/s
      Power consumption: 0.4 kW
      Price: 5 BTC (includes shipping)
Local electricity cost: 0.001 BTC/kWh → monthly power costs: 0.30 BTC
Current difficulty: 4 billion
Time to solve a block   = difficulty * 2^32 / (hash rate)
                        = 4 billion * 2^32 / 1 TH/s = 6.5 months per block
                        (0.153 blocks per month)
New bitcoins per block = 25 BTC
Avg. transaction fees per block = 0.5 BTC
Total mining reward per block = 25.5 BTC
Revenue per month = Total mining reward per block * blocks per month
                  = 25.5 BTC * 0.153 = 3.92 BTC

Scenario #1 - Difficulty increases by 100% per month
Month 1: Rev. = 3.92 BTC, Power costs = 0.30 BTC, Monthly profit = 3.62 BTC
Month 2: Rev. = 1.96 BTC, Power costs = 0.30 BTC, Monthly profit = 1.66 BTC
Month 3: Rev. = 0.98 BTC, Power costs = 0.30 BTC, Monthly profit = 0.68 BTC
Month 4: Rev. = 0.49 BTC, Power costs = 0.30 BTC, Monthly profit = 0.19 BTC
Month 5: (Power costs exceed revenue → turn off mining device!)
Total profits: 3.62 + 1.66 + 0.68 + 0.19 - 5 = 1.15 BTC (mining is profitable)

Scenario #2 - Difficulty increases by 200% per month
Month 1: Rev. = 3.92 BTC, Power costs = 0.30 BTC, Monthly profit = 3.62 BTC
Month 2: Rev. = 1.31 BTC, Power costs = 0.30 BTC, Monthly profit = 1.01 BTC
Month 3: Rev. = 0.44 BTC, Power costs = 0.30 BTC, Monthly profit = 0.14 BTC
Month 4: (Power costs exceed revenue → turn off mining device!)
Total profits: 3.62 + 1.01 + 0.14 - 5 = -0.24 BTC (better to just buy bitcoins)
```

If you decide to purchase Bitcoin-mining hardware, be wary. Anyone selling Bitcoin mining hardware has calculated that it would be more profitable to *sell to you* rather than use the hardware to *mine himself*. Carefully do your research on the vendor, the hardware details, and the shipping timelines. Receiving a mining device a few months later than you anticipated can mean the difference between a positive and a negative return on your investment (because the network hash rate will be higher).

---

11. At some rate varying from fast to unbelievably fast to slingshot-around-the-sun-to-go-back-in-time-and-save-the-whales fast.

Theoretical Hash Rate Limits

As computers become more powerful and energy efficient, and especially if Bitcoin adoption continues to increase exponentially, the network hash rate is expected to grow significantly. How high can it go? If more and more computers start mining and the price of a bitcoin remains fixed,[12] eventually the amount of bitcoins each miner earns won't cover the costs of electricity. Ultimately, it can be argued that the limit of the network hash rate depends on the energy efficiency of the mining hardware (see Table 8-1).

Table 8-1: Energy Efficiency of Different Forms of Bitcoin-Mining Hardware (Calculated as a Ratio Between Hash Rate and Power Consumption)*

Mining device	Hash rate (GH/s)	Power (W)	Energy per hash (J/GH)
Laptop with single-core CPU	0.0005	100	200,000
Laptop with efficient quad-core CPU	0.02	50	2,500
Medium-end GPU (400 cores)	0.1	200	2,000
High-end GPU (2000+ cores)	0.5	300	600
High-end FPGA	0.8	40	50
130 nm ASIC device	10.0	80	8
65 nm ASIC device	60	240	4
28 nm ASIC device	1,000	800	0.8

* Values are representative of typical mining devices; specific designs may vary significantly.

To determine whether Bitcoin mining is profitable using a certain type of hardware, we must combine three factors: the energy efficiency of the hardware, the cost of electricity, and the overall hash rate of the network. The graph in Figure 8-5 shows the relationship between these three factors.

The curves on the graph show how advanced the hardware needs to be, given the electricity costs. The lines on the right side represent instances of higher electricity costs. Clearly, if the electricity costs more, you would need a more advanced hardware setup to be profitable at mining. In this case, *more advanced hardware* means hardware that consumes less electricity for every joule of energy it consumes.

12. Well, let's just assume that's the case for now.

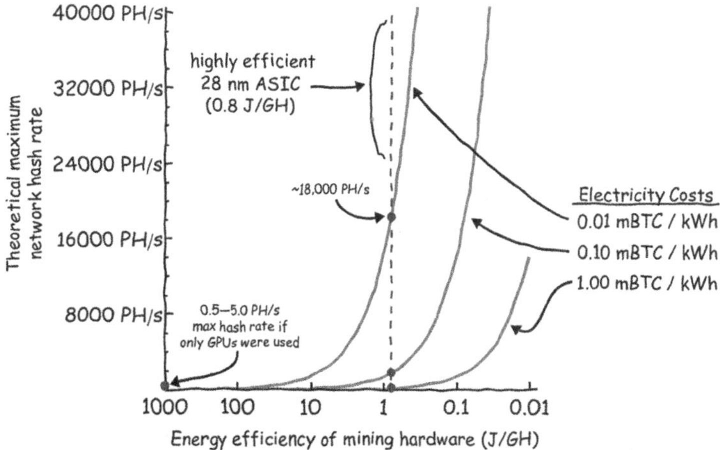

Figure 8-5: Profitability threshold curves for comparing hardware efficiency, electricity cost, and network hash rate on the Bitcoin network. Given your current electricity cost, a curve can be drawn that relates the efficiency needed by your mining hardware (in J/GH) to be profitable, for a certain network hash rate. If you can draw a point below *your electricity cost curve for your mining equipment, then you'll be able to mine profitably on the Bitcoin network.*

If bitcoins increase in value, the relative cost of electricity decreases, and the breakeven point for the network hash rate increases. If a mining device has an efficiency of 0.8 J/GH and electricity costs only 0.01 mBTC per kWh, the network hash rate at which mining would no longer viable would be 18,000 PH/s, corresponding to a difficulty of 2.5 trillion. So is it possible the hash rate could go even higher than it is today?

The ASIC designs in Table 8-1 show that the energy per hash drops as the feature dimensions decrease. If we assume that in the future high-efficiency 14 nm ASICs that use only 0.1 J/GH will exist, then at 0.01 mBTC/kWh the breakeven hash rate would be greater than 100,000 PH/s. Computer chips made with features smaller than 14 nm dimensions don't exist yet, but Moore's law[13] has persistently defied predictions by skeptics that computer chips have reached the smallest feature sizes possible. Clearly, the network hash rate could potentially be enormously higher than it is today.

Decentralization in Bitcoin Mining

Bitcoin's success depends on being a decentralized network. In its infancy, anyone could join the Bitcoin network as a mining node; however, now

13. Moore's law is an observation by Gordon E. Moore, cofounder of Intel, that the number of transistors on computer chips doubles approximately every two years. This has held true for over 40 years, largely because feature sizes on computer chips have continued to get smaller.

mining is done primarily by professionals with resources, expertise, and capital well out of reach of the average Joe. Is this trend *recentralizing* Bitcoin? This is a subject of debate among Bitcoin users, miners, and developers.

Another related subject we haven't discussed in detail yet is the limit to the number of transactions that can be included in each block. Obviously, a real, physical limit exists in the sense that an individual cannot include an infinite number of transactions in any block. However, a smaller limit is imposed as a rule in the Bitcoin protocol (i.e., although the physical limit might be in the range of millions of transactions per block, the rule-based limit is in the thousands of transactions range). The original purpose of this self-imposed limit[14] was to prevent the blockchain from becoming bloated with pointless transactions (i.e., spam), but some have argued that the limit serves a greater purpose, which is to maintain decentralization.

In addition to having a computing device that can perform SHA256 hashes very quickly, mining nodes *and* relay nodes must have sufficient storage space to store a full copy of the blockchain. If the blocks that make up the chain become much larger than they are now, not only will miners need faster computers, but their systems will also need the capability of storing substantial amounts of data (possibly in the form of large data centers). This would further increase the capital requirements of miners and inevitably lead some to abandon the profession. Fewer mining nodes would make the network more centralized by degrees. For this reason, some miners have advocated for limiting the number of transactions per block to a small number (although this would ultimately drive up transaction fees). Is such a desire justified?

Although it's a complicated issue, we can use the gold mining analogy to explain. Is gold a centrally controlled commodity? Very few people, by percentage, have the resources, time, and expertise to mine gold. However, no monopoly exists on gold mining; any well-financed venture can search for gold and attempt to mine it. Similarly, even though Bitcoin mining might no longer be viable for casual users and instead become a venture performed by companies and organizations, a single institution would never obtain sole control of Bitcoin mining. Nonetheless, it is best to keep a close eye on the future number of Bitcoin miners.

14. In this case, the limit was imposed by trusted developers of the core Bitcoin software. The protocols encoded in this core software are typically supported by a majority of miners and therefore usually determine the properties of the longest blockchain on the network.

THE STRANGE WORLD OF ALTCOINS
BBQ
LEFT TO RIGHT: APHRODITECOIN, LITECOIN, FEATHERCOIN, DOGECOIN, ETHEREUM, BBQCOIN, AND FLAPPYCOIN.
ONE OF THE FIRST QUESTIONS NEW BITCOINERS WILL ASK IS "WHAT'S TO STOP ANYONE FROM TAKING THE BITCOIN SOURCE CODE AND CREATING THEIR OWN COPYCAT CURRENCY?" AND THE ANSWER IS...
NOTHING!
ONE OF THE EARLIEST COPIES OF BITCOIN WAS LITECOIN
I USE A GPU-FRIENDLY MINING ALGORITHM!
LITECOIN BEGAT FEATHERCOIN...
SCIENCE PROVES I'M LIGHTER!
WEIGHT
BTC LTC FTC

A RECENT POPULAR UPSTART IS DOGECOIN...
SO MEME!
A RECENT FAD IS TO DESIGN ALTCOINS FOR SPECIFIC GEOGRAPHIC REGIONS, SUCH AS APHRODITECOIN.
GREETINGS FROM CYPRUS!
ALL THESE ALTCOINS RAISE A PERPLEXING ECONOMIC QUESTION: IN ESSENCE, THE KEY INVENTION BEHIND BITCOIN IS THE INVENTION OF DIGITAL SCARCITY...
THERE WILL NEVER BE MORE THAN 21 MILLION BITCOINS!
BUT IF ANY DICK, JANE, OR MOLLY CAN CREATE THEIR OWN ALT-CURRENCY, DOES ANY MEANINGFUL SCARCITY REALLY EXIST?
THERE WILL NEVER BE MORE THAN ONE BILLION ...UHM, RICHARDCOINS!
THERE WILL NEVER BE MORE THAN 1 TRILLION JANECOINS!
ANYONE WHO WAVES A MINING RIG EVEN BRIEFLY IN THE GENERAL DIRECTION OF A MOLLYCOIN WALLET IMMEDIATELY GETS ONE QUADRILLION ZILLION MOLLYCOINS!

TO UNDERSTAND HOW SOMETHING AS EASY TO REPLICATE AS BITCOIN CAN STILL REMAIN SCARCE, LET'S LOOK AT SOMETHING ELSE THAT'S EASY TO MANUFACTURE BUT STILL VERY EXPENSIVE: TOOTHPASTE!

EVER WONDER WHY YOU NEVER GET FREE TOOTHPASTE AT HOTELS?

THE REASON IS BECAUSE HOTELS HAVE LEARNED THAT ANYONE WILL USE "MAHOGANY GARDEN" SHAMPOO IN THEIR HAIR, BUT NO ONE WILL PUT THE POTENTIALLY POISONOUS CHEMICALS MAKING UP A SIMILAR BRAND OF TOOTHPASTE INTO THEIR MOUTH...

?

MAHOGANY GARDEN TOOTHPASTE

INSTEAD, A TYPICAL AMERICAN FEELS SAFE PUTTING ONLY ONE OF THE FOLLOWING FIVE HEAVILY MARKETED BRANDS IN THEIR MOUTH:

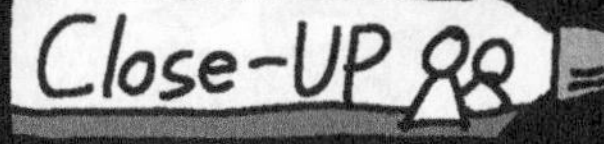

SINCE AN AVERAGE PERSON CAN'T KEEP TRACK OF 50 BRANDS OF TOOTHPASTE, THESE 5 BRANDS CAN COMPLETELY DICTATE THE SUPPLY. THIS IS WHY DRUGSTORES HAVE 99¢ SHAMPOO BOTTLES, BUT TOOTHPASTE NEVER IS BELOW $5.00

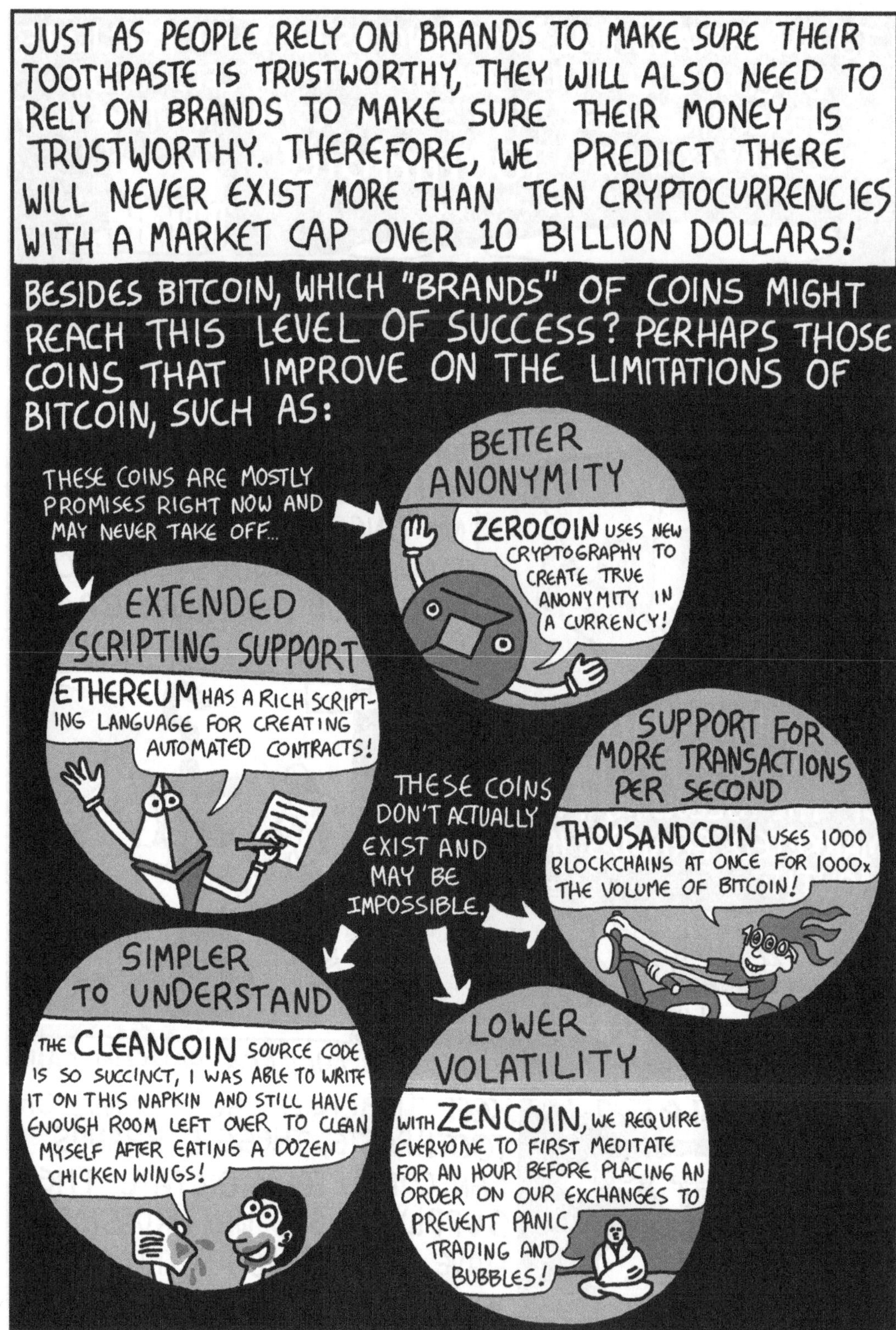
JUST AS PEOPLE RELY ON BRANDS TO MAKE SURE THEIR TOOTHPASTE IS TRUSTWORTHY, THEY WILL ALSO NEED TO RELY ON BRANDS TO MAKE SURE THEIR MONEY IS TRUSTWORTHY. THEREFORE, WE PREDICT THERE WILL NEVER EXIST MORE THAN TEN CRYPTOCURRENCIES WITH A MARKET CAP OVER 10 BILLION DOLLARS!
BESIDES BITCOIN, WHICH "BRANDS" OF COINS MIGHT REACH THIS LEVEL OF SUCCESS? PERHAPS THOSE COINS THAT IMPROVE ON THE LIMITATIONS OF BITCOIN, SUCH AS:
THESE COINS ARE MOSTLY PROMISES RIGHT NOW AND MAY NEVER TAKE OFF...
BETTER ANONYMITY
ZEROCOIN USES NEW CRYPTOGRAPHY TO CREATE TRUE ANONYMITY IN A CURRENCY!
EXTENDED SCRIPTING SUPPORT
ETHEREUM HAS A RICH SCRIPTING LANGUAGE FOR CREATING AUTOMATED CONTRACTS!
THESE COINS DON'T ACTUALLY EXIST AND MAY BE IMPOSSIBLE.
SUPPORT FOR MORE TRANSACTIONS PER SECOND
THOUSANDCOIN USES 1000 BLOCKCHAINS AT ONCE FOR 1000x THE VOLUME OF BITCOIN!
1000
SIMPLER TO UNDERSTAND
THE CLEANCOIN SOURCE CODE IS SO SUCCINCT, I WAS ABLE TO WRITE IT ON THIS NAPKIN AND STILL HAVE ENOUGH ROOM LEFT OVER TO CLEAN MYSELF AFTER EATING A DOZEN CHICKEN WINGS!
LOWER VOLATILITY
WITH ZENCOIN, WE REQUIRE EVERYONE TO FIRST MEDITATE FOR AN HOUR BEFORE PLACING AN ORDER ON OUR EXCHANGES TO PREVENT PANIC TRADING AND BUBBLES!

9

UNDERSTANDING THE DIFFERENT TYPES OF BITCOIN WALLETS

In Chapter 2 we recommended using the Bitcoin wallet program Electrum, which is free and open source, runs on most devices, and is ideal for beginners. However, *hundreds* of other Bitcoin wallet programs are available, ranging from simple to sophisticated, and new ones are being released constantly as developers compete to add new features and slicker interfaces. But beneath the slicker interfaces and occasionally gimmicky features, some fundamental differences between Bitcoin wallet programs exist. The goal of this chapter is to help you understand those differences so you can make an informed choice about the most useful Bitcoin wallet for your needs.

In this chapter, we'll occasionally use the terms *Bitcoin wallet* or just *wallet* to mean *Bitcoin wallet program*, despite the fact that a *Bitcoin wallet* normally refers to just a list of addresses and private keys.

Wallet Software Design Fundamentals

At a minimum, a Bitcoin wallet program needs to let a user send and receive bitcoins, as well as keep track of how many bitcoins are available to spend. In other words, a Bitcoin wallet program must be able to (1) create and broadcast transactions to the Bitcoin network, (2) generate new Bitcoin addresses, and (3) scan the blockchain to detect whether you've received any bitcoins at those addresses. The major differences between different wallet designs primarily involve these three functions and how they are implemented. The design choices that support these differences are as follows:

1. Offline vs. online transaction signing
2. Random vs. deterministic key generation (versus single key generation)
3. Full vs. simplified payment verification

These design choices have significant consequences for the computational resources required, the security of the stored bitcoins, and even the nature and effectiveness of backups. There are no right choices. Some users are better off using a wallet that requires only a single device and the least amount of computational power, whereas a large enterprise might prefer software that emphasizes security. In the following sections, we explain each design choice in detail so you can make an informed choice.

Offline vs. Online Transaction Signing

Bitcoin wallet programs need private keys in order to sign transactions before they can be broadcast to the Bitcoin network. In the simplest design, these private keys are found in the user's Bitcoin wallet, which is stored locally on the user's device in a *wallet.dat* file. This is the way the first Bitcoin wallet program, Bitcoin-Qt, worked. However, this design is vulnerable to attackers, who could attempt to remotely access the device over the Internet, copy the wallet file, and try to extract the private keys. A more secure design involves splitting the Bitcoin wallet and the software that manages it into two components: one with the private keys and the other without. The component *with* the private keys is usually stored in a highly secure location and is used for transaction signing. The component *without* the private keys can be stored anywhere, possibly in many locations at once, and is called a *watch-only wallet.*

As the name implies, you cannot directly spend money stored in a watch-only wallet. Instead, if you want to make a purchase, you would need to take an extra step to sign your transactions with the private keys. This second step is usually done via a second computer that isn't connected to the Internet (to prevent hacking attacks) and is used solely to store private keys and sign transactions with them as needed. This security technique, called *offline transaction signing*, was discussed to some extent in Chapter 3 as a strategy for securely storing large amounts of bitcoins, but it offers other benefits as well.

Watch-only wallets are particularly useful for point-of-sale terminals (i.e., cash registers) where the cashier needs to receive bitcoins from a customer but never needs to (and may not be authorized to) spend them. Importantly, because watch-only wallets do not store any private keys, if a point-of-sale terminal was stolen, the bitcoins it contained would remain secure. In addition, watch-only wallets can be safely installed on mobile phones or run from low-security web servers (requiring only a simple username and login for access) to allow users to monitor their funds without the risk of the wrong person gaining access to them.

Many Bitcoin wallet programs can be run in one of two modes: a *full mode* (where a single wallet program and computer are used for all steps) or a watch-only mode. If a wallet program advertises a *watch-only mode,* it typically implies that the same software can also be used for offline transaction signing. *Hybrid wallets* are also available in which some of the Bitcoin addresses are watch-only, whereas other addresses have their private keys stored on the online device. As a result, the same device can be used for spending from a low-security checking account and for monitoring a more secure savings account.

Depending on how new Bitcoin addresses are generated, watch-only wallets may or may not have to be synchronized with their offline component. Typically, a new Bitcoin address must be generated on the offline computer and then imported into the watch-only wallet (without importing the corresponding private key). However, with deterministic key generation (described in the next section), watch-only wallets can generate new Bitcoin addresses on their own without knowing the private keys that correspond to them.

NOTE *Deterministic key generation is very useful for point-of-sale terminals, because they won't run out of deposit addresses in situations that involve numerous customers.*

Random Key Generation vs. Deterministic Key Generation (vs. Single Key Generation)

All Bitcoin wallet programs provide new users with at least one randomly generated Bitcoin address and private key. How and whether additional addresses are generated is a design choice that can incite very strong opinions among Bitcoin developers. The original Bitcoin wallet program assumed that users would never reuse an address after spending bitcoins from it. Every time a user wanted to spend bitcoins, a certain amount would go to the intended recipient, but the rest would be moved to a new, randomly generated Bitcoin address called the *change address.* This approach helps protect the privacy of the user, because it is more difficult for an external observer to track an individual's bitcoins if the person continually changes addresses. It's not possible to distinguish the transfer of bitcoins to a change address from the transfer of bitcoins from one person to another. Not everyone likes this behavior, though; some think it's easier to have just one Bitcoin address (like having one email address) and aren't as concerned about privacy. So some Bitcoin wallet programs provide only a single address that is continuously reused. These *single key generation* wallet programs allow you to generate additional addresses manually, but the default behavior is to reuse existing addresses.

Among the Bitcoin wallet programs that constantly generate new addresses, differences in implementation exist. Recall that a private key is a 256-bit integer that is usually generated by some random process. From the private key, Bitcoin wallet programs can calculate the associated public key (which is a point on an elliptic curve; see Chapter 7 for the cryptographic details), which in turn can be converted into a Bitcoin address by applying the RIPEMD160 and SHA256 hash functions. To generate a collection of private key/Bitcoin address pairs, many programs use correspondingly as many random numbers. This is known as *random key generation*. Every time a user needs a new Bitcoin address, a new random number is used as the private key. The drawback to this approach is that backups need to be updated regularly—essentially, every time a new address is created. This is particularly important to keep in mind in the context of change addresses. If you send some of your bitcoins to a friend and the remainder of your balance is sent to a newly generated change address, potentially the majority of your funds are no longer backed up! Some unfortunate incidents have occurred in Bitcoin's history in which users of random key generation–based wallets deleted or lost their wallets shortly after their funds were sent to a new change address but before they updated their backup.

An alternative approach is *deterministic key generation*. With this approach, only the first private key is a randomly chosen 256-bit integer, which is known as the *master private key*, and it has a corresponding *master public key*. Whenever the user needs a new Bitcoin address, a new private key is chosen that is related to the master private key by a simple mathematical relationship (no randomness is involved). In the simplest implementation, the master private key is simply incremented by 1 to generate a new key (e.g., if the master private key is the number 47, subsequent private keys would be 48, 49, 50, etc.). The advantage of this approach is that a single backup, created when a user first creates a new Bitcoin wallet, is sufficient and never needs to be updated.[1] In fact, this is how Electrum works. Recall that in Chapter 2, Electrum prompted you to write down a 12-word mnemonic for backup purposes. That mnemonic was, in fact, a master private key.[2] All of the Bitcoin addresses in your Electrum wallet can be derived from this master private key.

---

1. An important exception is if the user imports a randomly generated private key (perhaps from a paper wallet) into his deterministically generated Bitcoin wallet. In this case, a new backup needs to be created because the imported key cannot be derived from the master private key.

2. The 12-word mnemonic is just one of an infinite variety of ways to encode a 256-bit integer. You can encode an integer in binary, hex, ASCII letters, lines of poetry, or ice cream toppings.

Combining Deterministic Key Generation with Watch-Only Wallets

Imagine the following scenario:

- Lisa owns a restaurant that accepts Bitcoin.
- All the waiters in the restaurant have Bitcoin wallets on their phones to accept payments.
- Lisa wants to be the only person who can spend the money sent to these wallets.

Clearly, it would be very convenient if Lisa could set up this system, but it seems like it would be a technical challenge: Every waiter would need the ability to create tons of new Bitcoin addresses on demand in their wallets, yet Lisa still needs to be the only person with access to the private keys that power each wallet.

However, when you combine deterministic key generation with a watch-only wallet, this type of system is actually straightforward: Surprisingly, it is possible for a watch-only wallet (running on every waiter's phone) to create many new public keys arbitrarily without having any knowledge about the private keys associated with them!

This is all Lisa has to do:

1. Create public and private keys on her computer using deterministic key generation.
2. Give a public key to each waiter along with a program that supports a watch-only feature as well as deterministic keys.
3. Waiters can then accept as many payments with their wallets as they like.
4. Only Lisa can spend the money in these wallets using her computer's wallet. Her computer is the only computer able to generate the corresponding private keys for all Bitcoin transactions in the restaurant.

Whether you run a restaurant, a bank, or any other business, having a payment mechanism whereby your employees can arbitrarily accept payments from customers but only you, the owner of the business, can *unlock* the money is a powerful feature.

The Math Behind Deterministic Key Generation with Watch-Only Wallets

So how is it mathematically possible to generate new keys using only public key information? To explain, we'll refer to the cryptography on how private keys and public keys are mathematically related. In Chapter 7, we explained that given a secret private key, d (let's call this a master private key), the corresponding (master) public key, Q, is determined by the point multiplication operation:

$$dG = Q$$

Recall that both G and Q are points on the elliptic curve, but that G is publicly known to everyone and is a hard-coded constant in the Bitcoin protocol (whereas Q is unique to you). The master Bitcoin address is then derived from Q using several hash functions and other formatting.

The *obvious* way to deterministically generate a *new* Bitcoin address is to first choose a new private key, $d_{new} = d + 1$, and then calculate the corresponding new public key, Q_{new}:

$$d_{new}G = Q_{new}$$

However, this method of generating a new public key requires you to know the master private key. So what if you don't know the master private key? Could you generate a new Bitcoin address with only the knowledge of a master *public* key? Yes!

We can rewrite the equation for Q_{new} as follows:

$$d_{new}G = (d + 1)G = dG + G = Q_{new}$$

Observe that the term dG can be rewritten as the master public key, Q:

$$Q + G = Q_{new}$$

As a result, we can calculate new public keys using only the knowledge of the master public key and the public constant G. Additional public keys can be generated by adding any number of G points:

$$Q + 2G = Q_{two}$$
$$Q + 3G = Q_{three}$$
$$\ldots$$

Of course, a danger of the deterministic key generation approach is that if your master private key falls into the wrong hands, all of the derived Bitcoin addresses would be compromised. Also, from a privacy standpoint, if someone sees your master public key (which becomes public information once you send bitcoins to the corresponding address), that person can derive your subsequent public keys in an attempt to track your spending.

Although we won't delve into the mathematical details, deterministic key generation allows for another, even more advanced Bitcoin wallet feature, *hierarchical deterministic wallets*, that may appeal particularly to large organizations. The master private key can be branched into sub-master keys, which can be further branched into sub-submaster keys and so on. Each has a property that allows any key at one level to access the bitcoins held at every level below it. For example, a bank manager may hold a level-two private key (the level-one key is held by the CEO), and his staff may each hold level-three keys. Everyone shares the same hierarchical wallet, but the manager has access to his own funds and those of his staff, and the staff can access only their own accounts. Hierarchical deterministic wallets might also be useful for families in which the parents want to give their children bitcoins but maintain access as well.

Full vs. Simplified Payment Verification

Bitcoin's central feature is that you don't have to trust an individual, third-party, or central institution. However, Bitcoin wallet programs must be able to verify that the transactions they receive are valid. In this context, it is important to distinguish between the blockchain (the immutable public document that correctly lists every valid Bitcoin transaction) and someone's copy of the blockchain, which is what you have access to. The former is an abstract concept, whereas the latter is the practical reality. When you connect your wallet program to the Bitcoin network, it connects to several nodes that will send your program transaction data, but you cannot assume that data is valid. If you ask a stranger on the Internet to pay you 2 BTC for an expensive watch you are selling, and a node you are connected to indicates you have received 2 BTC shortly thereafter, is it safe to mail the watch? A valid transaction needs to (1) have the correct digital signature and (2) use bitcoins that originated in a mining block reward and have not yet been spent. All Bitcoin wallet programs can verify the first need with complete certainty, but the second concern is addressed with varying degrees of certainty depending on the design of the program.

Bitcoin wallet programs can verify transactions either by keeping their own complete copy of the blockchain, which is referred to as *full payment verification*, or by using an abridged version, which is called *simplified payment verification (SPV)*.

Full payment verification wallets, also called *thick* or *heavyweight* wallets, require a complete copy of the blockchain. They can verify that bitcoins used in a transaction originated from a mined block by scanning backward, transaction by transaction, in the blockchain until their origin is found (and the wallets can check whether those bitcoins were ever double spent). These wallet programs are often active participants in the Bitcoin network in that they not only handle the user's transactions but they also verify and relay other people's transactions (in these cases, computers running such programs are called *full nodes*). All Bitcoin miners are also full nodes (i.e., they need a complete copy of the blockchain to mine).

One problem with full payment verification wallets is that they are very resource-intensive and take a long time to initialize. The blockchain, in its 5th year, was greater than 15GB in size and comprised 35 million transactions (by its 10th birthday, it may likely be 100 times larger). A fresh installation of a full payment verification Bitcoin wallet program can take several days (depending on bandwidth) to download the entire blockchain. Obtaining the blockchain requires connecting to other full nodes and checking to determine whose blockchain has the greatest proof-of-work total (by definition, this is assumed to be the consensus blockchain). For laptops and other home devices, running a full payment verification wallet may be merely inconvenient, but for some mobile phones, it is simply impossible. Fortunately, there is a way to make only a slight compromise in trust but in return achieve more computationally efficient transaction verification.

SPV wallets, also called *thin* or *lightweight* wallets, cannot check whether transactions are valid; rather, they can check whether full nodes, specifically miners, have validated them. The goal of a thin wallet is to check that a transaction has been verified by miners and included in some block in the blockchain. It's similar to having an accountant balance your checkbook instead doing it yourself. This method works reliably as long as miners, who are adding blocks to the blockchain, act honestly and allow only valid transactions to be included (which is a safe assumption as long as no individual miner is in control of more than 51 percent of the hashing power of the network). But without a copy of the blockchain, how does a thin wallet know whether or not a received transaction was included in a block? The transaction can *claim* it was included in block #24371 on the blockchain, for example, but how would you know whether the claim was true or false? One strategy would be for your wallet program to connect to several full nodes and ask to download block #24371 along with all of its other transactions. Then your wallet can comb through the transactions in that block and identify whether the transaction under investigation is present. However, if your SPV wallet program has to check several hundred transactions a day and each time you need to download an entire block (with all of its transactions), from an efficiency standpoint, this strategy is hardly better than just downloading the entire blockchain.

The ingenuity of SPV rests on its ability to verify, through the magic of hash functions, that a transaction was included in a block without looking at any of the block's transactions. To do so, SPV wallets need to download the headers of every block in the blockchain. Recall from Chapter 8 that each block in the blockchain contains two parts, a long list of transactions and a short summary of the block's contents (the header). Importantly, the header contains a hash of all the transactions within that block, structured in such a way that any Bitcoin wallet program can easily check whether a transaction belongs to a particular block by considering its hash value. This hash structure is called a *Merkle tree.*[3] Using this Merkle tree design, thin wallets can safely confirm that transactions they receive have been included in the blockchain without downloading the full blockchain. Downloading just the block headers requires only a fraction of the memory that's needed for the entire blockchain; therefore, SPV wallets can easily run on your smartphone and other inexpensive mobile devices.

A Bitcoin wallet app that uses SPV can also offer many but not all of the same security guarantees as a full wallet.

Being able to run a resource-hungry Bitcoin wallet on a smartphone is an impressive feat of engineering. SPV wallets use advanced computer science technology but make a few compromises in flexibility. Table 9-1 summarizes how we'd rate SPV wallets and compare them to full wallets using a variety of factors.

---

3. More details on Merkle trees can be found in Satoshi's original white paper.

Table 9-1: Rating SPV Wallets vs. Full Wallets

Factor	Simplified payment verification wallets	Full payment verification wallets
Speediness of initial installation and network synchronization	★★★☆☆	★☆☆☆☆
Speed of new payments (zero confirmation transaction)	★★★★★	★★★★★
Security for new payments	★★☆☆☆	★★★☆☆
Security for confirmed payments	★★★★☆	★★★★★
Overall security	★★★★☆	★★★★★
Efficiency of storage use	★★★☆☆	★☆☆☆☆
Ability to inspect arbitrary Bitcoin addresses	☆☆☆☆☆	★★★★★
Ability to import private keys	★★☆☆☆	★★★★★
Effect on overall health of Bitcoin network	★★★☆☆	★★★★★

Let's examine each feature in this table in more depth:

Speediness of initial installation and network synchronization

After initial installation, SPV wallets and full wallets need to download blockchain data from other nodes on the Bitcoin network. However, an SPV wallet only has to download block headers and some data specific to Bitcoin addresses it's responsible for maintaining. Hence, an SPV wallet can synchronize and be ready for use in less than an hour, whereas full wallets might take many hours to initialize.

Speed of new payments

For SPV wallets and full wallets, new (but still unconfirmed) transactions made on the network are quickly broadcast to all peers. If someone sends money to an address managed by your wallet, you'll be notified within a few seconds, no matter your wallet type.

Security for new payments

A full wallet that can access a complete blockchain can quickly validate new transactions, ensuring that it is sending money from a valid and adequately funded source address. An SPV wallet cannot do this and instead relies on its network peers to ensure its transactions are legit. In theory, if someone sends you a payment and is in cahoots with one of the (supposedly) random peers your SPV wallet interacts with, this sender could send you fraudulent payments. A full wallet is immune from this type of attack.

Security of confirmed payments

Even if a transaction is 100 percent valid, just because a transaction is broadcast doesn't mean it will make it into the blockchain, especially if the spender creates an additional transaction that attempts to double-spend the money to another address. For this reason, it's best to wait for three to six block confirmations on larger purchases. SPV and full wallets can validate transactions by tracking these confirmations. While a full wallet can directly prove that a transaction that has been mined into a new block is truly valid (i.e., sent from a fully funded address), an SPV wallet cannot. Therefore, if a miner includes a bad transaction in a new block, an SPV wallet could still be fooled. But it is very unlikely a miner would ever do this: Mining blocks is extremely costly, and by design a block with bad transactions would be immediately abandoned by any other full nodes on the network that take the time to perform validation on the block. As a result, a miner would never receive a reward for mining a block containing bad transactions. Hence, a confirmed payment sent to an SPV wallet is quite secure, although the security of a full wallet is still the gold standard.

Overall security

All in all, a properly programmed SPV Bitcoin wallet can offer security for your bitcoins and bitcoin payments that is quite good, though it can never match the security guarantees of a full wallet. If you're running an SPV wallet on your smartphone and receive a payment, you can rest assured that once this payment has been confirmed by a few blocks, the balance and other information reported in the SPV wallet can be trusted to be accurate.

Efficiency of storage use

As discussed earlier, storing the blockchain of a full wallet consumes many gigabytes of disk space. However, an SPV wallet requires less than a gigabyte of storage and can run efficiently on a modern smartphone.

Ability to inspect arbitrary Bitcoin addresses

Because a full blockchain contains the balances of all Bitcoin addresses in existence, a full wallet lets you easily check balances and other details of any address, even those you don't own (if the full wallet programmers choose to include this ability in their app). An SPV wallet is completely ignorant of all Bitcoin addresses other than those it is directly responsible for and is unable to provide such information.

Ability to import private keys

If you want to import an existing Bitcoin address (and associated private key) into a full wallet, the full wallet is able to incorporate the address and the funds linked to it within seconds. An SPV wallet has no easy way to import such a key, because it has no information about any historical transactions involving this address. Therefore, if you import a private key into an SPV wallet (given there is an option to do this), you can expect to wait several minutes as the wallet queries its peers for historical data involving the new address.

Effect on overall health of Bitcoin network

For the Bitcoin network to remain healthy, all the participating nodes need to cooperate in validating new transactions and blocks. As discussed previously, SPV wallets are limited in terms of validation capability. Also, SPV wallets usually don't accept incoming TCP connections and may not participate in broadcasting third-party transactions/blocks to peers. For this reason, having a large percentage of SPV nodes on the Bitcoin network could potentially have repercussions on the overall health of the network. At this time, there is little evidence of any negative effects. But as the blockchain grows year after year, the percentage of nodes that can't perform full validation may increase, and problems may arise. Nonetheless, improving storage capacity and faster network speeds will likely continue to allow people to cope with the growing blockchain, and definite benefits will be gained by running a full node. Hopefully, this will give many people incentives to run full nodes in the years to come to sustain the health of the network indefinitely.

In short, SPV wallets have some limitations, but as long as you understand these limitations, these wallets are suitable for storing your money. However, if you are storing large amounts of Bitcoin, it may be wiser to use a full wallet, given the additional security guarantees. But for storing some spending cash on your smartphone, SPV wallets are an ideal solution.

Other Common (and Not So Common) Bitcoin Wallet Features

In addition to features dictated by the underlying design of different wallet architectures, some Bitcoin wallets have a variety of other basic and advanced features. Some basic features you should expect to see include password protection, the ability to make backups of your private keys, QR code scanning and generation, and the ability to generate and import paper wallets.[4] A somewhat advanced feature that is common to many Bitcoin wallets is the ability to sign messages with your private key. Recall that Chapter 7 discussed how digital signatures are used to sign Bitcoin transactions with your private key. The same digital signatures can be used to sign arbitrary messages, and many Bitcoin wallets make this an easy-to-use feature because it is useful when you need to prove you are the owner of a particular Bitcoin address (for example, if you are trying to get preapproved for a loan from a bank and it wants you to prove you have bitcoins as collateral).[5]

---

4. Generating and importing paper wallets is the same as generating and importing private keys, and some Bitcoin wallets use one phrase or the other.

5. You think that sounds unlikely? Just wait!

Other advanced features you might see in some Bitcoin wallet programs include multi-signature transactions, in which multiple private keys are required to spend bitcoins from one Bitcoin address, and a feature called *coin control*, which provides fine-grained control over which bitcoins you use for making any specific purchase (see "An Advanced Bitcoin Wallet Feature: Coin Control" below). The number of advanced features available is too extensive to list here (and the number of features keeps increasing), but now you understand why so many Bitcoin wallet programs exist!

AN ADVANCED BITCOIN WALLET FEATURE: COIN CONTROL

Imagine you have three nickels in your pocket, and you walk into the Very-Cheap-Candy-Store to buy a chocolate that costs a nickel. Your nickels are *fungible*, meaning that each of your three nickels is equally valuable and useful as payment for the chocolate. Well, at least you think they are. But perhaps you didn't notice that each nickel has a different image engraved on the reverse side, and one of them is a 1913 Liberty Head V nickel (of which only five exist in the world and are valued at about $4 million each). When you pay for your chocolate, you use the nickel with the rare image, and the store owner recognizes it! To your alarm, he calls the police because the nickel you gave him once belonged to his friend (Warren Buffet? Richard Branson?) and it was stolen. After several hours of interrogation, you convince the police that you had no idea you were carrying a stolen nickel and explain that you've learned a valuable lesson about choosing your coins carefully before paying with them. This short tale is the basis for the coin control feature offered by some Bitcoin wallets.

If you have received bitcoins from multiple sources to the same Bitcoin address, then the bitcoins from each transaction can be distinguished from each other (each group of bitcoins is called an *unspent output*). With a Bitcoin wallet that supports coin control, when you send a payment from your wallet, you can choose to spend only the bitcoins you received from your employer, rather than the ones your friend gave you, even if the bitcoins are all sitting at the same address.

In most cases, it doesn't matter which coins you use to pay for something. However, in some situations you are legally obligated to choose a specific funding source for an expense. For instance, in most places in the United States, a landlord is required to place a tenant's security deposit in a separate bank account to ensure the money is not mishandled and can be spent only in appropriate ways. Someone may have similar obligations when managing Bitcoin funds for other people.

Additionally, because all Bitcoin blockchain information is public, if you receive and send payments from the same pool of Bitcoin addresses that comprise a wallet, your income source and purchases can theoretically be associated surreptitiously. Through the use of coin control, you can choose payment addresses that prevent this association, giving you more privacy.

Future Wallets

Future Bitcoin wallet programs may offer such features as automatic bill payments, cash flow statements, tax reporting, and tighter integration with traditional financial accounting software. Also, continued technical innovation could enable wallets to execute more complicated transactions, such as escrow transactions, or sending bitcoins to accounts that can't be spent until some external criterion is met (such as the year being greater than 2020). No doubt we will see many of these exciting features in Bitcoin wallets in the next few years.

Which Wallet Is Right for You?

Considering the preceding discussions, which Bitcoin wallet should you use? Well, keep in mind that you can use more than one. In fact, if two different Bitcoin wallets use *the same private key*, they can both spend the *same bitcoins*. You can have a lightweight, no-blockchain wallet on your mobile phone and a more sophisticated Bitcoin wallet on your home server, both managing one pool of bitcoins.

However, in practice many users keep distinct pools of Bitcoin in separate Bitcoin wallets (i.e., each wallet has its own set of private keys), because it's easy to move bitcoins between them.

A common setup that works well for personal use is to store a small number of bitcoins in a lightweight Bitcoin wallet on your phone or laptop, which travels with you, and store your savings in a separate Bitcoin wallet that is more secure (with such features as cold storage and offline transaction signing). In short, keep a few bitcoins in your hot wallet and save the rest in your cold wallet, which is similar to carrying a wallet with spending cash in your pocket and keeping your life savings in a bank account (except Bitcoin lets *you* be *your own* secure bank).

Additional Wallet Considerations

So far we've discussed Bitcoin wallets in terms of their functionality, features, and underlying design, but other considerations should be taken into account as well: Is the Bitcoin wallet open source? Has it received a security audit? Does it have a large user base? Because Bitcoin wallets manage money, it's imperative that you be more careful when choosing a wallet than when choosing other apps, such as games or office software. Be sure to research the Bitcoin wallet program you plan to use before storing significant amounts of money in it. Check with friends or colleagues to see whether they have had good experiences with the program.

Additionally, consider merchant integration. If you want to use bitcoins for transactions at certain stores or restaurants, check whether your Bitcoin wallet software is compatible with their point-of-sale systems. Any wallet app or program with a substantial user base will probably work well, but if you want to be the guinea pig for the latest and greatest Bitcoin wallet, expect to run into a few hiccups when you're trying to make a purchase.

Fortunately, it's easy to try many different wallets and fund them with a few cents of bitcoins to determine how they work and what features they offer. We suggest you experiment with several before you decide on your favorite.

10

BITCOIN 2030

So let's suppose Bitcoin is a runaway success. What would the world look like in 2030?

In the year 2030, 20 million bitcoins are in circulation; all but 1 million of the 21 million maximum have been mined.

Unfortunately, the future didn't work out well for Crowley: He didn't pay close attention to Chapter 3 and lost all his bitcoins in the infamous WhatsMyInstaSnapAppBook.com hack in 2019. Consequently, he's spending his days as a real estate agent and driving semitrucks cross country on the weekends for a living.

So exactly what would 20 million bitcoins look like? Well, unbeknownst to Crowley, if the 20 million bitcoins were each the size of a penny and were stacked as tightly as mathematically possible, they would almost exactly fill the inside of Crowley's US standard-sized, 53-foot semitrailer!

What Will a Bitcoin Be Worth in 2030?

Most likely, bitcoins will be worth *zero* in the year 2030: Despite the currency's early extraordinary success, 2030 is just too far in the future and too many events could trigger its demise. However, we can predict what the value of a bitcoin would be *if* Bitcoin achieved mainstream adoption.

For the rest of this chapter, let's imagine a world in which 1 billion people use bitcoins regularly. That number doesn't include everyone, because traditional currencies will still be used as well. So how many bitcoins might a typical Bitcoin user own in this future world?

Given that 20 million bitcoins would be in use in 2030, on average each person would own 0.02 bitcoins. Of course, wealth is never evenly distributed, and in all likelihood the top 1 percent would own more than 50 percent of the bitcoins (unfortunately, Bitcoin is unlikely to solve this problem on its own). Therefore, the typical Joe would own approximately 0.01 bitcoins, most likely referred to at this time as 10,000 microbitcoins.

Referring back to the example of a semitrailer of penny-sized bitcoins, the typical Joe's savings would consist of a fragment of a penny, about the size of a grain of sand a cubic millimeter in size.

As discussed in Chapter 6, the role that Bitcoin could fulfill that would produce the highest possible value per coin is as a store of value, in which case the typical Joe might store $1,250 of his savings in Bitcoin. If this extreme scenario were true, calculating the value of a single coin would be $1,250 divided by 0.01, or a ludicrous $125,000 per coin.

Bitcoin Mining in 2030

Using bitcoins to buy morning coffee, lunch, car fuel, and some online products, an average user might make 10 transactions a day.[1] A billion people making 10 transactions each per day is a substantial number of transactions! In fact, the number would be just over 100,000 transactions per second, which is 25–50 times more than the number VISA processes today. If transaction fees remained low (a must if many people adopt the currency)—let's say a penny each—the result would be $100 million dollars a day in transaction fees!

Although mining rewards in 2030 will be less than two bitcoins per block (based on the current schedule), if bitcoins have appreciated significantly in the interim, the mining rewards might still be considerable.

But most transactions might be off-chain transactions. (*Off-chain transactions* are Bitcoin transactions that are not handled by the blockchain but are instead handled by the ledgers managed by Bitcoin wallet vendors, in order to save on transaction fees for smaller payments.) Consequently, those 10 billion transactions per day may be only 1 million transactions per day as recorded on the blockchain. However, no matter how they are processed and reconciled, any payment system used by a billion people will generate many billions of transactions daily.

1. Note that we are not including micropayments, which Bitcoin makes possible and can number in the thousands per user per day. In this scenario, we are just referring to buying-things-that-cost-a-dollar-or-more transactions.

Mining would be very competitive, and the profit margins would be extremely slim. Only those with the most energy-efficient miners and cheapest electric power could stay in business. Assuming that the most efficient mining technology requires 0.1 J/GH, that electricity costs $0.10 per kWh, and that $100,000,000 a day in transaction fees is generated, the break-even hash rate would total more than 500 exahashes/s (500,000 PH/s)! Even assuming that mining technology is 100 times more computationally compact than it is currently, the amount of ASIC mining hardware required to achieve that level of mining power would fill around 5,000 small apartment buildings.

At a hash rate of more than 500 EH/s and an energy efficiency of 0.1 J/GH, a much greater amount of electric power will be needed to devote to mining. Over 50 GW would be used for Bitcoin mining, which is a bit less than 5 percent of the power produced by the United States today and about 0.3 percent of the global power output. Of course, if the expense of electricity increases, the network hash rate would drop. Bitcoin mining doesn't require a specific hash rate to function; however, the cheaper the electricity, the more Bitcoin miners will operate.

At this point, we've had fun speculating about the price of a bitcoin in a world dominated by this currency and discussing the infrastructure that would likely evolve around it. But what might life be like for an average bitcoiner in the year 2030?

A Day in the Life of a Bitcoiner in 2030

Let's follow Crowley as his day unfolds. It all starts when Crowley wakes up in the morning. Crowley wears his sleep-optimizing bracelet at night, which uploads his pre-waking vital signs anonymously to the Internet. Using this information, machine-learning systems across the world use bitcoins to bid on the time Crowley's alarm clock should go off, given his physical condition and sleep/wake cycle. The winning bid is the one that lets Crowley sleep the longest.

Because Crowley likes to take long, hot showers in the morning, he used to run out of hot water. But recently, a resident in his apartment building installed an industrial-grade hot water heater and is now selling hot water to other tenants to help with the cost. A chip in Crowley's hot water faucet automatically dispenses bitcoins directly to a chip in the hot water heater. As Crowley turns the shower knob clockwise, more bitcoins are dispensed and more hot water streams from the shower head.

As Crowley leaves his house, he beams a few satoshis from his wristwatch to one of the robotic lawnmowers mowing his lawn. A lawnmower repair shop down the street builds these mowers and provides them for free. Each lawnmower collects its own earnings and uses the bitcoins to pay programmers on the Internet to improve its AI algorithms so it can earn more. In addition, the mowers visit the lawnmower repair shop to get upgrades and pay there with their bitcoin earnings as well.

Today, Crowley misses his bus on his way to work. Apparently, the winning alarm clock bidder failed to detect Crowley's hangover this morning and cut the time too close. Usually, his bracelet would now dispense 20 satoshis to the winning bidder as a reward; however, because the bracelet calculates that Crowley has missed his bus, it draws upon a 100 satoshi insurance pool from an escrow account that the winning alarm-clock bidder had to set up as part of the bidding process. As a result, the winner *loses* money on today's bid (the programmer has some algorithm debugging to do).

With the satoshis from the escrow account, the bracelet starts an impromptu Bitcoin auction with all nearby parked, self-driving cars to determine if any are willing to rent to Crowley. After entering the winning car, Crowley is off to work.

Today, Crowley's real estate client is buying a house. Ever since the 2023 Digital Real Estate Reform Act, all houses are managed by simply tracking ownership of a single, specific satoshi assigned to each property. This satoshi acts as a *colored coin*, much like a title search in 2014. In effect, if the satoshi is handed to another person, the new person is assigned legal ownership of the property.

In 2030, Crowley just asks his Bitcoin wallet to do a title search by tracking the ownership of the satoshi linked to the house throughout the blockchain. Not only is this equivalent to an exhaustive title search and guaranteed to be 100 percent accurate, but his wallet software does this search instantaneously and for free.

WHAT IS A COLORED COIN?

One of the defining features of money is that it is fungible: If you want to buy a candy for a nickel and you have several nickels in your pocket, you should not have to think about which nickel to use—any of them is fit for this job. However, since the Bitcoin blockchain is public and we can therefore track the history of a single coin across time, it is possible to create a different type of money that is not fungible—a type of money where different coins may be tagged with different sorts of "colors."

For instance, suppose you are setting up a concert in a theater that can seat only 400 people. One way to make sure no more than 400 people show up on the day of the concert would be to hand out 400 milibits of Bitcoin to your 400 closest friends and then simply tell all of those people, "Please come to my show! However, if you can't make it to the show that day, feel free to trade or sell these milibits to anybody. They're yours to use as you see fit!"

Then, on the day of the concert, you would ask anyone who shows up to send one of these 400 milibits back to you. By analyzing the blockchain, you could theoretically follow each milibit through the past and verify each was among the 400 you initially sent out. There is nothing special about these original 400 milibits, other than the fact that you decided to arbitrarily give these 400 a special extra value (entry into a concert). This is referred to as *coloring* these coins. The benefits of this process would be (1) that no more than 400 people can show up to your concert with valid tickets and (2) your friends would have complete freedom to do whatever they wanted with the coins they were given. This same system could also be used to track ownership of more significant assets; for instance, to determine who owns the title on a house.

Of course, in practice it would be painful to track each of these coins in the blockchain yourself. However, software exists to automate the process of coloring and tracking bitcoins in this way. The most established protocol and tools for doing this share the name of "Colored Coins" and are available at *http://coloredcoins.org/*.

To complete the sale of the house, the buyer and seller simply enter a multi-signature transaction: In a single transaction, the buyer sends 150 microbits of bitcoins (the cost of the house) to the seller's address, and the seller sends the single-colored satoshi to the buyer. By using a single transaction, no sale can happen until both parties have signed the transaction with their private key. The transaction also contains a 1 percent commission that is sent to the real estate agents' addresses.

Because the blockchain was used to track property ownership, the entire title insurance and closing costs for the house (sans agent commission) is just the transaction fee, which may cost less than a penny.

After his workday is done, Crowley sends some money to his mom, who is a Nile crocodile. Her village, like every village in Burundi in the year 2030, has a Bitcoin booth that converts bitcoins to Burundian francs for a mere 0.5 percent commission. Of course, anyone can buy most items directly using bitcoins anywhere in the world nowadays, so that commission is not a necessary expense.

Instead of catching the bus, Crowley decides to get some exercise on this beautiful day and get dinner on his walk home. Unbeknownst to Crowley, a woman named Sofia who lives on the street he's walking down has just made a big salad for her family and realizes she's made too much and will have leftovers.

For this reason, she takes a picture of the leftover salad and uploads it to a food-sharing website. On that site, reviewers are paid with bitcoins to supply estimates of the tastiness of this salad. Within a few seconds, Crowley's phone rings because earlier he had put in a request for a meal of at least an 8 out of 10 rating in tastiness for no more than 15 satoshis that he could obtain on his way home, and Sofia's salad meets his request!

When Crowley rings Sofia's doorbell, an NFC chip in the doorbell communicates with Crowley's wristwatch to establish a contract for the dinner salad: Automatically, the doorbell sends Crowley's wristwatch a bill for 15 satoshis for entry into Sofia's impromptu restaurant.

How does Sofia know she can trust Crowley in her house? Crowley subscribes to an anonymous rating service, which for a 1 satoshi fee guarantees to Sofia that Crowley's trustworthiness score is 9.5 out of 10. This rating service is built into the Bitcoin blockchain in the form of a script. Users pay small fees to be part of the rating service, and the rating service (a computer program) uses these fees to pay for its online ads. In effect, it is a financial entity without an owner, living in cyberspace and paying for its own resources. This type of entity, called a *distributed autonomous corporation*, is made possible by blockchain technology.

After a long day at work, finally at home, Crowley relaxes in his recliner in front of the tube. In the middle of his favorite movie (*Harry Potter and the Forked Blockchain*), a pizza commercial appears. "Darn!" he exclaims. "That was a healthy salad I had for dinner today, but I could really go for a pizza chaser."

The reason this commercial suddenly interrupts Crowley's movie is not coincidental. Just at that moment, a pizza van driving by his house enters an automatic Bitcoin ad auction with Crowley's TV, earning the right to show its pizza commercial!

All Crowley has to do is simply open his mouth: In response, the gesture-recognition system in Crowley's TV automatically sends 8 satoshis to the pizza van.

In short order, the pizza van places a slice of pizza on a conveyor belt that extends from Crowley's house.

Within seconds, a robotic arm reaches out from the base of Crowley's recliner, grabs the slice of pizza from the conveyor belt, and stuffs it into Crowley's mouth.

You might have thought that a world built entirely on decentralized Bitcoin transactions would be a horrific dystopia. But after reading the awesome description of a day in the life of a typical bitcoiner in the year 2030, where everything operates via Bitcoin, we're sure your worries have been conclusively put to rest.

The Bitcoin End Game

In 1687, Isaac Newton published his *Principia*, arguably the single greatest piece of intellectual writing in the history of mankind. This book made

Newton famous because for the first time in history, someone had discovered simple mathematical formulas that could precisely describe the motion of the planets and other objects under the influence of gravity.

As great as this achievement was, the *Principia* had hidden within it another idea of even greater significance: the idea of infinitesimal calculus.[2] Most of the technology on which modern society depends—computers, cell phones, and even atom bombs—could have existed in a world without a theory of gravitation; however, it is highly unlikely this technology could have existed in a world without calculus.

In 17th century Europe, not everyone could appreciate the value of calculus. Newton had crafted this very abstract innovation almost solely as a tool to solve the far more romantic and poetic problem of explaining the motions of the planets for the first time.

Certainly, it is far too early to estimate where and whether Satoshi Nakamoto's Bitcoin whitepaper will appear in the annals of important scientific publications. But one fact is clear: In the same way that Newton had to first discover calculus to explain the motions of the stars, so Satoshi had to first discover the idea of a distributed anonymous ledger, the blockchain, to invent the idealistic notion of a fully distributed cryptocurrency.

However, unlike calculus and the laws of gravitation, the concepts of a blockchain and cryptocurrency are inextricably linked; they are yin and yang. A distributed form of money simply cannot exist without the security provided to it by the blockchain. Similarly, a blockchain cannot be created without giving people incentives to create it, and the only possible incentive that could work is a distributed form of money!

2. There remains some dispute as to how much credit Gottfried Leibniz deserves as a co-inventor of calculus.

So therein lies the genius of Satoshi Nakamoto: A person who was able to imagine two distinct technologies that on their own were clearly impossible and impractical. Sometime in the mid-naughts when Satoshi formulated his original whitepaper, for the first time in the world a person was able to clearly realize that although both technologies were impossible on their own, if you combine the two ideas into one enmeshed system, they become not only possible, but actually practical!

The true future of Bitcoin is evident: The technology of the distributed asset ledger combined with an incentive-producing currency is certain to remain with us for all time.[3] It is a mechanism that allows for great gains in efficiency in many situations in which trust previously had to be delegated to a central arbiter. Although there is no question that governments and central authorities will continue to exist and play a meaningful role in the world's future, much of the current work performed by these governments and other authorities is also needlessly repetitive and mundane.

Just as robots have helped the world reduce menial physical labor, so cryptocurrency technology now gives us the tools to automate the menial labor of bureaucracy. Optimistically, the entirety of humanity will benefit as a result.

---

3. However, it may not survive as "Bitcoin." It is possible that the blockchain technology could be adopted by other cryptocurrencies in the future, and those currencies could overtake Bitcoin in popularity.

HELLO MONEY! A SIMPLE JAVASCRIPT PROGRAM

One factor that makes Bitcoin so exciting is that *anyone* can write computer programs to link directly into the Bitcoin network and perform financial transactions. This appendix explains how to write a simple JavaScript program that watches a wallet and indicates when bitcoins have been sent to the wallet. In Appendix B, we'll create some more advanced programs in Java that expand on this idea.

The Meaning of "Easy"

Writing programs that manipulate money in Bitcoin is easy. However, as we walk through this process, it might not seem very easy to you.

But imagine, instead, if we built our app or service using a traditional e-commerce system. Roughly, here's what those steps would look like:

1. Incorporate your business to receive a DUNS[1] number.
2. Get a corporate account at your bank.
3. Have your account verified by a merchant services provider (Intuit, PayPal, Stripe, Apple, etc.).
4. Set up an account via the provider with your DUNS number to get access keys.
5. Acquire proprietary library software from the provider (you'll probably need to update this library regularly to maintain your software).
6. Redirect your customers to a special provider to authorize payments.
7. Write your code.
8. Have your finished app reviewed by the payment provider.

Here is the main step needed to get a Bitcoin-based, e-commerce system up and running:

1. Write your code.

Having to complete just this one task is what we mean when we use the term *easy* when programming with Bitcoin.

Three Ways to Write Bitcoin Software

To write Bitcoin-enabled software, you can use three different approaches:

1. Use a merchant service.
2. Connect to a local Bitcoin wallet program (typically the original Bitcoin wallet application based on Satoshi's initial code, named bitcoind).
3. Create a program that inserts itself directly into the Bitcoin network.

Using approach #1, you would connect to a web API over the Internet. That API would be supplied by a third-party company to manage your bitcoins. Companies that supply these APIs for sending and receiving bitcoins are typically called *merchant services*.

For example, if your website sells widgets and you want people to buy your widgets with bitcoins, using a merchant service may be a simple, no-fuss way to get your website working quickly. An additional benefit of a merchant service is that it may also offer services to automatically convert Bitcoin to/from other currencies as part of a transaction. Many companies supply these APIs, and BitPay is a common choice. But you can find a more extensive list of companies on the official Bitcoin foundation website.[2]

---

1. *Data Universal Numbering System*, a government-assigned code that is unique to every business in most of the world and identifies that business for financial purposes.

2. *https://en.bitcoin.it/wiki/How_to_accept_Bitcoin,_for_small_businesses#Merchant_Services*

However, this approach has some drawbacks. First, these vendor APIs arguably go against the spirit of Bitcoin, because using an API middleman makes you beholden to an external party; serious Bitcoiners prefer to retain 100 percent control over their money. Second, these APIs are mostly designed only for common use cases, so they don't allow the flexibility and innovative app development that we want to foster with this book. Third, the design of these APIs tends to change frequently, making it difficult to provide you with current information. For these reasons, we won't spend much time discussing vendor APIs in this book.

Approach #2 involves connecting to a local Bitcoin wallet and basically running the wallet on autopilot. Two of the Bitcoin wallet programs based on Satoshi's original code—Bitcoin Core and bitcoind—can be remote-controlled using a special protocol called JSON-RPC, as we will discuss shortly. Because these two programs are the gold standard in Bitcoin wallets, it is very enticing to utilize them for custom programs. Programs written to automate Bitcoin Core and bitcoind are easy to understand, and libraries exist in all popular programming languages, simplifying their use. You can use this approach in JavaScript, Ruby, PHP, Python, and many other languages. Unfortunately, the main drawback of using a local Bitcoin wallet program and controlling it from your own code is that this process often clunky and inefficient, as you'll see in the first programming example.

NOTE *Bitcoin Core and bitcoind share the same code. This common code is called the* Bitcoin reference client, *or just* Bitcoin. *It was the first implementation of* the *Bitcoin protocol and eventually was split into two variants: Bitcoin Core has a friendly graphical interface (UI), and bitcoind is a more stripped-down version with a text-based interface.*

Approach #3 involves going right to the metal and inserting your Bitcoin-enabled program directly into the Bitcoin network. You can do this in languages such as Java, C++, or Go or any language that has a fully implemented Bitcoin client library available. This approach is more robust and less resource-intensive than approach #2, but it is more technically complex.

However, if you're a programmer who believes in the Bitcoin ethos, being able to write an app that is a real *first-class citizen* in the Bitcoin network—a true Bitcoin node participating in the Bitcoin system—is motivating. The reason is that absolutely no limitations restrict what your app can do (as long as your app obeys the rules of the network.) In Appendix B, we'll write some programs that use this approach.

General Security Notes on Bitcoin Programming

An important disclaimer we need to mention here is that in this appendix, we'll write programs that send and receive only a few pennies. The techniques and example discussed are useful for learning the basic concepts of Bitcoin programming *but are in no way appropriate for writing programs that manipulate substantial sums of money*. If you plan on writing serious Bitcoin applications, you'll need to do the following:

1. Learn the basic concepts from the sample programs in this chapter.
2. Use this knowledge to study and understand the underlying source code for the Bitcoin libraries used in this chapter.
3. Follow the forums used by the developers and other library users to stay current with any security risks involved when using these libraries.

Most important, be aware that we're using community-maintained source code in our examples; if a clever black hat hacker[3] manages to insert some rogue code into the official library repositories, *he or she can steal all your money*. Even if you understand the library code perfectly, you run the risk of jeopardizing the safety of your money. For example, as you're downloading this library code from the Internet, a black hat hacker has many opportunities to perform a man-in-the-middle attack[4] and insert rogue code into a doctored version of the library that is incorporated into your program. As a result, the hacker can steal all your money.

Additionally, as mentioned in earlier chapters, hackers can steal your bitcoins in many other ways that aren't specific to Bitcoin programming. In a few years, if the current popularity of Bitcoin continues, we suspect most computer viruses will include code that immediately empties any Bitcoin wallets they find.

The bottom line is that you need to understand the grave risks your money might be exposed to if you plan on creating more advanced Bitcoin programs; you'll be able to safely protect your money only if you have a comprehensive and firm understanding of Bitcoin technology that goes beyond the introduction we give in this chapter. Please proceed with caution!

Some Upbeat Notes on Bitcoin Security

Now that you've endured some fire and brimstone to prevent you from losing money, we'll point out a few facts that should make you feel confident about Bitcoin security:

- The core Bitcoin network has so far maintained a record of almost perfect security. Most of the security risks involved in using bitcoins are due to careless acts that people executed on their own computers and could have been avoided.

3. Black hat hackers, as opposed to white hat hackers, are hackers who have no moral qualms about profiting from and harming their targets.

4. If you don't understand what a man-in-the-middle attack is, first, be aware that almost anything you do on the Internet is at risk of this assault, especially if you're connecting from a public Internet connection you don't fully control. Second, stop reading this chapter now and immediately read the Wikipedia page on this subject at *https://en.wikipedia.org/wiki/Man-in-the-middle_attack*.

- Despite the risks we've discussed so far in this chapter, established programming practices exist that mitigate all of these risks. You will be able to write secure Bitcoin software if you study this book, follow general guidelines on secure software development, and keep up-to-date on the latest security concerns discussed on Bitcoin development forums.
- As you are learning to write programs that use bitcoins, make sure you use a computer that doesn't contain Bitcoin wallets with substantial amounts of bitcoins in them. By doing so, you can learn to write Bitcoin software and avoid any dangers: You can't accidentally lose bitcoins (or have them stolen) on your development machine if you store your coins elsewhere.

Writing Your First Bitcoin Program in JavaScript

By convention, the first program a programmer writes when learning a new technology is a *Hello World* program: It's the simplest program possible in that it just prints the message *Hello World!* on the screen. Essentially, it indicates to the novice that your initial code seems to be working at the outset.

However, the Bitcoin programs we need to write must perform two main tasks: receive money and send money. In this chapter, we'll focus solely on receiving money and write a program called *Hello Money!*. In Appendix B we'll write a *Bye-Bye Money* program to send money.

Why Use JavaScript?

JavaScript is arguably the most well-known programming language in use today, because most developers who build software for the Web must learn it sooner or later (it is the only language that can natively run in a standard web browser). However, the JavaScript code we create will not run in a web browser: This is because web browsers have strong protections called *cross-domain restrictions* that shield them against communicating with external programs and websites. These restrictions limit what you can do with JavaScript within a web browser, making it difficult to interact with any external wallets (which is no surprise, because you wouldn't want your wallet emptied by visiting a malicious website).

However, currently you can also run JavaScript on a server, as is commonly done using the Node.js library. When run on a server, no such restrictions apply, and we can write simple programs that run in a console and can interact with Bitcoin Core and bitcoind.

Bitcoin Core vs. Bitcoind

As discussed earlier, the programming techniques described in this chapter will work with either of the wallet apps, Bitcoin Core or bitcoind. The only substantive difference between the two programs is that Bitcoin Core has a graphical UI; basically, it is just bitcoind with a frontend attached to it. Because of the friendliness of the graphical UI, we'll use Bitcoin Core for the example in this chapter. However, bitcoind is slightly less resource-intensive and can more easily run on computer servers via a terminal console. Consequently, it's best for you to use bitcoind if you actually deploy a finished program that uses the concepts in this chapter.

Preparing Your Machine for JavaScript Bitcoin Programming

You'll need a few tools to ready your machine before you begin programming, so let's get them now. The instructions provided here assume a Windows development environment; skip ahead to "For Mac Hackers" on page 219 or "For Linux Folks" on page 219 if you're using either of those platforms.

Installing Node.js

You first need to download an installer for Node.js from the *http://nodejs.org/* website. When you run the installer for Node.js, it will also install the Node Package Manager (npm) that we'll rely on next.

Installing node-bitcoin

Now you'll need a JavaScript library that connects to Bitcoin Core and bitcoind. We'll use the node-bitcoin library. To install node-bitcoin, go to a command prompt and enter **`npm install bitcoin`**. This command invokes the (previously installed) Node Package Manager, which downloads everything in the library in a simple step.

Starting Bitcoin Core

If you haven't already, download Bitcoin Core from its official website at *http://bitcoin.org/en/download.*

Next, you need to fire up Bitcoin Core in server mode. The wallet app will open an extra socket that we'll use to connect to the wallet from our JavaScript program. To do this on Mac and Linux machines, go to the Bitcoin Core installation directory from the console and run **`./Bitcoin-Qt -server`**. On Windows machines, open a command prompt, go to the *C:\Program Files (x86)\Bitcoin* directory, and enter **`bitcoin-qt.exe -server`**.

The first time you run Bitcoin Core in server mode, it will ask you to create a file named *bitcoin.conf* in a specific location and add a user ID and password to this file. Follow the directions as suggested because we'll use the userid and password shortly. Then, restart Bitcoin Core.

If you already have Bitcoin Core (previously called Bitcoin-Qt) installed but are following this tutorial for the first time, then you will need to locate your previously created *bitcoin.conf* file. For Windows users you might want to look in *C:\Users\<username>\AppData\Roaming\Bitcoin\bitcoin.conf.* For Mac users, try */Users/<username>/Library/ApplicationSupport/Bitcoin/bitcoin.conf.* For Linux users, try */home/<username>/ .bicoin/bitcoin.conf.*

NOTE *Gotcha for Windows users: If you try to create the* bitcoin.conf *file with Windows Notepad, be aware that Notepad will (oh so helpfully) tack on a* .txt *extension, which Windows will also (oh so helpfully) keep completely hidden from you for your own protection (a prime example of why most hackers these days try to avoid using Windows). To circumvent this problem, put quotes around the name* bitcoin.conf *when you enter it into the Save As dialog in Notepad.*

At this point, as is usual for a Bitcoin wallet, Bitcoin Core will take several hours downloading the blockchain before it's ready for the next steps—a perfect time for an extended lunch break!

For Mac Hackers

If you're using a Mac and are comfortable using a terminal, you can run specific commands to automatically search for, download, and install the required programs.

On Mac, download homebrew, a command-line tool that will handle the entire process for you:

```
# Get homebrew and if you haven't already
ruby -e "$(curl -fsSL https://raw.github.com/Homebrew/homebrew/go/install)"
brew tap phinze/homebrew-cask
brew install brew-cask

# Get node.js and bitcoin stuff
brew cask install bitcoin
brew install nodejs npm
npm install bitcoin

# Run bitcoin-qt in server mode
~/Applications/Bitcoin-Qt.app/Contents/MacOS/./Bitcoin-Qt -server
```

For Linux Folks

If you're using flavors of Debian Linux, such as Ubuntu, you'll just use the PPA feature to install the libraries:

```
sudo add-apt-repository ppa:bitcoin/bitcoin
sudo apt-get update
sudo apt-get install nodejs npm bitcoin-qt
npm install bitcoin
bitcoin-qt -server
```

With a working Bitcoin Core server, we're now ready to start programming.

Hello Money!

Okay, let's write our first Bitcoin app. Simply type the following complete program into a file named *hellomoney.js*:

```
var bitcoin = require("bitcoin");

var client = new bitcoin.Client({
    host: 'localhost',
    port: 8332,
    user: 'myUsername',
    pass: 'myPassword'
});

var previousBalance = 0;

function mainLoop() {
    client.getBalance('*', 0, function (err, balance) {
        if (err) {
            console.log(err);
        } else if (balance > previousBalance) {
            console.log("Hello Money! New balance: " + balance);
            previousBalance = balance;
        } else {
            console.log("Nothing's changed.");
        }
    });
}

setInterval(mainLoop(), 5000);
```

Before we start running the app, let's analyze what the code does line by line.

Part 1: Initializing the Connection with Bitcoin Core

```
var bitcoin = require("bitcoin");❶

var client = new bitcoin.Client(❷
   {
      host: 'localhost',
      port: 8332,
      user: 'myUsername',❸
      pass: 'myPassword'❹
   });

var previousBalance = 0;❺
```

The first line indicates that we're using the node-bitcoin library ❶. Next, we establish a connection to the Bitcoin Core server that we set up ❷. Because we'll be running the app on the same machine that Bitcoin Core is installed on, our host is set to `'localhost'`. By default, the bitcoin server will run on port 8332.

Important: On the next two lines ❸❹, input the user ID and password that you entered into the *bitcoin.conf* file. *Replace the placeholders shown here with your own.* Then, we create a variable to keep track of the previous balance in our program ❺, which we start at zero.

Part 2: The Main Loop

Now we'll write a loop that checks the balance in our wallet and reports to us when it has changed. The basic steps follow:

1. Ask Bitcoin Core for the current balance in its wallet.
2. If the balance is higher than the previous balance, print a message, and update the previous balance to the current balance.
3. Set a timer that completes the entire procedure again every five seconds.

The following `mainLoop` function carries out the preceding steps:

```
function mainLoop() {
    client.getBalance('*', 0, function (err, balance) {❶
        if (err) {
            console.log(err);❷
        } else if (balance > previousBalance) {❸
            console.log("Hello Money! New balance: " + balance);❹
            previousBalance = balance;❺
        } else {
            console.log("Nothing's changed.");
        }
    });
}

setInterval(mainLoop, 5000);❻
```

First, the function asks Bitcoin Core for the balance ❶. As we do this, we create a *callback function*, which reads `function(err,balance) {}`. A callback function is called at some future date. In this instance, it will be called when we receive the resulting balance from Bitcoin Core.

NOTE *If you've never worked with Node.js before, you may need some time to learn how to read this type of programming idiom. The philosophy in Node.js is that whenever your program has to wait on an external process (in this case the Bitcoin Core program), it makes you create callback functions, as opposed to stopping the program dead as you wait for a result to arrive. This is called* asynchronous programming *and enables your program to do other tasks while waiting for data to come in.*

When the balance becomes available, we first check whether an error has occurred and display it if one has ❷. Next, we check whether the new balance is higher than the previous balance ❸. If so, we print a message ❹ and update the previous balance ❺. Finally, we create a timer that runs every 5000 milliseconds with the `setInterval` function to repeatedly call `mainLoop` ❻.

The Bitcoin Core JSON-RPC API

The `mainLoop` function operates by *talking* with Bitcoin Core. This talking protocol is formatted as JSON-RPC, or JavaScript Object Notation – Remote Procedure Call. Simply put, JSON-RPC describes a structure with which two computers (or two programs on a single computer) can write messages to each other in a way that's easy for computer programmers to integrate into their code.

In our small app, we use only a single command to communicate with Bitcoin Core—the `client.getBalance` function. But many more commands are available that let you manipulate Bitcoin addresses, modify the wallet, analyze transactions, and complete most other tasks you'd want to do in a Bitcoin program. To learn which functions are available in the JSON-RPC interface, browse to the official API function list at *https://en.bitcoin.it/wiki/Original_Bitcoin_client/API_calls_list.*

Running the Hello Money! App

To try out our shiny new `Hello Money!` program, run the following command in a console from the directory containing *hellomoney.js*:

```
> node hellomoney.js
```

Next, simply send 0.001 bitcoins to the wallet managed by Bitcoin Core from another wallet. To do this, you'll need to use one of the public addresses, which you can find by clicking Receive in Bitcoin Core. The way we've written the app, it will count money that has arrived in your wallet only if it has received a confirmation on the blockchain. (In the next section, we'll write a `Hello Money!` program that detects money immediately on arrival, without requiring confirmations.)

Because confirmations typically take about 10 minutes, you'll need to wait a bit before you see the following:

```
> node hellomoney.js
Hello Money! New balance: 0.001
```

Congratulations! You've written a program that can watch a Bitcoin wallet and detect when money has been sent to it. If you then send additional money, the app will create messages to report on these new deposits as well.

Limitations of Writing Bitcoin Programs That Use JSON-RPC

By using JSON-RPC, we were able to write a program in JavaScript in no time that could report money sent to a Bitcoin wallet. However, if you're an experienced programmer (or have an advanced understanding of the Bitcoin protocol), you'll identify many problems with our example app.

One problem is that the app uses *polling* to detect when money has arrived. Polling constantly checks the status of Bitcoin Core by interrogating the software every five seconds. This process is similar to asking: "Do you have money yet? Do you have money now? What about now?" As you might imagine, repeatedly asking the same question like this not efficient.

If you're writing a production-quality application, it's therefore best to write it using *pushing*. Pushing involves specifying that our app is waiting for money and that it would like to be notified when money has arrived. But because of the way our connection with Bitcoin Core is set up, enabling pushing is rather difficult. After all, Bitcoin Core is primarily meant to be a wallet app in which no pushing to external programs is needed. Automating Bitcoin Core with JSON-PRC is a bit of a hack, and for this reason, we may run into limitations, such as needing to use inefficient polling.

NOTE *In more recent versions of Bitcoin Core and bitcoind, a feature called* walletNotify *allows for pushing, but the way it works is rather complicated—enough so that we recommend you avoid using it. Instead, we would suggest you use BitcoinJ instead of Bitcoin Core for pushing, as we will discuss in Appendix B.*

Another problem with our app is that we're just checking a crude *balance* amount to determine when money was sent to our wallet. However, the Bitcoin blockchain can sometimes trigger situations that cause the balance of a wallet to jump in ways that are unexpected and could make our app produce incorrect results.

For instance, suppose our wallet receives some money with one confirmation, but the blockchain suddenly forks, unconfirming the transaction that was tied to that money and causing the wallet to suddenly lose much of the confirmed money. Then, within the same five-second window, someone sends us more money. In this case, the balance in the wallet could actually *decrease*, even though we received some new money, and the *Hello Money!* message will never be triggered.

This is a very rare scenario, but if you're writing an app that manipulates large quantities of money, such incorrect behavior is intolerable. The solution to this problem is to use `client.listTransactions` (instead of `client.getBalance`). Then review these transactions to determine whether any new transactions involved sending money to the wallet in the last five seconds, which is what our app is looking for. However, this is too complicated to add to our simple `Hello Money!` program.

An additional problem is that Bitcoin Core (and bitcoind) requires large amounts of blockchain data and computational resources to run, even though our little app doesn't need most of this power. Is there any way of reducing these resource requirements? As you'll see in Appendix B, we can do this by writing a program that runs directly on the Bitcoin network.

B

BITCOIN PROGRAMMING WITH BITCOINJ

In Appendix A, we dabbled with JavaScript code that could perform some basic actions with a Bitcoin wallet by automating a preexisting wallet. In this appendix, we'll write far more powerful programs that directly insert themselves into the Bitcoin network. As discussed previously, Bitcoin programs written this way—meaning those that do not rely on APIs from external companies and avoid dependencies on separate wallet programs—are usually the smartest solution for serious Bitcoin development projects.

The Best Programming Language for Connecting to the Bitcoin Network

If you're an experienced programmer, most likely you have a favorite programming language you would prefer to use to write your Bitcoin programs. However, only a few mature libraries currently exist that can connect directly to the Bitcoin network. One is the C++ reference implementation with which all the first full clients of the Bitcoin system were written.[1] Large enterprise companies interested in supporting bitcoins should use this library. However, working with C++ is difficult for novices.

Another mature library is written in Java and is called bitcoinJ.[2] Because Java is easier to work with than C++, it is the library we'll use. (The bitcoinJ library can also be used easily from languages built on top of the Java Virtual Machine, such as Scala or Clojure.)

Currently, the options for other languages are rather limited. By searching the Internet, you *will* find Bitcoin libraries for other languages, such as Ruby, C#, and Python. However, most of these libraries are either in extremely early development or simply use the more limited JSON-RPC interface, which was discussed in Appendix A.

NOTE *Some serious attempts are being made to offer full Bitcoin client support within the Go programming language. However, at the time of this writing, these libraries are either still in early development (such as gocoin[3]) or are missing major features (such as btcd[4]).*

No matter which library you choose, keep in mind that you must be vigilant about security. Essentially, when you use any of these libraries, you'll be giving the library authors the keys to your Bitcoin kingdom. As we warned previously, technically it would be relatively easy to introduce rogue code into one of these libraries to steal all your money!

Installing Java, Maven, and the BitcoinJ Library

Let's ready your computer to do Java and bitcoinJ programming. The following steps should work on any major OS: Windows, Mac, or Linux.

Step 1: Installing Java

The Java programming language is maintained by Oracle Corporation. Your computer may already have Java installed, but if you've never done Java development, your computer may only contain the Java JRE (Java Runtime Engine), which can run Java programs but is not adequate for developing them. Instead, you need the Java JDK (Java Development Kit). To download the JDK, do a Google search for *Java JDK*. The first link (which should be a link on the official Oracle website) should direct you to the right place to access the download.

1. The C++ reference implementation is available at *https://github.com/bitcoin/bitcoin/*.

2. BitcoinJ is available at *http://bitcoinj.github.io/*

3. *https://github.com/piotrnar/gocoin/*

4. *https://github.com/conformal/btcd/*

NOTE ***Linux developers:*** *Some versions of Linux may install the OpenJDK version of Java by default. At the time of this writing, this unofficial Java variant is missing some components that this tutorial depends on. Instead, look online for information about installing the Oracle JDK on your version of Linux and make it the default Java version on your system.*

Step 2: Installing Maven

Maven is a packaging tool for Java. Essentially, you specify which libraries your program needs, and Maven automatically downloads them from the Internet and makes them available to your program. This is analogous to the Node Package Manager used in Appendix A.

You can download Maven and find instructions for installing Maven on each OS at *https://maven.apache.org/*. Just follow the instructions at the main Maven website to install it or search Google for tutorials. Because more than a million other people have had to install Maven, if you run into installation problems, just type your problem into Google. It is very likely you'll get helpful information on how to solve your problem.

NOTE ***Windows users:*** *At the time of this writing, detailed instructions for installing Maven on Windows are cleverly hidden at the very bottom of* http://maven.apache.org/download.cgi. ***Mac/Linux users:*** *You can use your package managers here:* `brew install maven` *for Mac and* `sudo apt-get install maven` *for Debian Linux.*

To ensure Maven is properly installed, a version message should display when you type `mvn --version` from a console.

For typical Java programming, we could stop here because any needed additional libraries could be downloaded through the Maven package system. However, because we're writing programs that work with money, the bitcoinJ maintainers require all developers to take a few extra precautions and install a couple of additional tools that directly relate to security issues.

Step 3: Installing Git

For security reasons, we'll install Git, which is a popular source code management tool. But it also offers features for securely downloading source code from online repositories that we'll rely on. Download Git from *http://git-scm.com/*.

NOTE *Once again, Mac and Linux users can use their package managers:* `brew install git` *and* `apt-get install git`*, respectively. Do you see a pattern?*

Step 4: Installing BitcoinJ

BitcoinJ is a Bitcoin library that can "talk bitcoin" and can connect directly to the Bitcoin network. By calling functions in this library, we can send and receive bitcoins in real time.

We'll build bitcoinJ directly from its authoritative source. Navigate to a directory from the console where you want to install the bitcoinJ library (your *Home* directory would be a good place).

NOTE *A new subdirectory will be created, so other existing files in this directory will not be affected by this installation.*

Enter the following into your console (on Windows you may need to use the special Git Bash console that was installed when you installed Git):

```
> git clone https://github.com/bitcoinj/bitcoinj.git❶
> cd bitcoinj
> git checkout cbbb1a2❷
> mvn install❸
```

The first line downloads the bitcoinJ code from the authoritative website ❶. Then, we use git to switch to an older version of this library using the `git checkout` command ❷. During this tutorial, this command will shield us from any problems that might be caused by newer versions of the library. However, when you've completed the tutorials, you can switch to the newest version of bitcoinJ (`git checkout master`) to experiment with its shiny new features. The last line installs the package into the local Maven package repository ❸. When we reference bitcoinJ from our programs, Maven will fetch it from this repository (instead of grabbing it from the Internet), and we can be confident we're using an uncorrupted version of this library.

Now we can finally start programming!

Creating a Starter Project for hello-money

In Appendix A, we created a JavaScript program called `Hello Money!` that detects when money is sent to a Bitcoin address. Now, we'll write a more sophisticated program with Java and bitcoinJ that accomplishes the same task. From the console, navigate to a directory where you want your new program to live, such as your computer's *Home* or *Documents* folder. A subdirectory will be created in this place.

Now type the following to have Maven create an empty starter project:

```
mvn archetype:generate -DgroupId=hellomoney -DartifactId=hello-money
   -DarchetypeArtifactId=maven-archetype-quickstart -DinteractiveMode=false
```

These commands create a directory called *hello-money* at the current location with the `hello-money` starter project.

NOTE *If Maven prompts you for answers during this process, just keep pressing* ENTER *to use the default setting.*

Next, we need to inform Maven that this program will use a couple of external libraries. We do this by editing the file *pom.xml*, which should now exist in the new directory. Also in this file should be a section named `<dependencies>` where we'll add bitcoinJ as a new dependency. After the previous dependency (i.e., *after* the line that reads `</dependency>` singular), add the following:

```
    <dependency>
      <groupId>com.google</groupId>
      <artifactId>bitcoinj</artifactId>
      <version>0.8</version>
      <scope>compile</scope>
    </dependency>
```

Now we'll add a plug-in called `exec-maven-plugin` to our program. A *plug-in* is a special type of library. The `exec-maven-plugin` will make it easier to run our finished program from the command line.

At the very bottom of the projects in *pom.xml* (i.e., *after* the line that reads `</dependencies>` plural), add the following lines:

```
<build>
  <plugins>
    <plugin>
      <groupId>org.codehaus.mojo</groupId>
      <artifactId>exec-maven-plugin</artifactId>
      <version>1.2.1</version>
      <configuration>
        <arguments>
        </arguments>
        <mainClass>hellomoney.App</mainClass>
      </configuration>
    </plugin>
  </plugins>
</build>
```

Now we're ready to run this *empty* program for the first time as a test. To do this, execute the following lines from the console in the program's directory:

```
> mvn install❶
> mvn exec:java❷

Hello World!
```

The first line ❶ loads all the necessary libraries into the project and builds the program into a Java bytecode file. The second line ❷ actually runs the program.

If the program runs successfully, you should see `Hello World!` printed on the screen. This means Maven has successfully created a functioning Java program and that we're now ready to start writing the core Bitcoin code.

Writing the Code for hello-money

The entirety of the code for our `hello-money` program follows. To add this to the project, open the file *src/main/java/hellomoney/App.java* and replace its contents with this program:

```
package hellomoney;
import com.google.bitcoin.core.*;
import com.google.bitcoin.store.*;
import com.google.bitcoin.discovery.DnsDiscovery;
import java.io.File;
import java.math.BigInteger;

public class App
{
    public static void main( String[] args ) throws BlockStoreException
    {
        NetworkParameters params = NetworkParameters.prodNet();
        Wallet wallet = new Wallet(params);
        ECKey key = new ECKey();
        System.out.println("Public address: " +
            key.toAddress(params).toString());
        System.out.println("Private key: " +
            key.getPrivateKeyEncoded(params).toString());
        wallet.addKey(key);
        File file = new File("my-blockchain");
        SPVBlockStore store=new SPVBlockStore(params, file);
        BlockChain chain = new BlockChain(params, wallet, store);
        PeerGroup peerGroup = new PeerGroup(params, chain);
        peerGroup.addPeerDiscovery(new DnsDiscovery(params));
        peerGroup.addWallet(wallet);
        peerGroup.start();
        peerGroup.downloadBlockChain();
        wallet.addEventListener(new AbstractWalletEventListener()
            {
                public void onCoinsReceived(Wallet wallet,
                      Transaction tx, BigInteger prevBalance,
                      BigInteger newBalance)
                {
                    System.out.println("Hello Money! Balance: "
                         + newBalance + " satoshis");
                }
            });
         while(true){}
    }
}
```

Next, run the command `mvn install`, which checks the syntax of this new program code and builds it into a program file. If the build works, the message `BUILD SUCCESS` should appear (along with tons of other esoteric messages).

Before we run the program, let's walk through it step-by-step to see what it does.

Declarations at the Top of the Program

The first line in the program declares the name of the package:

```
package hellomoney;
```

Next, we declare all the libraries the program will reference:

```
import com.google.bitcoin.core.*;
import com.google.bitcoin.store.*;
import com.google.bitcoin.discovery.DnsDiscovery;
import java.io.File;
import java.math.BigInteger;
```

Three of these references are for Bitcoin classes: First, we'll use the core libraries to access basic Bitcoin classes (such as classes for wallets and keys). Second, we need classes for storing the blockchain (called a *block store* in BitcoinJ lingo). Third, we need to use the `DnsDiscovery` class, which helps us find other nodes participating in the Bitcoin network. We import the `java.io.File` class because we'll be writing our block store to a file, and we import the `java.math.BigInteger` class to work with, well, big integers.

Now let's define the Java class that holds the program:

```
public class App
{
    public static void main( String[] args ) throws BlockStoreException
    {
```

The program code is stored in a new class called `App`, which contains a single member function `main`. We mentioned this `hellomoney.App` class in the *pom.xml* file, declaring it as the *main class* of the program.

Let's look at individual lines in the main function.

Initializing Our Java Objects

Here is the code that initializes the Java object we need from the bitcoinJ library.

```
        NetworkParameters params = NetworkParameters.prodNet();❶
        Wallet wallet = new Wallet(params);❷
        ECKey key = new ECKey();❸
        System.out.println("Public address: " +❹
            key.toAddress(params).toString());
        System.out.println("Private key: " +❺
            key.getPrivateKeyEncoded(params).toString());
        wallet.addKey(key);❻
```

We start by fetching the network parameters for the main, production Bitcoin network ❶. Although only one true Bitcoin network is actually used for transactions, it's difficult to test the Bitcoin system thoroughly with real money; therefore, Bitcoin developers also maintain a second Bitcoin network called *TestNet* for testing only. The `NetworkParameters` structure contains information about the genesis block (the first block in the blockchain) as well as information about the maximum number of coins and several other assorted details, which may differ between the main Bitcoin network and the TestNet. By having all this information packed in the `NetworkParameters` data structure, it's easy to connect our program to another network besides the main Bitcoin network, such as the TestNet, as desired.

Next, we create a new, empty wallet that we'll set up to receive our coins ❷. As discussed earlier, Bitcoin wallets contain one or more Bitcoin addresses, and each Bitcoin address consists of a public and a private key. Here ❸, the bitcoinJ library creates a new key pair for us. Then, we print out the public address and private keys that were generated ❹❺. Finally, we add our new key pair to the wallet ❻.

WARNING *Usually, when using bitcoinJ, you should reuse the same wallet every time the program runs and load/save it every time the program starts/stops or your program can lose track of money. This is not an issue for the simple* `hello-money` *program. However, before you build more sophisticated bitcoinJ programs, read "Gotchas When Using Wallets in BitcoinJ" on page 239.*

Not only does a Bitcoin app need a wallet, it also needs a blockchain. The following lines initialize a new blockchain for us:

```
File file = new File("my-blockchain");❶
SPVBlockStore store = new SPVBlockStore(params, file);❷
BlockChain chain = new BlockChain(params, wallet, store);❸
```

Because blockchains consume lots of space, we'll write it to a file named *my-blockchain* ❶. Next, we create a block store, which is an object that manages the data for our copious blockchain data ❷. BitcoinJ offers several block store types, all with different feature and performance trade-offs. In this example, we'll use an `SPVBlockStore` object, which is usually the best choice for most apps.

So what are the trade-offs you need to know about? Well, the biggest performance challenge any app that works with bitcoins has to deal with is that the official Bitcoin blockchain is larger than 10GB in size. Do most Bitcoin apps *really* need all 10GB of the blockchain?

To answer this question, let's consider why the blockchain exists. At a simplified level, a Bitcoin blockchain is responsible for two main jobs:

1. Figuring out how much money everyone on the network has
2. Figuring out whether new transactions broadcast across the network are valid

For the first task, the blockchain allows us to examine all the historical blocks in the blockchain and compile comprehensive data about every Bitcoin address ever used and how much money each contains. For the second task, it allows us to examine new blocks of transactions created by the network and then to verify that these blocks have the appropriate hashing information that proves they are correctly mined blocks according to the latest difficulty requirements.

But consider the first job of the blockchain: Do most apps need to discern how much money is in every wallet in existence? No, most apps only need to identify the amount of money in *one* or a small number of wallets. Therefore, not all 10GB of data are needed. The prescient Satoshi, in his original Bitcoin whitepaper, was able to see that in this case, an optimization called *Simplified Payment Verification (SPV)* was possible.

NOTE *We also covered SPV a bit in Chapter 9, when comparing different types of Bitcoin wallets.*

Here's a quick refresher of how SPV works: If you know you're interested in a single wallet ahead of time, you can just tally up how much money is in that one wallet as you pull the entire historical blockchain off the Bitcoin network. At that point, you only need to store header information of blocks and can ignore information in older blocks entirely in most situations, which is what `SPVBlockStore` does. In doing so, the `SPVBlockStore` (as of 2014) is less than 1GB in size, less than a one-tenth the size of the official blockchain, and this is why we use `SPVBlockChain` to store our data.

Once we've created the block store, we can use it to create a `BlockChain` object ❸. Notice that when we create this `BlockChain` object, we must pass in our wallet as created. Because we're not downloading all 10GB, the blockchain object needs to know ahead of time which wallets (and their addresses) are important to us so it can select the right blockchain data to download.

NOTE *Even though `SPVBlockStore` is much smaller than the full blockchain, it can still take a long time for your app to download all the needed data from the network—usually, about 20 minutes. However, it will write this data to a file, and an `SPVBlockStore` object is smart enough to check the supplied file to see whether any data has already been downloaded since the last time the program was run. If so, it downloads only new data that has arrived after the program was last run.*

Connecting to the Bitcoin Network

With a wallet and a place to store the blockchain data, we can now connect to the actual Bitcoin network. A Bitcoin node connects to the Bitcoin network by connecting to several semirandom peer nodes. Here is the code that fires up a connection to several peers:

```
PeerGroup peerGroup = new PeerGroup(params, chain);❶
peerGroup.addPeerDiscovery(new DnsDiscovery(params));❷
peerGroup.addWallet(wallet);❸
peerGroup.start();❹
peerGroup.downloadBlockChain();❺
```

First we create a `PeerGroup` object ❶ that manages these connections. Next, we choose some random peers to connect to. We do this by adding a peer discovery algorithm to the PeerGroup ❷. The DnsDiscovery class basically uses the URLs of some well-established and trusted nodes as a starting point to discover peers that are willing to accept new connections. Then we add our wallet to the PeerGroup object ❸.

Now we're finally ready to inject the app into the Bitcoin network! We do this by calling PeerGroup.start ❹, which will find and connect to some nodes and perform the appropriate handshake operations via network sockets. And, like any Bitcoin node, we request that the peers send us the blockchain so we can become a fully functional node ❺. As mentioned previously, this step will take a while to run, but only the first time we run the program.

Listening for New Money

One last feature we need to add to the hello-money program is a hook to detect when money has arrived:

```
wallet.addEventListener(new AbstractWalletEventListener()❶
    {
        public void onCoinsReceived(Wallet wallet, Transaction tx,❷
           BigInteger prevBalance, BigInteger newBalance)
        {
            System.out.println("Hello Money! Balance: "
                + newBalance + " satoshis");
        }
    });
```

The bitcoinJ wallet object has an addEventListener member function, and we can create an anonymous class of type EventListener, which intercepts and listens to different events that might happen to a wallet ❶. In our app, we're interested in the onCoinsReceived function ❷, which will be called every time money is received by this wallet. Let's explore in more detail exactly what this means.

Because the program lives directly in the Bitcoin network, it can listen to the *bitcoin firehose*, a stream of data that contains every Bitcoin transaction happening anywhere in the world in close to real time. Each transaction is examined to see whether it involves receiving money into any Bitcoin address contained in our wallet. In our app, the wallet contains only one address. As soon as this transaction arrives (even before it has been incorporated into a mined block), our function onCoinsReceved will be called.

NOTE *In the* hello-money *program, we won't worry about capturing confirmation events on the money received; we'll only listen for the transmission of new, unconfirmed transactions. However, if we were interested in confirmations, we could capture them via the* onTransactionConfidenceChanged *function. Because we're running a full Bitcoin client, we can do what we want, whereas in Appendix A we were* forced *to look only at confirmed transactions due to the limitations of the JSON-RPC interface.*

The onCoinsReceived function has four parameters passed into it ❷: the wallet object, a transaction object, the previous balance in the wallet, and the new balance. The bitcoinJ library uses the Java `BigInteger` class to encode Bitcoin balances, because this numerical type can handle very large integers precisely. If you've written financial software before, you'll know why the `BigInteger` class is used (or you may recall how the bank heist was done in the movie *Office Space*). The fact is that it's very easy to botch a financial transaction due to rounding errors, and using big, precise integers prevents this problem. Hence, bitcoinJ performs all Bitcoin math using satoshis, the smallest unit of bitcoins, which are worth one one-hundred-millionth of a bitcoin.

NOTE *Because we added the event listener* after *we downloaded the initial blockchain, the* `onCoinsReceived` *function will be called* only *when new transactions appear as the program is running. If we had declared it before downloading the initial blockchain, the design of* `bitcoinJ` *is such that* `onCoinsReceived` *would also have been called on relevant historical transactions.*

Finally, we put the program into an infinite loop, so the program continues running as we wait for money to arrive:

```
while(true){}
```

Running and Testing the hello-money Java Program

We're ready to run and test the program! As before, we first compile and then run the program:

```
> mvn install
> mvn exec:java
```

Some messages should then appear as your program connects to the Bitcoin network and downloads the blockchain. The first time the program is run, this may take a while:

```
Public address: 16YavT6SmJCuJpZgzRa6XG9WefPEu2M45
Private key: L3eoA1rXiD8kWFUzdxw744NWjoZNB5BGsxhzVas6y5KJgVteZ4uD
Downloading block chain of size 265184. This may take a while.
Chain download 1% done with 262532 blocks to go, block date Feb 1, 2009 5:09:55 PM
Chain download 2% done with 259880 blocks to go, block date Feb 22, 2009 11:32:14 PM
Chain download 3% done with 257228 blocks to go, block date Mar 18, 2009 9:59:38 PM
Chain download 4% done with 254576 blocks to go, block date Apr 11, 2009 4:27:52 PM
Chain download 5% done with 251924 blocks to go, block date May 4, 2009 9:23:54 AM
...
Done downloading block chain
```

After the blockchain has finished downloading, you can test the `hello-money` program and send it some tiny sum from your favorite wallet app. Simply send 0.0002 BTC to the public address and record the private key (we'll be using this money in the follow-up example program later in this appendix). The program should detect when the money arrives and display a message like this:

```
Hello Money! Balance: 20000 satoshis
```

The new balance in the wallet should display in satoshis (divide by 100,000,000 to see that this number is indeed 0.0002 BTC).

You've successfully written a bitcoinJ program that creates a Bitcoin wallet and reports on any money received. Now let's write a second program that uses the newly stored money!

Bye-Bye Money

Now, let's write a brand-new program that can *send* money from an arbitrary Bitcoin address. To create a new bye-bye-money program, run the following from your top-level program directory:

```
mvn archetype:generate -DgroupId=byebyemoney -DartifactId=bye-bye-money
   -DarchetypeArtifactId=maven-archetype-quickstart -DinteractiveMode=false
```

Then, make the exact additions to the *pom.xml* file as we did in the hello-money example, except for the line that reads <mainClass>hellomoney.App</mainClass>. Change that line to <mainClass>byebyemoney.App</mainClass>. (These steps are analogous to those we followed for our hello-money program in "Creating a Starter Project for hello-money" on page 228.)

Just as before, open the file *src/main/java/byebyemoney/App.java* and replace its contents with the following program:

```
package byebyemoney;

import com.google.bitcoin.core.*;
import com.google.bitcoin.store.*;
import com.google.bitcoin.discovery.DnsDiscovery;
import java.util.concurrent.ExecutionException;
import java.io.File;
import java.math.BigInteger;

public class App
{
    public static void main( String[] args )
        throws BlockStoreException, AddressFormatException,
                   InterruptedException, ExecutionException
    {
        NetworkParameters params = NetworkParameters.prodNet();
        Wallet wallet = new Wallet(params);
        DumpedPrivateKey key = new DumpedPrivateKey(params,
              "L1vJHdDqQ5kcY5q4QoY124zD21UVgFe6NL2835mp8UgG2FNU94Sy");
        wallet.addKey(key.getKey());
        BlockChain chain = new BlockChain(params, wallet,
              new MemoryBlockStore(params));
```

```
        PeerGroup peerGroup = new PeerGroup(params, chain);
        peerGroup.addPeerDiscovery(new DnsDiscovery(params));
        peerGroup.addWallet(wallet);
        peerGroup.start();
        peerGroup.downloadBlockChain();
        BigInteger balance = wallet.getBalance();
        System.out.println("Wallet balance: " + balance);
        Address destinationAddress = new Address(params,
                "1BTCorgHwCg6u2YSAWKgS17qUad6kHmtQW");
        BigInteger fee=BigInteger.valueOf(10000);
        Wallet.SendRequest req = Wallet.SendRequest.to(
               destinationAddress,balance.subtract(fee));
        req.fee = fee;
        Wallet.SendResult result = wallet.sendCoins(peerGroup, req);
        if(result != null)
            {
                result.broadcastComplete.get();
                System.out.println("The money was sent!");
            }
        else
            {
                System.out.println("Something went wrong sending the money.");
            }
    }
}
```

Many of the lines in this new program are shared with our previous hello-money program, but let's look carefully at the new parts.

Importing a Private Key

To send money from our program, we need to import the private key of the Bitcoin address from the previous example. Here is the code that does this:

```
        DumpedPrivateKey key = new DumpedPrivateKey(params,❶
                "L1vJHdDqQ5kcY5q4QoY124zD21UVgFe6NL2835mp8UgG2FNU94Sy");
        wallet.addKey(key.getKey());❷
        BlockChain chain = new BlockChain(params, wallet,❸
                new MemoryBlockStore(params));
```

In the first lines, we're explicitly adding a new, preexisting private key to our wallet ❶❷. This is the key associated with the Bitcoin address that received the money in the hello-money program. You need to replace the private key shown on this line with the private key you wrote down when running the previous example. Also, in this new program we're not using the SPVBlockStore function; instead, we're using bitcoinJ's MemoryBlockStore ❸ function for variety. This block store won't create a file, but by using it, our program will need to redownload the blockchain every time the program runs. (This also guarantees that bitcoinJ will assign the correct balance to the wallet. We'll discuss why in "Gotchas When Using Wallets in BitcoinJ" on page 239.)

Sending the Money

Now let's look at the code that actually sends the money:

```
BigInteger balance = wallet.getBalance();❶
System.out.println("Wallet balance: " + balance);❷
Address destinationAddress = new Address(params,❸
     "1BTCorgHwCg6u2YSAWKgS17qUad6kHmtQW");
BigInteger fee = BigInteger.valueOf(10000);❹
Wallet.SendRequest req = Wallet.SendRequest.to(❺
     destinationAddress,balance.subtract(fee));
req.fee = fee;❻
Wallet.SendResult result = wallet.sendCoins(peerGroup, req);❼
```

First, we get the balance contained in the wallet ❶ and display it ❷. Next, we declare the destination address the money should be sent to ❸. In this example, we input the main donation address for the Bitcoin Foundation; feel free to substitute a public address of one of your own wallets.

Nowadays, it's best to include a transaction fee when sending bitcoins, which we declare to be 10,000 satoshis ❹. Next, we create a SendRequest object ❺, which is a structure to hold the basic information about what we're sending and includes the destination address and the amount to be sent (which is the balance minus the fee). Then, we set the fee on this object ❻ and send our money ❼!

Ensuring the Money Transmission

If we try to send more money than we have, if the fee is inadequate, or if the Internet connection drops out at the wrong moment, the money might never be accepted by the network. Therefore, we need to write code that waits and ensures that the money we sent is transmitted to the network. Here's what we'll add to do this:

```
result.broadcastComplete.get();❶
System.out.println("The money was sent!");❷
```

The first line of code ❶ retrieves a Java *future* object, which indicates that the send transaction has been properly broadcast to the network. (A standard in Java, futures retrieve information about a separate execution thread—in this case the thread that monitors communication with the Bitcoin network.) If this line completes without throwing an exception, we display a message indicating that the money was sent ❷.

Running bye-bye-money

We can run bye-bye-money in the usual way (remember to input your own private key):

```
> mvn install
> mvn exec:java
```

EXCEPTION TYPES IN BITCOINJ

One feature we skimped on in this example is error handling: The main function simply rethrows a variety of different exceptions for operations that can go wrong as we attempt to send our money. These include the following exceptions:

- `BlockStoreException`: This is thrown when the block store cannot be created (most commonly, this happens with block store types that write to a file when something corrupts the file).
- `AddressFormatException`: This is thrown when the format of the address is incorrect.
- `InterruptedException`: This is thrown when network connection problems occur.
- `ExecutionException`: This is thrown when we're using a future object and an exception occurs in the other thread (as happens when we check for completion of the transaction broadcast).

In a more sophisticated Bitcoin app, you should catch all of these exception types separately and add more descriptive error messages for your app's users.

Because this program churns through the blockchain in memory, you'll need to wait a few minutes or more for it to complete (even when you rerun it). If the program is successful, you'll see the message *The money was sent!*, and the money should arrive at the destination wallet. You can also access a blockchain information site (such as *http://blockchain.info/*), enter the source or destination address, and see that the details of the transaction are part of the public record.

Congratulations! You now understand the basics of writing a Bitcoin application!

Gotchas When Using Wallets in BitcoinJ

To the novice, the way wallets and the `BlockChain` object work in bitcoinJ can be very confusing. If you don't fully understand bitcoinJ's behavior, bitcoinJ can also report incorrect wallet balances.

This happens because bitcoinJ is optimized around the concept of an SPV blockchain. The performance benefits of SPV blockchains were discussed earlier, but because they contain only limited blockchain data, you need to follow a few basic rules to ensure they work properly for you in bitcoinJ:

1. If your app's wallet already has money in it, bitcoinJ needs to know the amount *before* the blockchain is downloaded from the network.

2. After the blockchain is loaded, bitcoinJ will perform the necessary tasks to ensure the wallet's accuracy as new transactions appear on the network.
3. If you use a block store type that supports saving to a disk file, your app is responsible for saving the wallet to a file, as well (it is also responsible for loading the block store and wallet data).

As you saw when we constructed a `BlockChain` object, bitcoinJ expects the app to pass in a wallet object. This allows the wallet to be updated when relevant *historical* transactions are found in downloaded blocks and allows rule #1 to be enforced: *Be sure not to add additional keys to your wallet after the fact and expect your wallet to work without redownloading the blockchain.*

Similarly, when we initialized the `PeerGroup` object, we called `addWallet()` to add our wallet to the peer group. By doing so, bitcoinJ keeps the wallet balance in sync with any *new* transactions that appear in the Bitcoin network as the program is running, enforcing rule #2.

To make sure rule #3 is adhered to, you can use the `Wallet.loadFromFile()` and `Wallet.saveToFile()`functions. A `Wallet.autoSaveToFile()` function is also available that can help with loading and saving the block store and wallet data. To learn how to use these functions properly, look at the example programs in the bitcoinJ repository.

If you keep the previously listed three basic tenets in mind, you'll avoid most of the pitfalls that accompany mastering bitcoinJ.

Conclusion

We hope you've enjoyed this tour of bitcoinJ programming, and we look forward to seeing any awesome new apps that you build. After all, the app you build just might completely reinvent how people interact with their money in the Internet age!

INDEX

Note: Page numbers in *italics* refer to comic pages

Numbers & Symbols

μBTC (microbitcoins), 9
51 percent attacks, 167

A

`addEventListener` function, 234
addition, and elliptic curves, 147–148
`AddressFormatException` exception type, 239
`addWallet()` function, 240
Adleman, Leonard, 133–134
alternative coins (altcoins), 64
  comic on, *181–184*
Andresen, Gavin, 113–114
anonymity, Bitcoin ATMs and, 62
anonymity by default, 124
anonymous rating service, 208
application specific integrated circuits (ASICs), for mining, 174
arbitrage, 64
Armory Bitcoin Client, 41
ASICs (application specific integrated circuits), for mining, 174
ask order, 63
asymmetric key cryptography, 133
asynchronous programming, 221
ATMs, Bitcoin, 62
Austrian economics, 126
authentication
  password for, 40
  two-factor, 36, 53–54
Authy app, 58–59
average net worth, 121–122

B

Back, Adam, 120
bank account
  linking to Coinbase, 59–60
  linking to exchange, 65
bid orders, 63
`BigInteger` class (Java), 235
BIP38 encryption, 40
BIPs (Bitcoin Improvement Proposals), 40
bitaddress.org, 38
Bitcoin, 1
  in 2030, 199–212
  beginnings, 112–116
  benefits of using, 3
  cap on total supply, 26
  complexity of, 4–5, 27–29
  cryptocurrencies as side chains, 121
  energy costs of, 124–125
  future role, 121–123
  how it works, 8–9
  motive for creating, 2–3
  potential of, 116–127
  risk of destruction, 118–119
  safety and security, 31, 61
  units, 9–10
  value growth, 114, 116
Bitcoin addresses, 10–11, 139
  generating
    with Bitcoin wallet program, 19
    with master public key, 190
  sharing, 156
  SPV wallets vs. full wallets, 193–195
Bitcoin ATMs, 62
Bitcoin classes (Java), 231

bitcoin.conf file, 218
Bitcoin Core, 38, 214
  initializing connection, 220–221
  JSON-RPC API, 222
  programming techniques and, 217–218
  starting, 218–219
  version 0.1, 113
bitcoind, 214
  programming techniques and, 217–218
Bitcoin exchanges, 52
  intermediaries, 53–54
  live exchanges, 71
Bitcoiniacs, 53
Bitcoin Improvement Proposals (BIPs), 40
BitcoinJ, 226
  exception types, 239
  installing, 227–228
  issues for wallets, 239–240
Bitcoin network, 169
  code for connecting, 233–234
Bitcoin sellers, finding, 67–68
Bitcoin software applications
  in JavaScript, 217
  security notes on programming, 215–216
  writing approaches, 214–215
Bitcoin wallets. *See* wallets
BitPay, 214
Bitrated, 70
Bitstamp, 64
BitTorrent, 119, 127
black hat hacker, 216
blind signatures, 111
block
  anatomy of, 171–175
  number of transactions included in, 180
blockchain, 19–26, *96*, 165
  distribution, 138
  forking, 23–25
  importance of, 211
  initializing, 232
  lottery, 21–23
  orphaned, 24–25
  reasons for, 232–233
  recording transactions, 161, 170
  size of, 191
  storing, 33
Blockchain.info, 37
block depth, 25
block difficulty, 172–173
block hash, 138
block header, 171
  data in, 172
  and SPV wallets, 192, 193
`BlockStoreException` exception type, 239
Bosselaers, Antoon, 140
brain wallets, 45–46
broadcast-only node, 169
BTC, 9
BTC China, 64
BTC-E, 64
BTCquick, 53
Buffett, Warren, 110
buttonwood exchanges, 71
buying bitcoins, 49–71
  with Coinbase, 58–61
  from currency exchange, 62–66
  methods, 51–52
  from middleman, 52–57
  person-to-person, 67–71
`bye-bye-money` program, 236–239
  ensuring money transmission, 238
  running, 238–239
Byzantine Generals' Problem, 2–3, 164–165

C

C#, 226
C++, 226
calculus, 211
callback function, 221
cap on total bitcoin supply, 26
Cavirtex, 64
change address, 187
charities, accepting bitcoins, 18
Chaum, David, 111
Circle, 53
`client.getBalance` function, 222
`client.listTransactions` function, 223
client-server architecture, 119

Coinbase, 36, 53
buying bitcoins with, 58–61
linking bank account to, 59–60
registering at, 58
coin control, 196
cold storage, 47
vs. hot storage, 33–34
collision, hash functions, 132
colored coins, 205, 206
comic
on altcoins, *181–184*
on Bitcoin, *73–108*
commodities, spread for, 65–66
computer viruses, threat to wallets, 216
confirmed payments, security, 194
confirming transactions
in *Hello Money!* app, 222
infinite loop of, 164
contracts, 55–56
convenience, of storage, 35
credit cards, 111, 112
vs. Bitcoin transactions, 57
issuers, 125
cross-domain restrictions, 217
cryptocurrencies, 129
competition with Bitcoin, 119–121
cryptography, 129–159
Bitcoin need for, 137–139
elliptic curve, 141
methods in Bitcoin, 139–141
overview, 130–137
and rounding errors, 151
security for Bitcoin, 157–158
currencies
Bitcoin advantages over existing, 117–118
converting to bitcoins, 55–57
decentralized, 1
ideal, 117
stateless, 2
currency codes, standard for, 9*n*
currency exchanges, 50
buying bitcoins from, 62–70
opening, 114
transferring dollars to account, 65
Cybercash, 111

D

Data Universal Numbering Service (DUNS), 214*n*
decentralization, in mining, 179–180
decoding, cryptography, 134
decrypting messages, 130
deflation, dangers of, 126
`<dependencies>` section, 229
deterministic key generation, 187–190
combining with watch-only wallet, 189
difficulty target, 171
DigiCash, 111
bankruptcy, 112
digital currencies, 1, 64
dangers of decentralized, 123–127
discussions on government role, 116
history, 110–112
digital signatures, 11, 91, 131–132, 135–136
authorizing transactions with, 137–138
using elliptic curves, 154–155
discounts, for limit orders, 66
discrete logarithm, 131–132
distributed autonomous corporations, 208
distributed computing projects, Bitcoin as largest, 115
distribution of bitcoins, 162
divisibility, of currency, 117
`DnsDiscovery` class, 234
Dobbertin, Hans, 140
dollar bill, life span of, 118
dollars, converting to bitcoins, 55–57
double SHA256 hash, 171
security and, 156
double spending, 25, 167
Draper, Adam, 110
DUNS (Data Universal Numbering Service), 214*n*
durability, of currency, 118

E

e-cash, 111
ECDSA (elliptic curve digital signature algorithm), 146–153
  signing Bitcoin transaction with, 153–156
  verifying signature with, 155
e-commerce, building app using, 214
e-gold, 112
Electrum wallet, 14–16, 38, 188
elliptic curve cryptography, 141
  calculating sum of adding two points, 149
  pseudocode for summation and multiplication, 158–159
elliptic curve digital signature algorithm (ECDSA), 146–153
  signing Bitcoin transaction with, 153–156
  verifying signature with, 155
encoding, cryptography, 134
encryption, 130
  BIP38, 40
  paper wallets, 39–40
  password for, 40
energy costs, of Bitcoin, 124–125
error handling, Bitcoin programming, 239
escrow services, 68, 69
  face-to-face bitcoin purchase with, 69–71
  face-to-face bitcoin purchase without, 68
  setting up, 70
exchange intermediary, Coinbase as, 58
`exec-maven-plugin` plug-in, 229
`ExecutionException` exception type, 239

F

face-to-face bitcoin purchases
  with escrow, 69–70
  problems, 69
  without escrow, 68
fees, 26–27, 170, 238
  for Bitcoin transaction, 18
  for currency exchange, 63
  for middleman, 53
field programmable gate arrays (FPGAs), for mining, 174
Finney, Hal, 113
first bits scheme, 10*n*
FPGAs (field programmable gate arrays), for mining, 174
fragmented private keys, and multi-signature addresses, 41–42
fraud prevention, 125
Freenet, 127
Friedman, Milton, 110
full node, 191
full payment verification, 191
full wallets, 187
  vs. SPV wallets, 193–195
fungibility, of currency, 118

G

generator point, elliptic curve cryptography, 152
genesis block, 113, 165
German mark, 2*n*
Git, installing, 227
`git checkout` command, 228
Gnutella, 119, 127
gold, wealth stored as, 121
gold coins, 1
goods, first exchange for bitcoins, 114
Go programming language, 226
government
  digital currency companies and, 111–112
  risk of Bitcoin destruction by, 119
  stability, and Bitcoin, 126–127
graphics-processing units (GPUs), for mining, 174

H

hacker theft, likelihood of, 38
hardware, for mining, 174–175
  2030 requirements, 202
  energy efficiency of, 178
  profitability threshold curves for comparing, 179

hardware wallets, 42–43
hash, *98*, 132–133
    of transactions in block, 172
hash functions, 131
    for verifying information, 132–133
hash rate
    projecting future, 177
    theoretical limits, 178–179
Hayek, Friedrich, 126
health of network, SPV wallets vs. full wallets, 195
heavyweight wallets, 191
hellomoney.js file, 220
Hello Money! program, 217–218, 220–222
`hello-money` starter project
    creating, 228–229
    declarations, 231
    hook for detecting money arrival, 234
    running and testing, 235–236
    writing code, 230–235
hierarchical deterministic wallets, 190
Hill, Austin, 120
history of Bitcoin, 112–116
homebrew (command-line tool), 219
hosted wallets
    online services, 36
    vs. personal wallets, 34–35
hot storage, 47
    vs. cold storage, 33–34
hot wallets, personal, 37–38
human-readable Bitcoin addresses, 10*n*
hybrid wallets, 187

I

illegal activity, Bitcoin and, 124
impedance mismatch, 57
importing private key, 17, 39, 193, 194–195, 237
installing SPV wallets vs. full wallets, 193
integer factorization, 131
Internet bubble, 120
`InterruptedException` exception type, 239
irreversibility, of transactions, 25–26, 56
    superiority of, 57

J

Java, 226
    initializing objects, 231–233
    installing, 226–227
`java.io.File` class, 231
Java JDK (Java Development Kit), 226
`java.matho.BigInteger` class, 231
JavaScript, 213–223
    preparing machine for, 218–219
    writing Bitcoin program in, 217–218
jelly-filled donut incident, 141–156
JSON-RPC API (JavaScript Object Notation - Remote Protocol Call), 222
    limitations of writing Bitcoin programs using, 223
JSON-RPC protocol, 214

K

Kaminsky, Dan, 118
Keynesian economics, 126
Kienzle, Jörg, 110–111
Koblitz curve, 151
Kraken, 64
Krugman, Paul, 117

L

Landauer limit, 157
laptops, private keys on, 44
ledger, 11
length extension, 171*n*
liability, for stolen bitcoins, 34
lightweight wallets, 192
limit orders, 66
Linux
    installing Git, 227
    installing Maven, 227
    OpenJDK version of Java, 227
    setting up Bitcoin Core server, 219
live Bitcoin exchanges, 71
LocalBitcoins.com, 67, 68
    escrow service, 70

M

Mac OS
- installing Git, 227
- installing Maven, 227
- setting up Bitcoin Core server, 219

man-in-the-middle attacks, 216
market orders, 65–66
MasterCard, 112
master private key, 188
master public key, 188
- generating Bitcoin address with, 190

Maven
- empty starter project created with, 228
- installing, 227

mBTC (millibitcoins), 9
MD5 (message digest algorithm), 132
meeting places, for Bitcoin transactions, 68
`MemoryBlockStore` function (bitcoinJ), 237
merchant services, 214
Merkle trees, 192
mesh networks, 169
message digest algorithm (MD5), 132
microbitcoins (μBTC), 9
middleman, buying bitcoins from, 52–57
Miller-Rabin primality test, 90
millibitcoins (mBTC), 9
mining, 5, 20, 26–27, *96, 99,* 161–180
- in 2030, 201–202
- decentralization of, 179–180
- difficulty of, 173
- distributing new currency with, 167–168
- hardware, 174–175
  - 2030 requirements, 202
  - energy efficiency of, 178
  - profitability threshold curves for comparing, 179
- need for, 162–168
- nodes, 170
- pooled, 175–176
- practicality, 50
- preventing attacks with, 166–167
- process for, 168–176
- for profit, 176–177
- proof-of-work in, 138–139
- solving a block, 171

modular arithmetic, 131*n*
"m of n" private key, 42
money laundering, 112–113
Moore's law, 179*n*
Moxie Jean, 67
Multibit, 38
multi-signature addresses, and fragmented private keys, 41–42
multi-signature transactions, 57, 69–70
`mvn install` command, 230
My Wallet Service, 37

N

Nakamoto, Satoshi, 3, 110, 211
- identity, 113
- last comment, 114
- white paper on Bitcoin, 112

network effect, 120
`NetworkParameters` structure, 232
newbiecoins.com, 13
newly minted bitcoins, 26–27
Newton, Isaac, *Principia,* 210–211
node-bitcoin, installing, 218
Node.js library, 217, 221
- installing, 218

Node Package Manager, 218
nodes
- broadcast only, 169
- full, 191
- relay, 170

nominal deflation, 126
nonprofit organizations, accepting bitcoins, 18
NXT, 125

O

off-chain transactions, 201
offline transaction signing, 40–41
`onCoinsReceived` function, 234–235
online wallet services
- hosted, 36
- personal, 34, 37

Oracle Corporation, 226
orders, placing to buy bitcoins, 65
order of curve, elliptic curve cryptography, 152–153
orphaned blocks, 24–25

P

paper money, color copiers as threat, 110
paper wallets, 39
  encrypted, 39–40
passwords, 14, 40
  for brain wallet, 45
  function of, 40
  loss of, 37
Peercoin, 125
PeerGroup object, 233–234, 240
peer-to-peer architecture, 119
pegging, 120
pending transaction, 18
Perrig, Adrian, 110–111
personal wallets
  vs. hosted wallet, 34–35
  hot storage, 37–38
  online services, 37
person-to-person bitcoin purchases, 52, 67–71
point multiplication, 150, 158–159
point-of-sale terminals, watch-only wallet for, 187
polling, Bitcoin programming, 223
pom.xml file, 229, 236–237
pooled mining, 175–176
portability, of currency, 117
Preneel, Bart, 140
price discovery process, 120
privacy, 11*n*
  and criminals, 124
  multiple addresses and, 12
private currencies, 2
private key, 11–12, 150
  compromise of, 41
  extra protection for, 139
  fragmented, and multi-signature addresses, 41–42
  generating, 37
  importing, 237
  master, 188
  memorizing, 45
  parable on, 141–145
  reversing function of, 136
  security for, 39, 186
  signing transaction with, 156
  SPV wallets vs. full wallets, 194
  storing, 33
profit, mining for, 176–177
programming languages, for Bitcoin network connection, 225–226
proof-of-stake, 125
proof-of-work, 125, 166
  and blockchain, 165
  in mining, 138–139
protecting bitcoins, 61. *See also* security
protocol, for Bitcoin, 112
public information, transactions as, 11
public key, 150
  encryption, 91
  master, 188
  parable of, 141–145
  reversing function of, 136
  sharing, 156
public key cryptography, 133–135
public/private key pair, creating with ECDSA, 154
pushing, Bitcoin programming, 223
Python, 226

Q

quick response (QR) codes, for Bitcoin address, 10

R

Race Integrity Primitives Evaluation Message Digest (RIPEMD), 139–141, 188
radical decentralization, 126
random key generation, 187–190
randomness, for generating Bitcoin address, 39
relay node, 170
RelayRides, 67
remote servers, Electrum connection to, 15

retailers, acceptance of Bitcoin, 116
reversible transactions, 55–56
rewards, 170
  from Bitcoin-mining lottery, 22
  for transaction processing, 26
RIPEMD (Race Integrity Primitives Evaluation Message Digest), 139–141, 188
risks, to Bitcoin, 117–121
Rivest, Ron, 133–134
rounding errors, 235
  and cryptography, 151
RSA encryption, 133–134, 137
Ruby, 226

S

safety, of storage, 35
satoshi (bitcoin unit), 9
SatoshiLabs, 43
Satoshi Square, 71
savings, Bitcoin for, 121–122
scarcity, of currency, 118
Sean's Outpost, 18
Secure Hash Algorithm (SHA), 139–141, 188
  ASIC optimization to calculate, 174
security, 14, 118–119
  of Bitcoin exchanges, 63
  confidence in, 216–217
  double hash scheme and, 156
  SPV wallets vs. full wallets, 193–194
  of storage, 35
seed, in Electrum, 14, 15
sending money
  from Bitcoin address, 236–239
  code for, 238
`SendRequest` object, 238
settlement period, 55, 56
SHA (Secure Hash Algorithm), 139–141, 188
  ASIC optimization to calculate, 174
Shamir, Adi, 133–134
Shamir's Secret Sharing method, 42
shares, of mining reward, 176
side chains, 121
Silk Road website, 124
simplified payment verification (SPV), 191, 233
  vs. full wallets, 193–195
single key generation wallet programs, 188
smartphones
  private keys on, 44
  wallets on, 192
software as a service, 34
speed of payments, SPV wallets vs. full wallets, 193
spending bitcoins, 17–19
SPV (simplified payment verification), 191, 233
  vs. full wallets, 193–195
`SPVBlockStore` object, 232, 233
stateless currencies, 2
storage, Bitcoin, 31–47
  choosing method, 46–47
  hot vs. cold, 33–34
  of large amounts of bitcoins, 38–42
  private key, 33
  safety, security, and convenience, 35
  of small amounts of bitcoins, 35–38
  SPV wallets vs. full wallets, 194
  Trezor, 43–45
summation, pseudocode for, elliptic curve cryptography, 158–159
symmetric key cryptography, 133
synchronization, SPV wallets vs. full wallets, 193

T

Takhteyev, Yuri, 112*n*
tangent to curve, elliptic curve cryptography, 150
thick wallets, 191
thin wallets, 192
third-party service provider, as bank, 33
timestamp, for block, 172
Tor, 127
trade volume, of exchange, 63
transaction confirmation, 25
transaction fees. *See* fees

transaction history, verifying validity, 138
transactions
  authorizing with digital signatures, 137–138
  full vs. simplified payment verification, 191–195
  information in, 138
  off-chain, 201
  ordering, 166
  potential, in 2030, 201
  signing
    with ECDSA, 153–156
    offline, 40–41
    offline vs. online, 186–187
    with private key, 156
transferring dollars to exchange account, 66
Trezor, 43–45
true blockchain, 24
true ledger, 166
trust, 110, 111
two-factor authentication, 36, 53–54
  setting up in Coinbase, 58–59

U

unit of account, 123
units, Bitcoin, 9
unspent output, 196

V

valid transaction, 191
vendor APIs, 214–215
Visa, 112
volatility, of Bitcoin, 120

W

wallet file, 13, 33, 186
`Wallet.loadFromFile()` function, 240
walletNotify feature, 223
wallets, 12–19, *28–29*, 185–198
  acquiring bitcoins, 16
  BitcoinJ issues, 239–240
  brain, 45–46
  creating empty, 232
  future changes, 197
  generating, 38–42
  getting bitcoins into, 17
  hardware, 42–43
  online hosted services, 36
  paper, 39
  personal vs. hosted, 34–35
  running on autopilot, 214
  selecting, 197
  software design fundamentals, 186–195
    features, 195–196
    offline vs. online transaction signing, 186–187
    random vs. deterministic key generation, 187–190
  transferring coins from Coinbase wallet to, 61
  virus threat to, 216
  watch-only. *See* watch-only wallet
`Wallet.saveToFile()` function, 240
watch-only wallet, 186
  combining deterministic key generation with, 189
    math supporting, 189–190
  full vs. SPV, 191–195
  for point-of-sale terminals, 187
Windows development environment, JavaScript on, 218–219

X

XBT, 9

Z

zero point, elliptic curve cryptography, 152–153

UPDATES

Visit *http://www.nostarch.com/bitcoin* for updates, errata, and other information.

CPSIA information can be obtained at www.ICGtesting.com
Printed in the USA
BVOW10s1448041114

373595BV00004B/27/P